Praise for *A Course in Mysticism and Miracles*

"What is more interesting than listening to the mystics' description of their experiences? The answer, no doubt, is having such experiences yourself. If there is a book that can open that door for such experiences, it is *A Course in Miracles*, a modern spiritual classic. Open Jon's book to invite Divine insights to come through that door for you."

—Jerry Jampolsky, MD, author of *Love Is Letting Go of Fear*

"If you want to know about mysticism and miracles, this is the place to look."

—Marianne Williamson, author of *A Return to Love*

"I devoured this book almost in one sitting. I admit, shamefully, to have taken a dinner break, though reading it, I was amply nourished. Need I say more?"

—Mark Greenfield, PhD

"Who better to write a book on mysticism and miracles than Jon Mundy, one of the true mystics of our time who also happens to be one of the original contributors to *A Course in Miracles*. You'll love it!"

—Tom Carpenter, author of *Dialogue on Awakening*

"There have always been those mystics who have been able to see into the eternal. Jon has picked out for us a host of teachings from the worlds' mystical traditions and shows us how *A Course in Miracles* unwraps these teachings for a more psychologically refined, modern mind."

—Beverly Hutchinson McNeff, founder and president of the Miracle Distribution Center, Anaheim, CA

"Jon Mundy is one of my favorite authors; his books stay close to me while others come and go. In this masterful work Jon brilliantly brings Big Picture truths down to earth and makes the divine practical. You will rarely find a better blend of wisdom, heart, inspiration, and vision. Read it and leap!"

—Alan Cohen, author of *A Course in Miracles Made Easy*

"A tour de force! Jon Mundy shows us what it's like to be a true mystic and a student and teacher of *A Course in Miracles*. His many years of experience shine throughout these pages and will help readers accelerate the journey on their spiritual path. I highly recommend this important book."

—Gary Renard, bestselling author of The Disappearance of the Universe trilogy and *The Lifetimes When Jesus and Buddha Knew Each Other*

A COURSE IN

MYSTICISM

AND

MIRACLES

Begin Your Spiritual Adventure

JON MUNDY, PhD

Author of *Living A Course in Miracles*

WEISER BOOKS
An OPEN CENTER Book™

This edition first published in 2018 by Weiser Books, an
imprint of
Red Wheel/Weiser, LLC
With offices at:
65 Parker Street, Suite 7
Newburyport, MA 01950
www.redwheelweiser.com

ISBN: 978-1-57863-601-3
Library of Congress Cataloging-in-Publication Data available
upon request.

Cover design by Jim Warner
Cover photograph Shutterstock © Andrey Tiyk
Interior by Frame25 Productions
Typeset in ITC Stone Serif

Printed in Canada
MAR
10 9   8 7 6 5 4 3 2 1

The most beautiful and profound emotion we can experience is the mystical. He to whom this emotion is a stranger, who can no longer wonder and stand rapt in awe, is as good as dead. To know that what is impenetrable to us really exists . . . is at the center of true religion.

—Albert Einstein

To my teacher Ken Wapnick, PhD

Contents

Preface

*Mysticism is the pursuit of a spiritual and intangible quest;
the finding of a "way out" of illusion or a "way back" to
absolute truth. It is an intimate personal adventure. Mysticism
is the art of arts. It is the most romantic of adventures.*
—Evelyn Underhill, *Mysticism*

Why pick up this book? Why read any further? Maybe you already know something of the mystical. Maybe mysticism, for you, means remembering something you already know. When you read the teachings of the world's great wisdom literature and know of the wisdom of *A Course in Miracles*, a conversation naturally emerges regarding the similarities between the teachings of the Course and a host of teachings from different mystics and philosophers across the ages. Spend some time reading the Course and you'll soon say: "Who wrote this?" It is clear that no "body" wrote it. It came through the mind and the hands of Helen Schucman, a professor of medical psychology at Columbia University. Having known Helen, however—as brilliant as she was—these sentences are not her ordinary way of speaking or being.

In the 2016 movie *Arrival*, when aliens land on Earth, the first thing they must do is establish a means of communication. Not only are they confronted with a language barrier—as there would be, say, between someone who speaks Chinese and someone who speaks English—there is also a tremendous gap between the *way* the aliens think and the way those they find on Earth think. This boundary must be crossed before real communication can begin. Twentieth-century philosopher Ludwig Wittgenstein once pointed out that, although we cannot even begin to imagine how a lioness thinks, if her eyes are fixed on a gazelle, we have some idea of what she has in mind. So it is that mystical "thinking" also transcends "words" and our current ways of seeing, understanding, and being. Yet we can still grasp its meaning.

About *A Course in Miracles*

A Course in Miracles presents itself as "a manual for a special curriculum, intended for teachers of a special form of the universal course. There are many thousands of other forms, all with the same outcome" (M–1.4:1 *see reference key on page xiv.*). The Course is but one of many thousands of spiritual paths—indeed, thousands upon thousands. There have always been those, like 13th-century Persian mystic Jalaluddin Rumi, who have brought us different spiritual truths. In fact, many of the ideas contained in the Course are reflected in the teachings of a host of different thinkers and traditions that both pre-date and are contemporaneous with it. This is especially true for those who engage in what is called non-dualistic thinking—Gnostics, Neoplatonists, Advaita Vedantists, Zen Buddhists, Sufis, Kabbalists, Transcendentalists, those who expound New Thought philosophies like Christian Science, Unity, and Religious Science, and, more recently, those who favor the work of Mari Perrone in *A Course of Love*. Interfaith work and/or what is also called Interspirituality is clearly the wave of the future. In the end, no religion wins. God wins, which means everyone wins, as our will must ultimately be the same as that of God. Everything not of God is illusory—what the Course calls "the dreaming of the world." The Course, like all mystical teachings, calls upon us to awaken from all dreaming.

Since its release in 1976, *A Course in Miracles* has come to be regarded as a great work of art and a 21st-century spiritual classic. More than three million copies now exist in twenty-seven different languages. What is unique about the Course is its incredibly high level of psychological sophistication. It is truly a document of the 21st-century—one that gives us ever-deeper insight into the working of the mind.

This book explains what mysticism is and identifies the basic characteristics of mystical experience—the loss of subject/object identity, a sense of timelessness, release of the ego self, and experiences of wonder, awe, reverence, freedom, happiness, and bliss. The Course is a manual for the awakening of mystic vision without dogma, rituals, and the fetters of traditional religion. While there are many dedicated teachers of the Course, there is no hierarchy within its followers—no bishops, no central organization, no chain of command.

This book contains quotes from and/or stories of more than 200 different individuals and sources. In the back of the book, you'll find an alphabetical listing of the mystics, philosophers, poets, and personalities discussed, along with a sentence or two about their lives and who they are or were.

Reference Key

Quotations and paraphrasing from *A Course in Miracles*, unless otherwise designated, come from the third edition, published by the Foundation for Inner Peace. The location of each quote or paraphrase appears immediately after the reference, followed by a listing of the chapter, section, paragraph, and sentence. For instance, in the example T–9.III.4:1, "T" means "Textbook"; "9" is the chapter; "III" is the section; "4" is the paragraph; and "1" is the sentence. For this purpose, the following key applies:

T references the *Textbook*

W references the *Workbook*

M references the *Manual for Teachers*

C references the *Clarification of Terms*

S references *The Song of Prayer*

In references the *Introduction*

A Course in Miracles is referred to throughout this text simply as "the Course." In a few instances, I have added bracketed words to clarify vague terms or pronouns cited out of context. Although some parts of the Course are delivered as poetry, here I cite them in prose form for clarity's sake. All Biblical quotations are from the King James version, the one referenced within the Course and one of Helen Schucman's favorite translations.

Acknowledgments

First, my thanks to my wife, my partner in life, my darling Dolores, who is ever-present in her love and devotion to the life we gladly share. Loving her is my greatest happiness. I am a very lucky man. The day I met Dolores was the best day of my life. She brought me my daughter, Sarah; and Sarah brought us her husband, Andrew; and the two of them together have brought us our delightful grandson, Bryson and our granddaughter, Avery Rose.

Fran Cosentino, my assistant from 2005 to 2017, helped in every stage of development. I am grateful to her for her editorial skills, diligence, and patience. Since June 2017, my new assistant, Eileen Katzmann, has added her editorial skills.

I'm grateful to *A Course in Miracles* students/teachers Lynne Matous, Gregg Matous, David Brown, Lorri Coburn, and Reverend Heather Harris for the many hours they spent looking over this book and making suggestions for improvements.

My thanks to my young friend Zhao Wang, who contributed significantly to Chapter 10 of this book. Zhao is a remarkable young woman who went through a disrobing of the ego that has left her very wise for her age. Thanks as well to my friend Rod Chelberg for his critical assessment of this manuscript. In addition to being a medical doctor, Rod is a seasoned meditator and, like Zhao, committed to the truth.

My friend Shanti Rica Josephs has, since 1972, been my steady rock—the one to whom I've been able to pour out my soul, the one who has consistently known the right answer.

Finally, my thanks to Christine LeBlond, my editor at Red Wheel/Weiser, Jane Hagaman (managing editor), and Laurie Trufant (copy editor) for their consistent wise guidance in the development of this book.

Introduction:
Why Mysticism *and* Miracles?

The part of your mind in which truth abides is in constant communication with God, whether you are aware of it or not.

W–49.1:2

Two early 20th-century mystics, G. I. Gurdjieff and Ramana Maharshi, both said that what is important in life is having a clearly defined living question. As *A Course in Miracles* expresses it: "The test of everything on earth is simply this: 'What is it for?'" (T–24.VII.6:1). We can think of this question as the "how" and the "why" of life. We thirst for the truth because only truth will satisfy the soul's deep longing for God. How did we get into these bodies? In this world? At this time? What are we supposed to do here? Does life extend beyond the limitation of our bodies or do we just have a birth, a dream, and then death?

There are people who say they know the answers to these questions. They have experienced "insights"—sometimes a momentary knowing, sometimes longer, deeper, more profound experiences that led to an inner conviction and a living awareness of eternal life. Some have experienced "awakenings" that have lasted for days and were so profound that they were not able to talk or eat. To go through such an "awakening" is to be transformed. When thus awakened, they often feel the need to share what they have seen, but find it very hard to put it into words. Likewise, you may experience an insight with such profundity that you stop for a moment and peek into eternity—through disciplined study and contemplation; through simply getting quiet; through falling in love; perhaps due to the death of a spouse; perhaps while fishing or driving; or perhaps for no clear reason at all. That is when your mind takes a picture of something you can never forget.

A Little Background

For over forty years, I simultaneously followed two professions: I was a parish minister and I taught classes in philosophy, religion, and psychology at several colleges. During the summer of 1970, I trained in yoga with Swami Vishnudevananda; in the summer of 1971, I left on a trip through India on which I spent time with Sathya Sai Baba, Muktananda, and Osho. While meditating in an underground man-made cave at Muktananda's ashram in Genishpuri, I was guided to go back to New York and assured that I would find what I was looking for there. The whole experience left me wanting something more. By this time, it was clear to me that God could only be found within, but I still needed to look for deeper clarity and understanding.

My first book, *Learning to Die,* appeared in 1973. Helen Schucman, the scribe of *A Course in Miracles,* and William Thetford, her supervisor at Columbia University School of Physicians and Surgeons, came to a lecture I was giving on mysticism and near-death experiences. At the time, I was one month shy of my thirtieth birthday and knew that my own experiences paled in the face of Helen and Bill's deeper understanding of the spiritual path. They were, however, quite kind. Helen welcomed my enthusiasm for mysticism and appreciated the fact that I was a theology student.

One spring Sunday in 1975, Helen sat me down with Bill Thetford and another of her colleagues, Ken Wapnick, in Ken's tiny studio apartment in New York. There, she told me how the Course had come to be and how it affected the other people in the room. After this initial meeting, Ken and I decided we would continue to get together for further discussions at General Theological Seminary, where I was living, teaching, and doing postgraduate work. From that night on, Ken became my primary teacher and "older brother" in this earthly journey. When he died, Ken left us a mountain of information in printed books, audio recordings, and video productions. Exploring this treasure is marvelous fun and I still listen to his many CDs as I drive. Ken left us more than words, however; he also left us an example—a demonstration of how to live in truth and find our way back Home. For those who knew Ken, one word describes him above all others: *kindness*.

Helen became a kind of informal therapist for me, helping me sort through my feelings and deal with my too-frequent romantic upheavals. A few weeks after our meeting, Helen met Judy Whitson, who later became the President of the Foundation for Inner Peace, which published the first edition of the Course. Judy and I had been friends since the 1960s and were both working with the American Society for Psychical Research. Judy arranged for the xeroxing of 300 copies of the Course—called the Criswell Edition—so a small group of us could start reading it and practicing the Workbook lessons prior to its publication in 1976.

Old News

What the Course says is not new.
It simply provides an expansive view. (Jon)

Israeli-American violinist Itzhak Pearlman once said: "An amateur practices until they get it right. A professional practices until they can't get it wrong." The more a student practices a musical instrument, the more perfect and beautiful the sound. Likewise, the more the principles of the Course are understood and applied, the deeper we experience a sense of divine order. The Course is sophisticated and erudite, unpretentious and profound. It tells us over and over that the path is incredibly simple. We, however, are not simple. Understanding the Course requires that we purify our thoughts and deliberately remove all blocks to an awareness of love's presence. It requires that we put aside all judgments, attack thoughts, defensiveness, and deceptiveness. Most of all, it requires practice, practice, practice—until you simply can't get it wrong.

Mysticism and the Ego

I once asked Ken why he thought the Course came to us when it did—during the last quarter of the 20th century. He said that he did not know for sure, but he was sure that it could not have appeared until after the work of Sigmund Freud, the father of psychoanalysis. Freud understood the ego very well and described in some detail how it works. Before Freud, men like German Idealist philosopher Johann Fichte maintained that a study of the ego was fundamental to philosophy and to the then newly emerging field of psychology, but no one before Freud had spelled out the workings of the ego in such detail and with such amazing clarity.

While there are similarities between the use of the word "ego" in the Course and in Freudian psychology, the usage is not the same. In the Course, the word is used in ways more akin to how it is used in non-dualistic, mystically oriented philosophy, in which the ego is a false self with no lasting reality. By contrast, Freud thought that we were damned to a life with the ego—absolutely stuck with it. There was no exit, no door to freedom.

In *The Future of an Illusion*, Freud writes: "The idea of God is an illusion based on an infantile emotional need for a powerful supernatural *paterfamilias*"—that is, a strong father figure. Freud's atheism kept him from seeing that God was the answer to this dilemma. By contrast, the Course teaches that "allegiance to the denial of God is the ego's religion" (T–10.V.3:1). If Freud had studied Eastern philosophy or mysticism, as did Jung, he might have seen the way out. The presence of God is an absolute ingredient in awakening. Without God, we're lost. Mystics are lucky. Although perhaps not yet realized, they know that the search for God is the only way to go. And it is in that search that we experience miracles.

This is much like the teachings of Meister Eckhart, a 12th-century Dominican often regarded as the greatest of the medieval Christian mystics. "The world," Eckhart tells us, "is an emanation from an ultimate, indivisible being with whom the soul is 'ultimately' united." Charged with heresy by the Inquisition, Eckhart spent the last two years of his life defending his mystical teachings and died before he could be executed.

(He is thus referred to as "Meister," not "Saint.") Eckhart epitomizes the teaching of all mystics in this admonition: "Become in all things a God seeker and a God finder, at all times and in all places." Albert Einstein, a mystic in his own way, put it more simply: "I want to know the Mind of God."

Viewed from the perspective of medieval mysticism, the Course is "the Philosopher's Stone"—the *Magnum Opus*, or "the great work"—that truly answers the riddles of the Universe. It represents a process by which we can learn of the truth of our being, find freedom from our insanity, and be reassured of eternal life. Like all mystical "systems," the Course is a path, a way, a process, and a passage. It is a story that tells us of the grand destiny and points the way to the path out of hell. Ultimately, the answer to the riddle we call life is simply a matter of a willingness to live in harmony with the Divine. That *is* the miracle. We are simply called upon to *remember*—or better, *re-cognize*—what we already know.

The True Mystic

At the core, everyone is a mystic. Everyone longs for God and our eternal Home. Once, when I was teaching a class on mysticism, I described a thinker as "a *true* mystic." A student asked what I meant, forcing me to contemplate the qualities I ascribed to mystics. I settled on four major characteristics that are common to them all:

- A true mystic looks for God above and beyond all worldly endeavors.

- A true mystic is willing to go through a deep inner cleansing of the soul, accept responsibility for decisions, and begin living in accordance with the Will of God—which is our own will.

- A true mystic dedicates his or her life to spiritual growth and to the process of being free of illusion in favor and recognition of reality.

- A true mystic is a lover of the Absolute.

Evelyn Underhill called true mystics "the heroes of our race."

PART I

The Mystical Path

We live in the appearance of things. There is a reality but we do not know it. To be everything, you must first be nothing. There must be no wanting, no needing.

—Kalu Rinpoche

Chapter 1

Mysticism and Miracles

Wholeness heals because it is of the mind. All forms of sickness, even unto death, are physical expressions of the fear of awakening. They are attempts to reinforce sleeping out of fear of waking. This is a pathetic way of trying not to see by rendering the faculties for seeing ineffectual. "Rest in peace" is a blessing for the living, not the dead, because rest comes from waking, not from sleeping. Sleep is withdrawing; waking is joining.

T–8.IX.3:1–6

No one becomes a mystic by reading a book. Reading a book doesn't hurt, however. *A Course in Miracles* is, in the first instance, a book. The right book can turn our minds and start the gears moving in a "wholly" new direction. Reading a mystic's writings helps us remember what we already know and provides a link to other mystics. Reading about mysticism is not the same as *being a mystic,* but it is a clear indication that our feet are on the path. With a little luck, we may be inspired to do the work required to develop a contemplative life. Mohammad said: "A scholar who writes about mysticism without mystical eyes is like a donkey carrying a load of books." Mysticism is available to all—including, or sometimes especially, children. You may not know how close mysticism is to you while driving your car, listening to music, taking a walk in nature, or sharing deeply with a loved one—but it is there.

Almost nothing brings me greater joy than listening to mystics describe their experiences. Mystics naturally enjoy meeting and being with other mystics. They do so freely and in a relaxed manner, being appreciative of whatever gifts their companions bring. Mystics may have any career: teacher, salesman, computer operator, car mechanic—you name it. They can be found among poets, writers, musicians, nature lovers, artists, healers, ministers, philosophers, psychologists, and craftspeople of all sorts. Libraries are filled with mystical poetry and stories, mystical philosophies, and studies on mysticism.

Many Are Called

"Many are called but few are chosen" should be, "All are called but few choose to listen." (T–3.IV.7:12)

Mysticism is an experience. It is something we live, not something we study or describe or investigate. These experiences can be found everywhere—in profound contemplation or in everyday life. Jeff Mills, a student of the Course, describes this simple mystical experience, which came to him as he was leaving his barber after getting a haircut.

I had not taken ten steps when I saw an elderly woman pass by who reminded me of my mom. All a sudden, I was overcome with an incredible sense of Oneness. I felt a spreading warm feeling in my chest. For a brief moment, it occurred to me to turn around and tell the barber about it, but what would I say? I leaned against the brick building while tears welled up in my eyes. I don't know whether coming across the woman triggered the event or whether it was coincidental, but I felt an incredible sense of connection—that all of us are connected to our Source and to each other. I realized there is nothing to fear because there is absolutely nothing outside of us. I felt so safe and joyful. After a couple of minutes, I headed to my car with a deep peace flowing through me.

Tell somebody who has never fallen in love what it's like to fall in love. You can try, but you can't really explain it—precisely because it is an *experience*. Magnify that experience tenfold and you may begin to understand something of what a mystical experience is. You may get just a glimmer of it. The Taoists tell us: "The Tao which can be described is not the Tao." The Buddhists put it this way: "The finger pointing to the moon is not the moon." How can you freeze the infinite? Although mystical experiences may fade, however, they are never forgotten; something consistently pulls us Home.

Mystical knowledge is not secret. It is a revelation—a "re-cognition"—of what already is. The word "mystic" derives from *myste*, meaning "to close the lips and eyes." Unlike the word "esoteric," which means "secret or hidden," the word mystical refers to knowledge that is not hidden, but simply not available to someone who is "sleeping"—unawakened or unaware. Mysticism is thus both an *experience* and an *ongoing developing awareness*. Mahavira, Buddha, Jesus, and Mohammad, as well as many other religious leaders, have always given the highest importance to the direct, personal experience of truth.

Something wonderful happens during a mystical experience. A feeling of unity and connectedness and a knowing transcend our ordinary sight. Something impels us to reach out in love for even greater love. Repeated experience with the mystical encourages our attention. Something pulls us to an even deeper seeing, knowing, and being. Fifteenth-century Italian polymath Leonardo da Vinci once wrote: "I awoke only to see that the rest of the world was sleeping." Mysticism is an awakening and the discovery of a state of mind that *transcends* what can be called the "ordinary mind" or the "sleeping mind" or the "dreaming mind." Mystical experiences are transpersonal—that is, they transcend the personal and lead to an understanding of something much greater than the bodily "me" that walks the Earth and has an identity as an individual.

While others may question the veracity of mystical experiences, mystics do not. Profound mystical experiences— what the Course calls "Holy Instants"—are transformative and life-changing. Once the door opens, you cannot shut it completely, and God's love will eventually flood your life. Seventeenth-century English dissenter George Fox, the founder of the Society of Friends, better known as the Quakers, said: "God can *only* be found experientially." We do not need the ideas of others or a book to learn about God. Holy women and men often spend a great deal of time in silence going within. "There is," Fox said, "something of the inward light in everyone, and *anyone* can make direct contact with God."

Mysticism is also a process of becoming. It is a churning, turning, cooking kind of thing. Like pebbles rolling around in a tub of sand, we must sometimes go through rough places to smooth things out. The door to Heaven is called forgiveness, and sometimes it takes a bit of work to find freedom from our judgmental minds. According to the Course, when we see the world without the contamination of the ego, we see only purity—only wholeness. Forgiveness means looking at the world of the ego without judging it. Even in the face of what appears as evil, mystics see only love. Thus, Jesus could go to the cross saying: "Father, forgive them for they know not what they do." He did not say that so God would know how to handle the situation. He said it so we would have a better understanding of how to handle much less severe situations when we feel ourselves to be persecuted.

Vast numbers of people have had mystical experiences. Immediate spiritual intuition can come to anyone, regardless of age, religious training, or spiritual inclination. And it can come at any time—perhaps when you are very relaxed, perhaps under dramatic circumstances like an automobile accident. Having a mystical experience does not make you a mystic, however. Mystical experiences are simply doors and windows to a wider awareness. They signal a stage in spiritual development that will, if nourished, grow ever more deeply into love. As one Course teacher and contemporary mystic put it: "The heart of mysticism is the transformation of human consciousness into divine consciousness."

In *No Boundary: Eastern and Western Approaches to Personal Growth,* Ken Wilber argues that the mystical traditions of the world provide access to a transcendental dimension that is available throughout all time. "The essence of mysticism," he claims, "is that in the deepest part of your true being, in the very center of your own pure awareness, you are fundamentally one with Spirit, one with Godhead, one with the All, in a timeless, eternal, and unchanging fashion." When we have a mystical experience, everything we see is the love of God and everything we experience is the love of God. Carl Jung expressed it this way: "Your vision will become clear only when you can look into your own heart. Who looks outside, dreams; who looks inside, awakens."

What Mysticism Is

I gathered these definitions while reading various sources on mysticism:

1. Mysticism is a direct experience of God and an awareness of truth.

2. Mysticism is knowledge that comes from the Self and not the ego self.

3. Mysticism is realizing there is no such thing as ego.

4. Mysticism is knowledge of the interconnectedness of all things.

5. Mysticism is the science and art of the spiritual life.

6. Mysticism is the science of self-evident reality.

7. Mysticism is an experience that brings aware-ness of higher truth.

8. Mysticism is a transcending of the ego world to experience Self.

9. Mysticism is direct union with the Divine by means of contemplation.

10. Mysticism is a belief in the power of spiri-tual access to ultimate reality.

11. Mysticism is about clearing the mind to access transcendence.

12. Mysticism is a realization that truth is imma-nent and transcendent.

13. Mysticism is being receptive instead of projective.

14. Mysticism is the awakening within the Self of divine reality.

15. Mysticism is the purification of perception and seeing through illusions.

16. Mysticism is an inner return to our divine Source in consciousness.

17. Mysticism is faith in a transformative "higher power" without dogma.

What Mysticism Is Not

"Mysticism is one of the most abused words in the English language," Evelyn Underhill tells us in her 1911 book *Mysticism,* which has become a classic. "It has been claimed as an excuse for every kind of occultism, for diluted transcendentalism, vapid symbolism, religious or aesthetic sentimentality and bad metaphysics." Underhill, perhaps the most brilliant and indefatigable researcher in the field of mysticism, devoted her life to the topic, writing over thirty books on it. Upon her death, *The Times* said that, in the field of theology, she was "unmatched by any of the professional teachers of her day." Underhill's insight is key and suggests that it is as important to understand what mysticism is *not*, as it is to understand what it is.

> **Mysticism is not vague.** Sometimes, experiences may be called mystical because the ideas involved may seem unclear. Mysticism is occasionally associated with the word "misty" because the words sound similar. There is, however, nothing misty, foggy, or hazy about mysticism. To mystics, the truth is clear.

> **Mysticism is not a mystery.** While there is an etymological connection between the words "mysticism" and "mystery," mysticism is not about secrets, although to the uninitiated, any mystical path may appear mysterious—like an unfamiliar language. Mysticism is also not something entirely within the realm of the intellect—not something open to conceptualization alone.

Mysticism is not magic. Underhill tells us in *Mysticism:* "Magic wants to get. Mysticism wants to give." Mysticism isn't about getting anything. It is not a display, nor is it about using secret incantations or hocus-pocus of any kind. It's not about sorcery or the use of rituals to achieve something. "Magic," the Course tells us, "is the mindless or the miscreative use of mind" (T–2.V.2:1). Magicians are illusionists. They hide the truth. Mystics reveal truth. They bring us clarity and freedom.

Mysticism is not evangelical. To be evangelical, you must feel that you are right and others are wrong. Mysticism, on the other hand, simply means aligning the mind with truth, which changes relationships, making them peaceful. It thus changes the world in a subtle and completely nonviolent way. As English scholar John Davidson points out: "Outwardly, mystics live a normal, straightforward existence, being good, kind, and honest with everyone, without feeling the need to convert others to their own point of view."

Mysticism is not occult. Occultists claim to have "secret" knowledge and paranormal abilities. Mysticism, on the other hand, is about awakening to the reality of who we are in truth. While mysticism may have some of the characteristics of parapsychological phenomena—clairvoyance, clairaudience, distant vision, telepathic or precognitive abilities—it is not about hearing voices, talking to the dead, predicting the future, seeing visions, reading minds, or walking on hot coals. In fact, occult powers and the desire for them can impede mystical-mindedness. "Mysticism is not an opinion," Underhill claims in her classic book. "It is not a philosophy. It has nothing in common with the pursuit of occult knowledge."

Mysticism is not self-promoting. Self-realization—enlightenment—is the only true result of a mystical experience, although practiced mystics have been known to develop any number of extraordinary powers of perception and intuition. In fact, it's inevitable that abilities like these will develop quite naturally as the side-effects of mystical development. But they are not the aim of it. Genuine mystical powers are not exhibited, promoted, or sold like commodities. Ramana Maharshi, a primary teacher of Advaita Vedanta, did not publicize himself as a guru; he never appointed successors and he never claimed to have disciples. He said regarding the development of psychic or occult powers: "The idea that the Master is one who has attained power over the various occult senses by long practice and prayer or anything of the kind, is absolutely false. No Master ever cared a rap for occult powers. He has no need for them in his daily life."

Mysticism is not retreat. Although mystics sometimes retreat from the outer world to develop a deeper awareness of inner reality, mysticism itself does not require retreat. Becoming a mystic does not require an escape from the so-called "real world." In fact, "practical mysticism" calls upon us to be very present and aware of whatever is going on in the world, without buying into its illusions.

Mysticism is not time-bound. Traditional religions place a major emphasis on the past—on sin, guilt, and fear—and an emphasis on what life is going to be like after death. Will we get to go to Heaven? Will we go to hell? Mysticism, by contrast, takes the focus off time by bringing us into the present and into the ever-present presence of God as the only living reality.

Ignitiation

"Ignitiation" is not a word found in any dictionary. The word "ignition" means "to set something on fire." The word "initiation" means "a rite of passage from one stage to another." To experience an "ignitiation" is thus to experience a "trial by fire" that instantly introduces a higher level of seeing, knowing, and being. Many of the mystics of the Middle Ages who were burned at the stake by the Catholic Church (and later also by the Protestants) experienced a literal ignitiation while being released from the confines of the body. Take, for example, John Huss, a 14th-century mystic who openly objected to the Pope raising money to fight wars and to the selling of indulgences—buying admission into Heaven by donating money to the Church. "By selling indulgences," Huss said, "the Church was selling its own soul." Huss was publicly strangled and then, not yet dead, burned at the stake. As the fire began to consume him, he cried out: "Christ, son of the Living God, have mercy on us!"

My own "ignitiation experience" was less spectacular, but no less enlightening. In 1976, I went through a dramatic ego-death experience under the guidance of Salvador Roquet, a Mexican psychiatrist who combined the insights of Western psychiatry with shamanism. It was through this experience that I came to understand what the Course meant when it said there is no world, no time, no body, no me, and no you as separate individuals. I give details of this experience, which I call "Holy Hell," in a previous book, *Eternal Life and A Course in Miracles*. The experience was *holy* because of what came out of it. It was *hell* in terms of the ego-shattering death I went through. Hell comes in the "fear" of dying—in resisting God and in thinking we can build a world without God.

Roquet realized that the psychiatric methodology of administering drugs to treat people's symptoms not only does not heal them, it keeps them in a dream-like stupor when what is needed for healing is awakening. Mystics must face reality, not run from it. Rather than putting us to sleep—as society does, as television often does, as repetitious religious rituals often do, as over-eating and over-drinking do—Roquet chose instead to wake us up. He encouraged us to accept responsibility as spiritual beings in the Universe. He asked us to say to ourselves—*and mean them*—the words given in the Course: "I am responsible for what I see. I choose the feelings I experience, and I decide upon the goal I would achieve. And everything that seems to happen to me I ask for, and receive as I have asked" (T–21.II.2:3–5).

Unlike psychotherapy, which is often a slow and unproductive process that reinforces the ego rather than providing

freedom from it, ignitiation is more direct. In my own ignitiation experience, we lay inside sleeping bags, blindfolded,
with earphones covering our ears. We were given a dose of
pure LSD, followed a half hour later by an intramuscular shot
of ketamine, a powerful muscle relaxant sometimes used to
cure depression. The ketamine made it impossible for us
to move. This combination of drugs induced a metaphoric
death experience that led to an awakening from the dream
world. This kind of ignitiation is not a gentle path, but nothing will wake you up faster. I do not recommend it, however,
since the Course provides a more gentle means of awakening: "Fear not that you will be abruptly lifted up and hurled
into reality. Time is kind and. . . it will keep gentle pace with
you in your transition" (T–16.VI.8:2).

Right Time, Right Place

Your passage through time and space is not at random. You cannot but be in the right place at the
right time. Such is the strength of God. Such are His
gifts. (W–42.2:4–6)

While working with Salvador Roquet, I clearly saw seven
things that all mystics see. We'll discuss each of them in this book.

The world is "made up." It is a concept—a
construct. We make up every aspect of the world,
which looks nothing like our real Home—Heaven.

As the Course expresses it: "This *is* an insane world, and do not underestimate the extent of its insanity. There is no area of your perception that it has not touched, and your dream *is* sacred to you. That is why God placed the Holy Spirit in you, where you placed the dream" (T–14.I.2:1–8).

Time is relative. This is Einstein's great discovery. Time can speed up; it can slow down; it can stop—in which case, there is no time! Heaven is eternal. The world is ephemeral. The Course sees time as "a trick, a sleight of hand, a vast illusion in which figures come and go as if by magic. Yet there is a plan behind appearances that does not change" (W–158.4:1–3).

The script is written. There are no accidents! As Einstein said: "God does not play dice with the universe." "When experience will come to end your doubting has been set," the Course teaches us. "For we but see the journey from the point at which it ended, looking back on it, imagining we make it once again; reviewing mentally what has gone by" (W–158.4:3–5).

We are not bodies. Bodies are temporal. In just a few years, neither your body nor mine will exist. It doesn't matter. And it doesn't matter—now! Life does not begin with the birth of a body. Life does not end with the death of a body.

There is no duality. There are no opposites. There is only Oneness. We are all already One with God. We are simply called to remember who we already are. We must each awaken to our own call. "God," the Course tells us, "has only *one* Son. If all His creations are His Sons, everyone must be an integral part of the whole Sonship. The Sonship in its Oneness transcends the sum of its parts" (T–2.VII.6:1–3). If you prefer, use the word Being or Beingness for Son. Since there is no division, there is neither male nor female.

Neither you nor I exist as individuals. We cannot and do not exist apart from God. Thinking we exist without God is merely dreaming.

All decision-making must be turned over to God. And the sooner, the better. It's the only way to be truly happy. "The power of decision is your one remaining freedom as a prisoner of this world," the Course teaches. "You can decide to see it right. What you made of it is not its reality, for its reality is only what you give it" (T–12.VII.9:1).

Lost and Found

All my life I sought for God and when I found Him I discovered that it was He who was seeking me. (Meister Eckhart)

Chapter 2

The Infinite Infant

Heaven lies all about us in our infancy.
—William Wordsworth

The prefix that introduces both the words "infant" and "infinity" means "not." Infinity means "not finite." The word infant comes from the Latin *fari*, meaning "not yet able to talk." An infant has thus not yet developed speech. We move from infancy to early childhood as we begin to label the world with words. Infants see the world with awe and wonder—without words, although we continue to pour words through them. Infants enjoy a state of relative (though rapidly evaporating) innocence, as the sense of "me" and "mine" and an awareness of the outer world become increasingly and, therefore, "seemingly" real.

As we grow, we progressively separate our "selves" out from others, from "things," and from the environment. Infants, on the other hand, are still a part of wholeness. They have not yet been imprinted with appropriate responses, although the conditioning is taking place a little more every day. Infants have not yet learned fear and shame. Having no past, they feel no guilt. They can "pee" on you or throw up on you without embarrassment. You can look them directly in the eyes and they will look directly back, because they have nothing to hide. Most adults can't do that, although lovers seem able to look longer into each other's eyes than most. I once witnessed two young lovers who sat directly across from each other on a bus. They did not talk; they did not take their eyes off each other; they did not notice the other passengers. This went on for the entire twenty-minute ride. Young lovers—and especially children—are more at "essence."

Words are the tools with which we create the world. They are also forms of delimitation. Once you have a name for something, you will never again look at it without labeling it. "You have made up names for everything you see," the Course tells us. "Each one becomes a separate entity, identified by its own name. By this you carve it out of unity" (W–184.1:2–4). A book once named is a book forever. This delimitation (or limitation) in form keeps us from seeing. We can't remember infancy because there were no words to freeze it into form and, thereby, frame the experiences. This wordless world is full of wonder. You can see it so clearly in a child's eyes. This wonder—this ability to be totally receptive to a limitless reality—is a quality shared by mystics.

Contemporary Hindu spiritual teacher Amma describes this quality in her book *For My Children:* "Look into the eyes of a child. You can see God there. You can see Krishna or Jesus or Buddha in the eyes of a child. But once the dormant or undeveloped *vasanas* [unconscious longings] start manifesting, the innocence will disappear." Infants and mystics are thus much alike in their innocence. The difference is that, one day, the child will long for more, while the mystic will be satisfied with wholeness. "You have not lost your innocence," the Course tells us. "It is for this you yearn. This is your heart's desire. This is the voice you hear, and this the call which cannot be denied. The holy Child remains with you. His home is yours" (W–128.12:1–6). "Go back the way you came," says Ramana Maharshi.

Sleeping Child

You are a child of God, a priceless part of His King-dom, which He created as part of Him. Nothing else exists and only this is real. You have chosen a sleep in which you have had bad dreams, but the sleep is not real and God calls you to awake. (T–6:IV.6:1–3)

Amazement and Imagination

In her book *Practical Mysticism,* Evelyn Underhill describes her childhood mysticism as "abrupt experiences of the peaceful, undifferentiated plane of reality, like the 'still desert' of the mystic." Young children can literally be overwhelmed with mystical experiences. Wonderful memories shine in the experiences of childhood, and some mystics never lose touch with those marvels. Children laugh a lot more than adults; for them, happiness is much more easily found. New discovery plunges them into jubilation, and they spend their lives in the wonderful world of imagination where cartoon characters are real. Santa Claus is real. Fairies are real. Angels are real. Unlike adults with fully formed egos, children don't know that they do not know. Perhaps they *can* talk to God.

Some of the best descriptions of the mysticism of childhood are found in the work of 17th-century English poet and mystic Thomas Traherne, who wrote of the glories of childhood and nature that enlighten the mind through beauty, and of the blissful congruence of being a child in the natural world. By introducing a child's point of view, Traherne brought a new dimension to literature, something unknown before his time. His poems, like those of his fellow English poets William Blake and William Wordsworth, express an uncomplicated, simple love of God. "Your enjoyment of the World is never right," he tells us, "till every morning you awake in Heaven; see yourself in your Father's Palace, and look upon the earth and air as celestial joys, having such reverent esteem of all, as if you were among the Angels." English novelist and poet C. S. Lewis called Traherne's writing the most beautiful books in English, and Trappist mystic Thomas Merton expressed deep gratitude for his work.

Here, Traherne describes his early mystical experiences:

The corn was Orient and immortal Wheat which never should be reaped, nor was ever sown. I thought it had stood from Everlasting to Everlasting. The dust and the stones of the street were as precious as Gold. The gates were at first the end of the world, the green Trees when I saw them first through the gates transported and ravished me; their sweetness and unusual beauty made my heart to leap, and almost mad with ecstasy, they were such strange and wonderful things; The men! O what venerable and reverend creatures did the aged seem! Immortal cherubims! And the young men glittering and sparkling angels and maids strange seraphic pieces of life and beauty. Boys and girls tumbling in the street and playing, were moving jewels. I knew not that they were born or should die.

Similarly, 19th-century Indian mystic Ramakrishna would, as a boy, go into ecstasy at the simplest occurrence in nature. At age fourteen, he was transfixed while watching white cranes flying before the dark clouds of a thunderstorm. To support himself, Ramakrishna became a temple priest. Having little interest in the material world, he meditated for hours each day. His relatives, growing weary of his seeming madness, tried to restore him to sanity by getting him to marry. Resisting domestication, Ramakrishna left the temple, discarded his possessions, and took a vow of poverty. He undertook the practices of Islam, Christianity, and various other faiths, thereby concluding that the goal of all religions is the remembrance of God.

Miracles or Murder?

Be lifted up, and from a higher place look down upon it. From there will your perspective be quite different. Here in the midst of it, it does seem real. Here you have chosen to be part of it. Here murder is your choice. Yet from above, the choice is miracles instead of murder. (T–23.IV.5:1–6)

Children can be so engrossed in imagination and play that they lose awareness of time and the world. Nineteenth-century Russian author Leo Tolstoy gives this description of the mystical awareness of childhood in his book *Childhood, Boyhood, and Youth*:

> The chatter of the peasants, the tramp of the horses and the creaking of the carts, the merry whistle of quail, the hum of insects hovering in the air in motionless swarms, the smell of wormwood, straw and horse's sweat, the thousand different lights and shadows with which the burning sun flooded the light yellow stubble, the dark blue of the distant forest and the pale lilac of the clouds, the white gossamer threads which floated in the air or lay stretched across the stubble, all these things I saw, heard, and felt.

In his book *Silence of the Heart*, American mystic Robert Adams tells of a profound spiritual awakening he experienced at the age of fourteen. Faced with a math test for which he had not studied, he said "God" three times, with an unexpected outcome:

> . . . the room filled with light, a thousand times more brilliant than the sun. . . . It was a beautiful, bright, shining, warm glow. Just thinking of it now makes me stop and wonder. The whole room, everybody, everything was immersed in light. All the children seemed to be myriad particles of light. I found myself melting into radiant being, into

consciousness. . . . It was not an out-of-body experience. This was completely different. I realized that
I was not my body. What appeared to be my body
was not real. I went beyond the light into pure
radiant consciousness. I became omnipresent. My
individuality had merged into pure absolute bliss.
I expanded. I became the universe. . . . It was total
bliss, total joy.

Child of Nature, Child of God

Seeing God in nature is the mysticism of farmers, gardeners,
campers, hikers, all lovers of nature, and all native people. It
is the parks that bring sanity to our cities. Central Park is literally the heart of New York City; Hyde Park plays the same
role in London, as does Hibiya Park in Tokyo. Cities without
parks suffocate. Transcendentalist philosopher Henry David
Thoreau went to the woods "to live deliberately, to confront
the essentials of life, and not learn when it came time to die
that he had not lived."

Nature mysticism is the simplest, oldest, and common-
est form of mysticism. It was the mysticism of the primitive, and so it is for anyone who wishes to take time to stop,
look, and listen to nature's soft whisper. Catholic monk and
author Wayne Teasdale wrote: "Natural mysticism is the
environment of childhood; it is what nurtures us. The child
is exposed to the cosmic revelation from birth and infancy.
This is the child's world, a world that has a fresh, magical,
numinous quality."

My childhood years were bathed in the delightful smells,
sights, and sounds of nature. I feel fortunate to have grown
up on a farm in Missouri during the 1940s and 1950s. There

is an immediacy about farm life that quickens the mind and opens many doors and windows. Weather permitting, all farm boys live life outdoors. There were several children of about my age living on nearby farms—Clifford, Ronnie, Malcolm, Freddie, and Donnie—and the Missouri woods along the Old Salt River were our playground. We worked hard and we played with enthusiasm. As the wheat came out of the hopper on the combine into the back of the truck, the heads of grain poured forth in glorious golden, rainbow colors. When the alfalfa was cut and winnowed, its sweet smell filled the air. We rolled around in it, absorbed in its sweet aroma. In the evening, we sat and listened to tree frogs, katydids, and crickets. On July nights, we stood mesmerized by the flicker of fireflies, the stars, and occasional northern lights. On one of these glorious evenings, I wrote this poem:

THESE SUMMER EVENINGS

Sitting—outside on a summer's evening.
After—a hard day of work.
Our bellies—full of mother's supper.
My father—smoking a cigar.
Talking—about nothing consequential.
Sometimes—not talking at all.
Sitting—watching evening fall.
Listening—to the katydids, tree frogs, and crickets.
And then—the moon, the stars, and the fire-flies.
Sleep—comes so peacefully these summer evenings.

Swiss scientist Albert Hofmann underscores the importance and universality of these visionary experiences, whether found in nature, or outside it. In his book *LSD: My Problem Child*, he writes:

> In studying the literature connected with my work, I became aware of the great universal significance of visionary experience. It plays a dominant role not only in mysticism and the history of religion but also in the creative process in art, literature, and science. More recent investigations have shown that many persons also have visionary experiences in early life, though most of us fail to recognize their meaning and value. Mystical experiences, like those that marked my childhood, are far from rare.

Mystical experiences are best understood in the present tense, as this makes the event more direct and more immediate. Less is lost to the past. Join me here in one of my own early mystical moments.

I am nine, maybe ten, and I'm standing behind our farmhouse. Nothing is happening, which is what makes it mystical. I am looking—seeing—taking in the loveliness of it all. Everything fits together in amazing unity, and I am a part of it. Kittens are playing in the yard, and free-range chickens are busy looking for bugs. It all fits together so wonderfully well. I feel the interconnectedness of it all. It is a bright, sunny perfect sort of a day. Suddenly, unexpectedly, I'm overwhelmed. Tears come to my eyes in awe-inspiring joy and I back up to take it all in. It is all so beautiful! Time stops and I snap an indelible picture in my mind. This is a moment that can never be lost—a little spark, a glimpse into eternity so clear that it can never be forgotten, because it is forever a part of eternity.

Truly Perfect

If nothing but the truth exists, right-minded seeing cannot see anything but perfection. (T–3.II.3:5)

Beyond our ordinary seeing, there is a seeing of wholeness, of perfection, of eternity. I did not have the words for it then—but I knew that I was happy and that everything was as it was supposed to be. It was a perfectly impeccable Holy Instant, beyond fault and flaw and the limitation of time.

Something similar happened again when I was fourteen. While hunting on the back reaches of our farm, I walked through an opening in a grove of trees near the bass pond. I stopped and stood perfectly still—and decided to play a game. I pretended that I didn't exist. Mindless eyes were recording the scene in the woods, like a video camera completely uninvolved in what was happening. And a delicious quietude settled on me—a feeling so peaceful that I knew I would spend the rest of my life looking to confirm this reality, this holy place where only love abides. In my childish way, I named this place "My Heavenly Spot." I wrote of this experience in an earlier book, *Missouri Mystic*. When my mother read the book, she told me that she used to visit the same spot in search of solitude. Almost forty years later, I brought my future wife, Dolores, to this miraculous place.

Chapter 3

Mystical Moments
and Holy Instants

*Sometimes a teacher of God may have a brief
experience of direct union with God. In this world,
it is almost impossible that this endure.*

M–26.3:1–2

One of the main characteristics of a mystical experience
mentioned by William James in his classic *The Varieties of
Religious Experience* is "transience." Mystical experiences are
transitory. They do not last. *A Course in Miracles* calls mystical moments "Holy Instants"—moments outside of time in
which we find ourselves living fully in the present. A Holy
Instant is any moment in which there is no judging and,
therefore, no separation. It is a taste of eternity that lies
beyond the illusion and transience of time.

Holy Instants are moments in which the truth dawns
clearly in the mind. The Course describes them as "the Holy
Spirit's most useful learning device for teaching you love's
meaning. For its purpose is to suspend judgment entirely.
Judgment always rests on the past, for experience is the basis
on which you judge" (T–15.V.1:1–3). Simply put, they are

moments outside of time in which we see through the eyes of Spirit instead of the ego and gain some new knowledge or understanding. There comes, in such moments, the *absolute conviction* that awakening has occurred and we feel blessed. The advantage of a Holy Instant is that, although it is impermanent, it whets the appetite and encourages further seeking for the permanent.

"Perception is a mirror, not a fact," the Course teaches (W–304.1:3). The ability to consistently hold a contemplative state necessitates the dropping of all judgment—all projection. Like a two-way radio, we cannot send and receive at the same time. We cannot be both projective and receptive at once. We cannot see things as they are when we consistently impose our definitions, evaluations, and judgments onto the world. "It is impossible to accept the holy instant without reservation," we learn in the Course, "unless, just for an instant, you are willing to see no past or future" (T–8.VII.4:1).

How Long Is a Holy Instant?

As long as it takes to reestablish perfect sanity, perfect peace, and perfect love for everyone, for God and for yourself. As long as it takes to remember immortality, and your immortal creations who share it with you. As long as it takes to exchange hell for Heaven. Long enough to transcend all of the ego's making, and ascend unto your Father. (T–15.I.14:1–5)

A Holy Instant is a moment outside of time when we see clearly. It is thus "a miniature of eternity . . . a picture of timelessness in a frame of time" (T–17.IV.11:4). Simply being present frees us from the trap of time. God knows us in the present—in the *now*. "He remembers nothing, having always known you exactly as He knows you now," the Course reminds us. "The holy instant reflects His knowing by bringing all perception out of the past, thus removing the frame of reference you have built by which to judge your brothers" (T–15.V.IX.1–2). The Course asks us to *resign now* as our own teachers and become aware of a wisdom that is greater than our own.

Holy Instants are not full experiences of eternity, but previews of a possibility. They are any instant in which there is no guilt—any moment when there comes a recognition in others and ourselves of a profound innocence. Only then is it possible to return the "mind" to "the Mind." You are not in charge, and you don't want to be. How nice it is not to direct. Sit back and let Spirit take the lead. "To learn to separate out this single second, and to experience it as timeless," the Course promises, "is to begin to experience yourself as not separate" (T–15.II.6:1–3).

Holy Instants are times "in which you receive and give perfect communication . . . in which your mind is open, both to receive and give. In these moments, you recognize that all minds are in communication. You seek to change nothing, *but merely to accept everything*" (T–15.IV.6:1–8).

Intuition and Insight

As mini-mystical experiences, Holy Instants are usually fleeting. And they can take on different manifestations that differ in subtle ways—from epiphany, to insight, to recollection, to a literal re-cognition. An epiphany is a sudden intuitive perception into the reality of the essence of something. It usually comes on suddenly, like a blaze of lightning, but is often preceded by a lot of contemplation. A Course student may study the Workbook lessons for a long time before enlightenment strikes.

As the mystic's way is a way of inner searching, sometimes awakening comes as an abrupt insight into something that was already there—literally an *in-sight*. Twelfth-century German mystic Hildegard of Bingen said that each of her great revelations was received *in an instant*. Fourteenth-century Bridget of Sweden said that her entire book was given to her *in a flash*. Likewise, Serbian-American electrical engineer Nikola Tesla said that his idea for alternating current came to him *in a flash*, while English physicist Stephen Hawking said that his greatest insight came to him one evening as he was getting into bed. Einstein called intuition "the only real valuable thing." Of course, Tesla, Einstein, and Hawking had already spent many hours in contemplation and study before their respective solutions suddenly became clear. German composer Wolfgang Amadeus Mozart said he received entire sonatas in an instant. He just had to write down what he heard in his mind.

Divine revelation comes in the same way. Revelation as a direct communion with God has nothing to do with words or time. Suddenly, we "know" something we have always known, but now we see anew. In *Mysticism,* Underhill calls it an "act of perfect concentration, the passionate focusing of the self upon one point." In the language of mysticism, she claims, this is "the state of recollection."

Spontaneous, intuitive inspiration is beyond the realm of the ego. Since we are "well-habituated" to the ways of the ego, it takes a great deal of work to free ourselves from its agitations. The Course is extraordinarily redundant, saying the same thing in many ways. We must often hear the truth from many angles before we see it clearly. When truth does become clear, however, it comes with remarkable clarity and suddenness, helping us to resist later temptations to be impatient or judgmental.

While insight is an affair of the head, intuition is more of a *gut-heart* experience. It is fast, automatic, natural, and not always available for inspection. It is also frequently emotionally charged. As we come to live a "natural" life, intuition develops "naturally," bringing us to an awareness of truth. Often, it's a *feeling* leading to an understanding of why certain events are occurring as they are. Ralph Waldo Emerson described it thus: "Whilst the doors of the temple stand open, night and day, before every man, the oracles of this truth cease never, it is guarded by one stern condition, this, namely; it is an intuition."

On the other hand, déjà vu—the French expression meaning "already seen"—describes a first-hand experience of timelessness or the simultaneity of experience. This minimystical moment provides insight into the unity or Oneness of all things. It represents a stepping outside of time. If you're with someone and you have an experience of déjà vu, resist the temptation to share it. The ego likes to brag. Wait until the experience stops. If you open your mouth, you will lose the experience by trying to bring it into form. Hang with it—you can always talk about it after the fact.

Nothing New

In the holy instant nothing happens that has not always been. Only the veil that has been drawn across reality is lifted. Nothing has changed. Yet the awareness of changelessness comes swiftly as the veil of time is pushed aside. (T–15.VI.6:1–3)

Atonement

Atonement, as described by the Course, is the process by which we remove the blocks we have built to an awareness of love's (God's) presence. This is the same goal sought in mystical processes described by most religions. There is a Self that is forever connected with God and thus, forever, a part of eternity. This Self has gotten covered over by an artificial self that we call the ego masquerading as the true Self. The self we create in the world, however, is not who we are in truth. Only by relinquishing this pretense of a self can we remember our eternal Home in God.

The ego is a charade, a pretext, a deception lacking in reality of any kind. Italian sculptor Michelangelo said: "The best artist has that thought alone which is contained within the marble shell; the sculptor's hand can only break the spell to free the figures slumbering in the stone." We are all, like Michaelangelo, seeking to free the Self that has been covered over by a veil of guilt, fear, and separation. All that a mystical experience does is to remove the veil we have created in the world by looking at the ego and recognizing it for what it is—nothing. When we choose the ego (separation), we create a fantasy world and thereby lose sight of the real world of Oneness. Our task is simply to undo the illusion.

---

1 + 1 = One

Revelation unites you directly with God. Miracles unite you directly with your brother. (T–1.II.1:5)

No one is excluded from Heaven, and the "Perfect Communication" of the Course is available to everyone. We remember "together." Every mind is already there, already included. In the outside world of time, space, and separation, however, survival is dependent upon exclusion, on limitation. Thus, we set out to destroy those "enemies"—those external, separate illusions—that seem to threaten our survival. In Atonement, however, "the past is gone, and with its passing the drive for vengeance has been uprooted and has disappeared. The stillness and the peace of *now* enfold you in perfect gentleness. Everything is gone except the truth" (T–16.VII.6:3–6).

A holy relationship of Atonement is simply the expression of the Holy Instant in this world. It is a moment of complete sanity in which the mind is host to God rather than hostage to the ego. Only by recognizing our own insanity can we begin to let it go.

Falling in love is often the first transcendent experience we can identify with as truly mystical. It doesn't matter with what or with whom we fall in love—another person, an animal, music, nature, a field of knowledge, a craft, an art, or an activity like dancing or swimming or playing an instrument. The soul longs to fall in love again and again. The trick is not to lose the awareness we gain in such moments. To fall in love is to remember God. In fact, everyone is already 100 percent love. All we need do is remember what is already there.

When we fall in love, we are flooded with a deep, intense feeling of joy. We feel transported. We feel a sense of emotional freedom, along with beautiful thoughts and images of our beloved. Our feet don't quite touch the ground. We are bathed in emotion. Falling in love is bigger than we are. The more we let it happen, the more it will happen. Still, be careful—fools do, indeed, rush in. Be watchful. The ego is tricky; it can kick back in and tempt we to be judgmental. Love is innocent and often also blind. True love is forever.

Dreaming

Dreams are altered states in which we temporarily abandon the rational mind. They are a way for the subconscious (whole) to communicate with the conscious (part). Freud called them "the Royal Road to the unconscious." The Course tells us that the Holy Spirit "has use for sleep, and can use dreams on behalf of waking if you will let Him" (T–8.IX.3:8). But dreams contain many of the ego's symbols, so they can sometimes be fearful and confusing.

I remember one dream I had while on a return flight to New York from the West Coast. Although I did not realize it because I was sleeping, the plane was going through a bit of turbulence. I dreamed that I was driving a car with my eyes closed. My hands, which were in my lap as I slept, were not on the steering wheel. It was very scary. I realized within the context of the dream that I had to stop the car, but I had no idea where I was or what was around me. I struggled to open my eyes and finally, with some effort, succeeded, only to realize that I was on an airplane, not in a car, and now quite awake and free of this fearful dream.

I took the dream as an interesting metaphor. All we need do is awaken and our nightmarish dream world will be gone. "Rest in the Holy Spirit," the Course teaches, "and allow His gentle dreams to take the place of those you dreamed in terror and in fear of death. He brings forgiving dreams, in which the choice is not who is the murderer and who shall be the victim. In the dreams He brings there is no murder and there is no death" (T–27.VII.14:3–8).

Although many dreams are ego-oriented and replay surface desires and anxieties, dreams can also grant us access to a larger world. Dreams are telling us something and, if we look carefully, we can learn from their guidance. Carl Jung called dreams "the small hidden door in the deepest and most intimate sanctum of the soul, which opens to that primeval cosmic night that was soul long before there was conscious ego and will be soul far beyond what a conscious ego could ever reach."

While "surface dreams" are concerned with daily anxieties or problem-solving, dreams are also metaphorical. If we listen and watch carefully, we can find lessons in our dreams—perhaps even the voice of God. In *Dreams: God's Forgotten Language,* John Sanford tells us to look carefully at the messages that come in our dreams. Dreams can also introduce us to our shadow when we do things in them we would not do in an awakened world. By looking at the dark side of ourselves, we can begin to relinquish some of the shadow's power over us.

Chapter 4

Modern Mysticism

The narrow path of the mystic's climb begins
where the philosopher's broad road leaves off.
—Evelyn Underhill, *Mysticism*

Except among American Transcendentalists and German Idealists, little general interest in "the science of mysticism" was evident prior to the latter part of the 19th century. The beginning of the 20th century, however, saw a flowering of interest in mysticism because of the newly developing field of psychology. At the same time, Catholic scholars became more interested in the experiences of some their most famous mystics, like 12th-century Saint Francis of Assisi and 16th-century Saint Teresa of Avila. A lot can be learned about mysticism and its relationship to psychology by following the works of scholars working in this crucial period.

The first book I ever read on mysticism was Richard M. Bucke's 1901 book, *Cosmic Consciousness,* which I found in our small town's local library when I was sixteen. On a buggy ride in England, feeling inspired by one of Walt Whitman's poems, Bucke had a great illumination—what he later called "cosmic consciousness"—in which he realized that the cosmos was "fully alive." Humans have immortal souls and the Universe is constructed in such a way that all things work toward the good. Love is the most basic force in the Universe.

Bucke described cosmic consciousness as "a transpersonal awareness of the universal mind and oneness with it. Mystical or cosmic consciousness is primarily an awareness of the life and order of the universe." A person with this consciousness is aware of immortality as something he or she "already" has. Bucke believed that the occurrence of mystical experiences had been on the rise throughout history, and this steady increase in divine revelation would one day obviate the need for organized religion and find a way to end all war.

Cosmic Consciousness

- An intuitive, non-intellectual, and ineffable awareness.

- An elevated moral awareness and an inability to hurt others.

- Freedom from sin, guilt, and fear.

- An awareness of immortality.

- Freedom from fear of death.

- A definitive peak experience and a moment of transformation.

- An intellectual illumination or revelation.

William James was a contemporary of Bucke who taught the first class in psychology as a separate science at Harvard in 1885. His *Principles of Psychology* was one of the first textbooks on psychology. In 1901, James delivered a series of lectures known as the Gifford Lectures, which were collected in print under the title *Varieties of Religious Experience*. Here, James closely echoed Bucke's description of cosmic consciousness in the characteristics he ascribed to mysticism. Mystical experiences, James wrote, are ineffable and beyond our capacity to express in words. They are passive, in that they seem to happen to or through us without our direction. They are transient—that is, time stops or the mystical experience seems to happen outside of time. And they have a "noetic" quality, in that, through them, we come to "know" something profound.

Building on these insights, Rudolf Otto, a professor of systematic theology at the University of Marburg, in his book *The Idea of the Holy*, coined the word "numinous" to define the mystical. Numinous comes from the Latin word *numen*, which means "a non-rational, non-sensory experience or feeling whose primary and immediate object is outside the self." According to Otto, mystical experiences all share five characterisitics: they induce a sense of "awe" or fullness; they feel overpowering; they impart a sense of energy or urgency; they carry a feeling of being "Wholly Other"; and they contain an element of fascination.

Same Flower, Different Garden

Whether the flower of mysticism blooms in India or in China, in Persia or on the Rhine, its fruit is one. (Rudolf Otto)

Like James, Evelyn Underhill described four characteristics she found common to all mysticism, although her descriptions vary slightly from James's. Mysticism, she argued, is an entirely spiritual activity, in no way concerned with adding to, exploring, rearranging, or improving anything in the visible Universe. The business and method of mysticism, she concluded, is love. It draws the whole being Homeward, always under the guidance of the heart. It is an experience of the whole Self. And most important—for Underhill, as for James—mysticism entails a definite psychological experience arrived at by arduous psychological and spiritual progress. Thus it is essentially practical, not theoretical.

"The disastrous feature of our civilization," French-German philosopher and physician Albert Schweitzer observed, "is that it is far more developed materially than spiritually." This observation is no doubt even more relevant today than when he made it 100 years ago. Schweitzer's interest in mysticism led him to appreciate the Pauline concept of "being in Christ" as the most important concept in Christianity.

In his book *Paul and His Interpreters: A Critical History*, Schweitzer distinguishes between three categories of mysticism.

Primitive mysticism: a view of union with Divinity brought about by esoteric ceremonies found in the most primitive of religions, including the rites and rituals still observed in Christianity, Judaism, and Islam. These attempts at "devotion," he concluded, are moving in the right direction, but fall far short of true mystical experience.

Pauline mysticism: a more advanced and intellectual form of mystical experience involving a mystical union with Christ, which is ultimately the same as being one with God.

Universal mysticism: a more developed form of mysticism found in the Greek mystery religions, in which a conception of the universal is reached by an actual experience of a relationship with the totality of Being. In its intellectual form, this concept of mysticism is found among Buddhists and Brahmins, in Platonism and Stoicism, and in the writings of 17th-century Dutch philosopher Spinoza and the 19th-century German philosophers Hegel and Schopenhauer.

No discussion of the development of modern mysticism would be complete without considering the work of Swiss psychiatrist Carl Jung, who must be included as a pioneer in the field of mystical studies. Although Jung claimed that he was not a mystic but a scientist, he dove deeply into what he called the "collective unconscious" and found there a wealth of information. Through a study of alchemy, he discovered a vast array of archetypal images, including patterns of thought and images present in the psyche of mankind. Unlike his contemporaries Underhill and Schweitzer, however, he never devised a list of characteristics of the mystical state. Nonetheless, he sounds much like a mystic when he writes, in *Man and His Symbols*:

> From the standpoint of the gods this world is less than child's play; it is a seed in the earth, a mere potentiality. Our whole world of consciousness is only a seed of the future. And when you succeed in the awakening of Kundalini, so that she begins to move out of her mere potentiality, you necessarily start a world which is a world of eternity, totally different from our world.

Romanian scholar Mircea Eliade, another major contributor to the study of mysticism, saw it as central to genuine religion. Influenced by Rudolf Otto, Eliade wrote extensively on what he called the "eternal return"—the belief that religious behavior, as a participation in sacred events, restores mythic time. In his 1954 *Cosmos and History: The Myth of the Eternal Return*, he argues that the perception of linear time is different from an awareness of sacred time, which he saw as cyclical.

Building on all these scholars and philosophers, humanistic psychologist Abraham Maslow made a major contribution to contemporary mysticism in *Religions, Values, and Peak-Experiences*, where he defined a mystical, or peak, experience as "one of those times when the entire pretense of the personality and all fear drops away, and we seem to be in touch with the whole universe."

In 1969, Sir Alister Hardy, author of *The Flame*, a book on the evolution of religion, founded the Religious Experience Research Center to investigate the nature of mystical experiences. Originally located at Oxford University, the Center is now located at the University of Wales. It sponsors lectures, publishes journals, and has a distance-learning program as well as onsite presentations. Hardy's organization has studied thousands of descriptions of mystical experiences in an effort to determine their primary causes. In one study, respondents were asked to identify what triggered their experiences. The results are given below as the number of mentions per 1,000 experiences, in descending order of frequency:

- Depression and despair: 183

- Meditation and contemplation: 136

- Natural beauty: 123

- Participation in worship, chanting: 111

- Literature, drama, film: 82

- Illness: 80

- Music: 56

- Crises in personal relations: 37

- Grief; death of a loved one: 28

- Sacred places: 26

- Visual arts: 24

- Creative work: 20

- Prospect of death: 15

- Silence, solitude: 15

- Anesthetic drugs: 11

- Physical activity: 10

- Relaxation: 10

- Childbirth: 9

- Happiness: 7

- Psychedelic drugs: 7

- Sexual relations: 4

Hardy's contribution to the scientific study of religion is reviewed in David Hay's book *Something There: The Biology of the Human Spirit*.

Since these pioneers, several good books on mysticism and a great deal of research and writing in the field have appeared. In addition, we now have the insights of various scholars who have done psychological analyses of the mystical state. Last, but not least, are the testimonies of thousands of individuals who have experienced mystical awareness. Together, these provide the ground of contemporary mysticism.

Mysticism as Perennial Philosophy

The term "perennial"—meaning "persistent" or "enduring"—was coined by 18th-century German philosopher Gottfried Wilhelm Leibniz. Perennial philosophy is also called *universal* because it shows up in all cultures—from Asia to Africa, from Europe to the Americas. The perennial view holds that, because there is one core of truth, when we study the diversity of mystical experience, we are looking at one phenomenon with many different expressions found in many different cultures over a vast period. Mystics and sages from a variety of different places and times record similar perceptions about the nature of the Self, reality, the world, and the purpose of existence. Aldous Huxley popularized this term in his book *Perennial Philosophy*.

Mysticism, when seen as perennial or universal, is the height of religion, because it includes all attempts to reach the beyond within the heart/mind/soul/Self. Regardless of how they are practiced, each of the great world religions receives its most sublime interpretations from the mystics. Lao Tzu, Buddha, Jesus, Nanak, Mahavira, and the founders of various other religious traditions were not institution-builders. They were mystics and teachers. As 19th-century Indian Swami Vivekananda expressed it: "Mystics in every religion speak the same tongue and teach the same truth."

Mysticism 101

By combining the insights of pioneers in modern mysticism, we can construct the following definition. Mystical experience is:

1. An experience of God.

2. An experience with intellectual, emotional, and sensory components.

3. An experience that includes personal transformation and fascination.

4. An ineffable feeling that cannot be described in words, only pointed to.

5. A noetic experience that includes an awareness of immortality.

6. A simple and yet profound existential state.

7. A transcendental moment that happens outside of time.

8. A passive event in which all control is gladly turned over to God.

9. A practical, not purely theoretical, event that leads to action.

10. A nonjudgmental event not aimed at changing or fixing others.

11. An experience in which there is no subject-object, only Oneness.

12. An "oceanic" experience in which all blends and melts into Oneness.

13. A perception of freedom from sin, guilt, and fear.

14. An existential sense of awe, wonder, joy, and bliss.

15. An event that leads to a state of enlightenment.

16. A state in which love, truth, and God are all that remain.

Chapter 5

Mysticism and Traditional Religion

*When the will is really free it cannot
miscreate, because it recognizes only truth.*

T–2.II.2:7

Free will is a gift from God. It is one of the things that make us divine. We must have free will because God is free; thus, as part of God, we must also be free. Mystics freely pursue the truth of God. And mystics are teachers. In a sense, they have to be, and it comes to them quite naturally. But, as the Course tells us: "Free will does not mean that you can establish the curriculum. It means only that you can elect what you want to take at a given time" (T-in.–1:4–5). Persian philosopher Zoroaster and the Indian founder of Jainism, Mahavira, were both mystics and teachers, as were Buddha, Jesus, and Mohammad. What they taught was *given* to them by divine inspiration—by mystical experience.

"Religions start from mysticism," writes Trappist David Steindl-Rast. "There is no other way to start a religion." Eventually, however, religions tend to lose their direct ties to the mystical experiences from which they grew:

I compare this to a volcano that gushes forth . . . and then . . . the magma flows down the sides of the mountain and cools off. And when it reaches the bottom, it's just rocks. You'd never guess that there was fire in it. So, after a couple of hundred years, or two thousand years or more, what was once alive is dead rock. Doctrine becomes doctrinaire. Morals become moralistic. Ritual becomes ritualistic. What do we do with it? We have to push through this crust and go to the fire that's within it.

Unlike traditional religions, however, mysticism has no hierarchy, no creeds, no laws or dogma. It has no required ways of believing and worshipping. There are no buildings, priests, ministers, or reverends—although priests, ministers, and reverends may very well be mystics. Indeed, it is the call of God that has drawn them into their profession. Mystics know that there are certain laws basic to happiness that are writ large in the Universe. When life is lived in accordance with God's laws, things work out. When life is lived in conflict with them, it takes a little longer. Italian mystic Aegidius of Assisi, a disciple of Saint Francis, once said: "I know a man who saw God so clearly that he lost all religion."

Rules, Regulations, and Freedom

The word "religion" comes from the Latin *religio,* which means "to constrain, to restrain, or to tie back." It also means "the observance of a rule." Catholic Holy Orders are grounded in sets of rules established to control their members. Monks' lives are strictly regulated by rules that define their diurnal activities—from waking to praying, from eating in silence to singing the offices, from working to worshipping.

Mystics, on the other hand, follow an inner guidance— naturally. While rules, laws, and required ways of living tend to make traditional religions concrete and inflexible— focused on the past—mysticism remains ever in the present. Where organized religions emphasize belief, mysticism follows intuition and revelation, avoiding dogma and doctrine. As we learn in the Course: "The higher mind thinks according to the laws spirit obeys, and therefore honors only the laws of God" (T–5.I.1:6).

No Errors

In the service of the right mind the denial of error frees the mind, and reestablishes the freedom of the will. When the will is really free it cannot miscreate, because it recognizes only truth. (T–2.II.2:6)

By the early Middle Ages, the Church had become so rule-bound that even the lowest of peasants resented being under the thumb of ecclesiastical power. In many places, the Church was more powerful than the local government; in fact, in numerous provinces in Europe, the Church *was* the government. By the time of the Protestant Reformation, the Catholic Church had become so top heavy with rules and governance that it was almost inevitable that its power structures would be questioned. Foremost among those who questoned the status quo were the mystics. But prophets always run afoul of the establishment. The Reformation was thus prefaced by the deaths of thousands of mystics who, in the name of truth, literally gave up their bodies to the "bonfires" of the Church. And when mystics become martyrs, it's almost inevitable that a following will spring up based on their teachings.

English author George Orwell, in his book *1984,* has one of his characters say: "Orthodoxy means not thinking, not needing to think. Orthodoxy is unconsciousness." Mysticism transcends beliefs precisely because it is a *direct* experience, not an orthodoxy or a doctrine. "All beliefs," the Course points out, "are real to the believer" (T–3.VII.3:3). When mystics describe their experiences, they are not repeating a catechism or a creed. The truth needs no orthodoxy, doctrine, or defense. Once there is an established church, there is a hierarchy, a system, and a set of rules. And in any hierarchical command, egos rule. Moreover, history shows that almost all hierarchies become despotic.

Nineteenth-century French author Victor Hugo observed: "Religions pass away, but God remains." A nonpracticing Catholic, Hugo called himself a "rationalist deist." Deism is the belief that God created the world with rational, universal laws (in Mind) and lets those laws play out without interference. While deists believe in God, they often do not follow any specific religion. According to Hugo: "The one most undeniable fact of Life is the reality of God." Mystics affirm the "undeniable fact" of God through intuition and heart-centered direct experience, but do so in a highly reasonable way. After all, the Course points out: "Reason will tell you that the only way to escape from misery is to recognize it and *go the other way"* (T–22.II.4:1). What could be more simple and reasonable? Be willing to look inside. See what is "really" going on. And, if you do not like what you see—go the other way. We need no external authority. (God works inside every mind, gently guiding us Home.)

Hugo developed an antipathy toward the Church's arrogance, its wealth, and its indifference to the plight of the poor. Not surprisingly, his books were condemned and placed on the *Index Librorum,* a list of books deemed to be heretical. Hugo predicted that the Church would one day suffocate under the weight of its own dogma. Christianity, he said, would one day disappear, but people would still believe in "God, Soul, and Heaven." "There is only one thing more powerful than all the armies of the world," Hugo famously said, "and that is an idea whose time has come."

Twentieth-century Islamic scholar Idries Shah, who wrote over three dozen books on the interconnection of psychology and spirituality, observed that most people feel comfortable with organized religion because it keeps them within the walls of habits. Mysticism, however, is freedom, and the Course is a pathway to that freedom. As Noble Laureate and philosopher Steven Weinberg points out: "With or without religion, you would have good people doing good things and evil people doing evil things. But for good people to do evil things, that takes religion."

No Pain, Only Gain

You cannot be hurt, and do not want to show your brother anything except your wholeness. Show him that he cannot hurt you and hold nothing against him, or you hold it against yourself. (T–5.IV.4:4–5)

wwwwwwwwwwwwwwwwwwwwwwwwwwwwwwwwwwwwwwwwwwwwwwwwwwwwwwwwwwwwwwwwwwwwwwwwwwwwwwwwww

It takes religion to inflict evil on others and justify it in the name of God. God is foremost and forever love. Jesuit mystic Anthony de Mello, best known for his best-selling books *Contact with God* and *The Song of the Bird,* sums up the role of established religion like this: "Religion is a fruitless effort to mark a pathway on the shifting sands of the desert. The infinite cannot be trapped, described, or noted. We are one with the infinite even as we pretend that we are not."

City with No Gate

Mysticism, unlike established religion, is completely free and open to anyone at any time. You join this invisible, non-dues-paying club by realizing that you are *already* a mystic. No other qualifications are needed. You may be male or female; nine or ninety; black, white, brown, or polka-dotted. There is no pledge you must make, no oath you must take, and no contract to sign. You don't even have to make weekly contributions! This is its power and its glory.

Mysticism is non-church, nondenominational, nonhierarchical spirituality. While a mystic may be a part of any religion, mysticism ultimately transcends all doctrinal perspectives. All "structures," all forms—even the seemingly solid ones—pass away when a greater truth is realized. Nineteenth-century Danish theologian Søren Kierkegaard even went so far as to claim that institutional religion subverted individual awareness and hampered the opportunity to experience the truth. Indeed, the goal of the mystic, he claimed, was to step away from all these illusions.

Likewise, mystic Jiddu Krishnamurti, who was born in India but spent most of his life in the United States, taught an interfaith perspective that transcended the man-made limitations of religion, nationality, ideology, and sectarian thinking. He disavowed ritual and dogma and refused to play the role of a guru. He urged his listeners to be a light unto themselves, telling them ". . . liberation is available, here—now." His primary teaching centered on freedom from the ego:

> Truth, being limitless, unconditioned, unapproach-
> able by any path whatsoever, cannot be organized;
> nor should any organization be formed to lead or
> coerce people along a particular path. The moment
> you follow someone You cease to follow Truth. I am
> concerning myself with only one essential thing: to
> set man free.

It is easy to get trapped in our own interpretations, judgments, and analyses—all of which keep us from seeing and from knowing God's plan for salvation. Although we can keep salvation hidden from ourselves, following God's plan is the most joyous journey Home—to a "place" we never left. We are *all, always,* headed Home, even if we are not aware of the journey. A mystic is simply someone who is actively looking for the truth. Now and then, mystics experience Holy Instants in which higher awareness is attained and through which, with time, a deeper more permanent state of being is realized.

Chapter 6

Mysticism as a Journey

You will undertake a journey because you are not at home in this world. And you will search for your home whether you realize where it is or not. If you believe it is outside you the search will be futile, for you will be seeking it where it is not.

T–12.IV.5:1–3

Why we are here? Life must be about more than earning money, raising a family, eating, sleeping, and dying. Are we simply strangers in a strange land, each ego dreaming its life away? A mystic is someone who *knows*—who senses deeply inside—that the world the individual ego sees is not reality. In myth after myth—from the biblical story of the prodigal son, to Bunyan's *The Pilgrim's Progress*, to Castaneda's *Journey to Ixtlan*—we hear the story of a seeker on a journey, and the destination is always Home, or Heaven. And where does the journey end? What is the end of the story? The end of the story is an awakening and the realization that Home, or Heaven, is a place we never left.

Mystics often describe their passage through the world as a process that involves different stages or levels of spiritual development. They chart their journeys by degrees and stations. We see it in Jacob's ladder extending to Heaven (Genesis 28:12) and in 13th-century Saint Bonaventure's "pilgrimage of the soul." Fourteenth-century Flemish mystic Jan Van Ruysbroeck, who emphasized the detachment, humility, and clarity of the mystic's path, noted three stages of progress in what he called the "Ladder of Attainment": the active life, the inward life, and the contemplative life. Fourteenth-century English mystic Walter Hilton likewise described a "ladder to perfection." If we study the various stages of spiritual development in the writings of the mystics, it is easy to see the similarities of these various stages in each spiritual path.

A Course in Miracles also speaks of a "ladder of separation," down which we have descended into illusion, and another ladder that leads us back across the "Bridge to the Real World." We make this journey through several different levels of perception to arrive at the place where there is just one Mind free of division.

Levels or stages of spiritual development are more clearly seen as we look backward over the path we have trod. As Danish philosopher and mystic Søren Kierkegaard explained it: "Life must be lived forward but it can only be understood backward." What was meaningless before becomes the lesson we needed to learn. Serious students develop a sense of astuteness, perspicacity, and discernment about what is essential and what they can let go of on their spiritual journeys. From an early point in life, some people are clear about being "called" and therefore are on a spiritual path. Others may have little or no awareness of any spiritual path until something happens—perhaps the death of a loved one, or a health issue that forces them to take a closer look at life.

Reality as Parable

A myth, or story, is a metaphor for life. Since we cannot see the ineffable with physical sight, we sometimes need symbolism to make it more clear. In mystical literature, the "translator" that makes the ineffable knowable is often the myth, the metaphor, the tale, the dream—the story.

The Gospel of Matthew tells us that Jesus never spoke to people directly, but always taught through stories called parables (Matthew 13:10–15). Twentieth-century German theologian Rudolf Bultmann spoke of the parables of Jesus as stories about *the other side* told in terms of *this side*. A story plants a seed; its theme remains after the story is told. Without parables, the teachings of Jesus would sound like those of many philosophers—profound, but unengaging. The meaning of his message is understood on a deeper level because of the illustrative quality of the parables he used to teach it. The imagery of the stories provides a hint of something more. We often hear more in poetry or music than we do in essays; we can intuit more from a surrealist work than we can from a realistic one.

Moreover, Jesus's life itself is a parable, a description of the pathway to the Kingdom. At an early age, he was sure of his destiny. Tormented, crucified, and given every reason to be angry, Jesus, like any true mystic, remained faithful to his clear perception of God's call. From Bethlehem to Golgotha, his is a Hero's journey. It is also your story and mine. It belongs to each one of us—unique and divine.

In the 1960s, I enjoyed reading the work of British-born American mystic Alan Watts, who was largely responsible for introducing the then-expanding New Age culture to Zen Buddhism. In his 1957 book *The Way of Zen,* Watts defines mythology as "an image by which we try to make sense of the world." Mythology and parables are both ways of sharing the ineffable, abstract truth of ultimate reality.

To decode this abstract truth, however, we have to look at what is going on beneath the story. We have to "demytholo-gize" the story to find out what it is saying on a psychological level. A myth is not "true" in any literal sense, but the "story" has an impact on the human psyche. I use the word "psyche" here in its broadest sense, to refer to the whole mental and psychological structure of a person—the heart, mind, soul, and spirit of which we are all a part. Because we are One, we all share truth on a psychic level—always.

Individuation and the Mystic Journey

In the spring of 1973, I was privileged to attend a seminar titled Hero Mythology taught by Joseph Campbell, who is regarded as the 20th century's greatest mythologist. Much of Campbell's work is based on Jung, who, in turn, built upon the work of Freud. But while Freud explored the unconscious, Jung looked deeper into the collective psyche of mankind to see what he could find in dreams, myths, fairy tales, and the esoteric sciences—alchemy in particular. Jung described spiritual growth as the *process of individuation*, the gradual integration and unification of the Self. Individuation, according to Jung, was a "coming to terms of the inborn germ of wholeness with the outer acts of fate."

All or Nothing

The Course gives us this simple prayer: "Let me remember that my self is nothing and my Self is All." (W–358.1:7)

While the goal of God remains the same for everyone, however, the spiritual pathway is highly individualized. And although the result of the mythic journey—namely, God realization—remains the same, each mystic's story has a unique expression in time. According to Campbell: "The adventure of the hero is the adventure of being alive." There is a unique path for each of us. If the path we are following in life isn't clear, then, he said, we must follow one of the world's prescribed paths; and that is always frustrating, as then you feel you're missing out on something.

What we're missing out on is meaning and purpose. The Course calls problems set up to be incapable of solution "favorite ego devices for impeding learning progress" and tells us that these diversionary tactics simply keep us from asking "the one question that is never asked by those who pursue them . . . *What for?*" This, the Course insists "is the question that *you* must learn to ask in connection with everything. What is the purpose?" Whatever it is, we are assured, "it will direct your efforts automatically" (T–4.V.6:6–10).

Mysticism is a journey, but it is not like just taking a train to a given destination. Mystical awareness comes slowly into flower. The flower possesses its beauty while still in the seed, but it must be drawn out. The mystical dimension comes as we let go, or surrender to a Mind that seems much greater than our own, even though we already know something of it. The mystical comes as we "forgive," "let go," and "surrender" the ego self to something much bigger than our "little self." As the Course explains it:

> Forgiveness is acquired. It is not inherent in the mind, which cannot sin. As sin is an idea you taught yourself, forgiveness must be learned by you as well, but from a Teacher other than yourself, Who represents the other Self in you. Through Him you learn how to forgive the self you think you made, and let it disappear. Thus you return your mind as one to Him Who is your Self, and Who can never sin. (W–121.6:1–5)

As light is key to the growth of a flower, the knowledge that comes with the disrobing of the ego is key for the mystical journey. Belief in the body and separation made the ability to perceive physicality possible. In other words, we must perceive *something* (an object) with *something* (physical senses), and the brain gives what we perceive meaning. Accordingly, perception involves an exchange, or translation. Pure knowing, however, needs no exchange between the perceiver, what is perceived, and its meaning. According to Ramana Maharshi: "Form is always limitation. Pure Being is unhampered by form." As we relinquish the ego world—as we begin to be progressively free of our illusions—we find truth. When the world of ego has been completely removed, then comes the realization of Self. When the mind, which is the cause of all cognition and all actions, becomes quiescent, the ego world disappears.

Pure being just *is* without a separate object of perception. Pure knowing comes, like Atonement, when we willingly let go of the misperception that seemingly changed us into a body and an ego—a "place" we mistakenly perceived as Home.

Joy in Sharing

God, Who encompasses all being, created beings who have everything individually, but who want to share it to increase their joy. Nothing real can be increased except by sharing. That is why God created you. Divine Abstraction takes joy in sharing. (T–4.VII.5:1–4)

As mystics, we are involved in an inner process of realization—an inner stirring or awakening. The deeper we dig, the greater our sense of *kismet*, an awareness of an inner fate that guides our lives. While the journey to God is inevitable for everyone, it slowly becomes clear to us that we are, indeed, on a journey and are headed Home. As seekers, we proceed and regress, proceed and regress. Something is gained when we move forward; something is gained when we retreat. Whether we are aware of the spiritual process or not, it is still there.

The more we become aware of the journey of realization— the more we make a living connection with it—the richer our lives become. The less aware we are of an inner life, the more our lives seem to lack meaning. If we walk through life mindlessly, we have a sense that we're missing out on something important. In Maya's house (the constantly changing world of time and space), there are many illusions. Thus, the journey is one of separating out the false from the true. The task is to discover why we came here and what our destiny must be. Life becomes meaningful as we give in to the urge toward creative self-realization and expression.

The Pilgrim's Progress

After the parables of Jesus, John Bunyan's *The Pilgrim's Progress* is perhaps the most famous Christian allegory. As required reading in Protestant schools in the 18th and 19th centuries, it was second in sales only to the Bible until the beginning of the 20th century. *The Pilgrim's Progress* is the story of a hero named Christian who goes off in search of the Celestial City (Heaven). He carries many burdens on his back and must go through a series of trials, including the Slough of Despond, the Valley of Humiliation, and the Valley of the Shadow of Death. As he goes through these various experiences, he sheds his burdens and finally arrives at the Celestial City completely naked (unburdened). We bring nothing with us into Heaven.

Christian's journey is mirrored in almost all mythological traditions. From ancient to modern times, we find stories of heroes and heroines who go in search of a greater destiny. The Hero leaves home, ventures into a strange land, encounters difficulties, and falls prey to a variety of forces and illusions. The good news is that the journey is not taken alone. "You will not take this journey alone," the Course assures us. "I will lead you to your true Father, Who hath need of you, as I have. Will you not answer the call of love with joy?"

(T–11.in.4:6–8). The Hero thus departs on the journey with a guide, who provides tools to help with the tasks that will be met along the way.

When we accept the call to journey, we can count on help. The life of Jesus is full of protective guides—angels and wise men who appear at his birth, for instance. In myths, a caring figure often appears—an old man or woman, a medicine man, a hermit, a shepherd, an escort, a shaman, a smithy, a ferryman or pilot, or other similar figures. Moses speaks directly to God. Cinderella has her fairy godmother. King Arthur has Merlin. Luke Skywalker has Obi-wan Kenobi and Yoda. Castaneda encounters Don Juan. Dorothy has the Good Witch. These guides are often encountered when the Hero is alone—off in the desert, on a mountaintop, or sitting alone in a room. Jesus tells his disciples that he must leave them, for if he does not, the Comforter, the Holy Spirit, cannot come to them. Obi-wan Kenobi becomes more powerful *after* he leaves his body.

In today's world, these guides may be an older friend, an uncle, a grandparent, a therapist or coach, a teacher or mentor, a minister or guru. Gail Sheehy notes in her book *Path-finders* that most people who become pathfinders have at least one strong role model who exerted a forward pull and offered guidance—someone who endorsed their quest and helped them toward realization. Children who have absent or undependable parents naturally gravitate toward other figures—perhaps a grandparent or a great-aunt or -uncle. The Course tells us that "the sight, the vision, and the inner Guide all lead you out of hell with those you love beside you, and the universe with them" (T–31.VII.7:7).

In addition to protective guides who call us to action and keep us safe on the path, we also have companions who join us on our journey Home. While guides are usually a generation or two older, companions are usually about the same age as the Hero and also in search of their destiny. We thus reach the Kingdom holding, on one side, the hand of someone who helped us and, on the other side, the hand of someone we have helped. The one who helps us the most is often the one we have the most trouble forgiving. Only when we realize the profound equality of everyone, including those we think of as sinners, will the Kingdom of Heaven begin to come more clearly into view.

In *The Pilgrim's Progress,* Christian has a companion named Faithful, who plays a dual role as companion and guide. The lesson is that we are here to help each other grow. In the Babylonian tradition, Gilgamesh and Enkidu are enemies until they get into a wrestling match that neither can win. Exhausted, they begin to talk and each learns that the "other guy" is not so bad. Eventually, they become friends and companions on the path.

Moses had his brother, Aaron, as companion. Jesus had John the Baptist. Spanish mystic Saint John of the Cross had Teresa of Avila. Peter Pan has Tinkerbelle. Pinocchio has Jiminy Cricket. Dorothy has the Tin Man, the Lion, and the Scarecrow, each of whom is in search of a different spiritual quality. And, like Dorothy in the parable of Oz, we all end our journey Home with the realization that we never left it. It was all a dream from which we can awaken.

Myths are filled with companions of all sorts—animals, dolls, puppets, teddy bears, cartoon characters, imaginary friends, or symbolic entities invented by our imaginations.

Animals are often found as companions in myth because they instinctively know things of a spiritual nature that humans do not. Animals know how to be still—how to shut down and quiet the mind—something mystics must learn to do. Eckhart Tolle writes: "I have lived with five Zen Masters, all of them cats." Cats do not care much for the outside world. It does not "weigh on them" as it does on so many humans. It's all a matter of perspective.

Dolls have a similar value as companions on our journey. Jungian psychologist Clarissa Pinkola Estés writes:

> The doll is . . . the symbol of what lies buried in humans that is numinous. It is a small and glowing facsimile of the original Self. The doll is a little piece of ourselves that carries all the knowledge of the larger soul Self. In the doll is the voice, in diminutive, of old La Que Sabe, "the One who knows." The doll represents the inner spirit . . . the voice of inner reason, inner knowing, and inner consciousness . . . the small being within. It is our helper which is not seeable, but which is always accessible.

Although we are assured of both guidance and companionship on our journey, know that you will also probably encounter what appear to be evil forces or opponents. Moses had to deal with the Pharaoh. Jesus had to face the Romans, the Pharisees, and the Sadducees. Dorothy encounters the Wicked Witch. Cinderella has her evil stepsisters to deal with. For Heroes like Martin Luther, Mahatma Gandhi, Martin Luther King, Jr., and Nelson Mandela, the evil force is often the establishment, the old order, the traditional tyrannical way of doing things. The stealthiest and most difficult opponent is always our own egoistic, fear-driven self that temporarily takes over as dictator.

There comes a point on the journey, however, when you cannot go back. (You are not in Kansas anymore, after all.) You must move forward and fulfill your destiny. The distractions are many and so you will stumble and fall—perhaps into an addiction, perhaps into debt, perhaps into a "dark night of the soul." But something will always happen to awaken you. Perhaps your guides will help; perhaps your companions will come to your aid. You may even crash and burn before you finally come awake.

Mysticism is an *inner* journey of transformation through which our highest potential can be and is fulfilled. We are called upon to live an ordinary life in an extraordinary way, imbuing all activities and relationships with aliveness, richness, and purpose. In Babylonian mythology, Gilgamesh and Enkidu must save their city. Moses must lead his people to the Promised Land. Jesus came to tell us about the Kingdom of Heaven. King Arthur must find the Holy Grail. Dorothy must find her way back home.

Original Freedom

The creative impulse in the world, so far as we are aware of it, appears upon ultimate analysis to be free and original, not bound and mechanical. (Evelyn Underhill, *Mysticism*)

The great mystic journeys of literature are all symbolic of the path of transformation, which is often portrayed as a dream, as it is for Dorothy in *The Wizard of Oz*; for Alice in *Alice in Wonderland*, and for the boy in the modern fairytale *The Polar Express*. We, like them, wake up only to find that we never left Home. For the Hero, destiny summons and awaits a response. The more the call is acknowledged, the less we seem to have anything to do with it. The more strongly the call is felt, the more fate seems to step in, heightening the sense of synchronicity. The journey may seem long and the tasks we are called to perform may seem Herculean, but incredible things happen when you accept the call and your destiny begins to unfold.

PART II

The Path of Miracles

Remember that no one is where he is by accident, and chance plays no part in God's plan. It is most unlikely that changes in attitudes would not be the first step in the newly made teacher of God's training. There is, however, no set pattern, since training is always highly individualized.

M–9.1:3–5

Chapter 7

The Miracle of Purification

It is through knowing who you are not that the
greatest obstacle to knowing who you are is removed.
—Eckhart Tolle

The mystical journey is often described as a passage through different stages of spiritual development. At the end of that journey, beyond Heaven's door, there are no more steps, no more stages, no more time, no more body—only eternal love. Regardless of how the stages are enumerated and described in different versions of the mystical path, the spiritual journey always starts with the miracle of awakening and a longing for truth. Something begins to stir inside and the heart wants to know more. As we have seen, awakenings may happen because of some alarming event like a negative medical diagnosis or the death of someone you love. An awakening may rise out of necessity or it may come as a "sobering" of a drunken ego overwhelmed with guilt.

Once awakened, we must prepare ourselves for the journey. We do this through purgation—the act of freeing ourselves from excess, from superfluous entanglements, from the overindulgence and sloth that can dominate life and serve as a block to the awareness of love's presence. Purgation—cleansing or purifying—thus stands at the beginning of every spiritual path.

First Things First

Miracles are everyone's right but purification is necessary first. (Principle #7 of the Course)

As we'll discuss more in chapter 14, the ego uses the body for attack, pleasure, and pride. In the hands of the Holy Spirit, on the other hand, the body is a learning device. We learn through communication, and the purpose of communicating is healing. We must heal *all* of our relationships before we can open Heaven's door. Since that door can only be opened in love, we cannot get into Heaven alone, but only together as One.

Since the body has a function in the world, it is best to fulfill that function. When its time is done, however, we can lay it gently aside and rest awhile from labors gladly done and gladly ended. "I do not want to share my body in communion because this is to share nothing," we read in the Course. "Would I try to share an illusion with the most holy children of a most holy Father? Yet I do want to share my mind with you because we are of one Mind, and that Mind is ours. See only this Mind everywhere, because only this is everywhere and in everything" (T–7.V.10:8–10). The ego stands at the center of all that is artificial and perishable. While the ego dreams, Spirit is slowly awakening us to eternal life.

Evelyn Underhill writes in *Mysticism* that "no mystic can omit the initial stage of purgation and a putting aside of the old for the new to be born." Those who know they are on a spiritual path begin to "let go" of the blocks. Sometimes purgation includes a catharsis, a confession—getting it off your chest. The fifth step in the twelve-step program of Alcoholics Anonymous is to admit to God, to ourselves, and to another human being the nature of our misperceptions. This helps to reduce the likelihood of falling back into denial.

No Stand-Ins

Seek not your Self in symbols. There can be no concept that can stand for what you are. (T–31.V.15:1–2)

Having built up a host of defenses against the truth, as we turn and look more deeply within, it's not surprising that we become more aware of the blocks we have placed between ourselves and others—and thus, between ourselves and God. Purgation means being willing to look at the blocks we need to release, so we can truly be healed. In his book *Vipassana Meditation*, William Hart likens the process to the surgical operation of lancing a pus-filled wound. In a similar vein, Trappist monk Thomas Merton says of his early experiences: ". . . my soul was broken up with contrition, but broken and clean, painful but sanitized, like a lanced abscess."

Those who awaken because of a "crash-and-burn" experience often undergo a profound purification. Of course, we don't like to hear that the lessons we must learn are those we have brought upon ourselves. But the Course tells us: "Trials are but lessons that you failed to learn presented once again, so where you made a faulty choice before you now can make a better one, and thus escape all pain that what you chose before has brought to you. In every difficulty, all distress, and each perplexity Christ calls to you and gently says: 'My brother, choose again'" (T–31.VIII.3:1–2).

Indeed, we can find our way Home only by accepting responsibility for everything that seems to come our way. This may entail a literal "letting go" of things, relationships, or status. British author Aldous Huxley, after watching his house burn to the ground, said that the experience left him with "a marvelously clean feeling." When he lost every "thing," his life turned more deeply inward. Indeed, for many mystics, the final goal is complete emptiness. The "letting go" may involve a political struggle, career ambitions, an unhappy marriage, an eating disorder, or an addiction to a drug or alcohol. No matter the target, the solution is always "undoing" rather than doing.

Fasting is often used as a means of purgation in mysticism. Fourteenth-century Italian Saint Catherine of Siena said she had little need for food because she found nourishment in the abundance of grace she received. Fasting for prolonged periods produces a change in blood chemistry as surely as does the ingestion of a psychotropic. It is a part of the puberty rights of many native tribes, including the vision quests of the Sioux Indians. Indeed, fasting is part of the training of mystics all over the world. Galen, a Greek medical scholar in the first century, even claimed that "dreams produced by fasting are clearer." "The overstuffed body cannot see," Don Juan of the Castaneda series explains. Revelation comes to Moses, Elijah, and Daniel after long periods of fasting, while both the Koran and the Old Testament stress its importance. Fasting heightens mental clarity and removes unnecessary weight and toxins. It helps us retain energy and sharpens the senses. Fasting is not a required step in the development of a contemplative life, however. It is simply a tool, a means of bringing an abused body back into balance.

Solitude and Silence

Solitude and silence are both types of purgation. The soul is overwhelmed by "the city"—by a constant bombardment of news and media, by ego games, and by the noise of politics. On the other hand, the soul is nourished in solitude. It craves silence. Solitude gives us time to work, think, or rest without distraction. Many holy men lived in seclusion during the first centuries of the Christian Church. Before there were monasteries, individual hermits lived in caves. Seclusion makes it easier to concentrate, maintain mindfulness, and become contemplative. While mystics often spend time alone, however, they can also be highly "connected" because, lacking blocks to the awareness of love's presence, they love everything. Paradoxically, solitary mystics can be the most connected individuals.

Zoroaster was alone in the mountains when he received his revelation. Moses was alone in the wilderness when he saw the burning bush and heard God's voice. Buddha was sitting alone under the Bodhi tree when he experienced his enlightenment. Only after that did he begin to teach. Jesus spent forty days and forty nights in the wilderness, where he was tempted by the devil (the ego). "After that, he began to preach" (Matthew 4:17). Mohammad was sitting alone in a cave when he heard the word "Recite" and then received the Koran. "Something equivalent to the solitude of the wilderness is an essential part of mystical education," Underhill maintains.

Rumi tells us to listen to the voice that doesn't use words. Catherine of Siena spent three years in hermit-like seclusion in a little room, which can be seen to this day. She lived in her own small house, entirely cut off from the life of her family. She found, she said, "the desert and solitude in the midst of people." Likewise, Thomas Merton tell us: "It is in deep solitude that I find the gentleness with which I can truly love my brothers. The more solitary I am, the more affection I have for them. Solitude and silence teach me to love my brothers for what they are, not for what they say."

Shhhhhh!

The whole of life is diseased. If I were a doctor and I were asked my advice I would say, "create silence." (Søren Kierkegaard)

Retraining your mind to think with Spirit instead of ego is like starting a body-building regimen for someone who has been sick. Daily, gentle workouts are the most helpful. Try beginning and ending each day free from distractions. If you can avoid it, do not wake up with an alarm—especially a radio alarm. Try to begin each day by reading a lesson or a section from the Course or some other inspirational material. If you have time, do some stretching or some yoga, or simply meditate. Avoid immediately turning on the television or the computer. Doing so jolts you back into the world.

Thoreau acknowledged the value of this gentle awakening when he wrote: "Morning is when I am awake and there is a dawn in me." His contemporary, Harriet Beecher Stowe, understood it as well: "Still, still with Thee, when purple morning breaketh, when the bird waketh, and the shadows flee, fairer than morning, lovelier than daylight dawns the sweet consciousness, I am one with Thee."

As we get older, the spiritual path takes on increased meaning as many of the externals of life seem less significant. A friend of mine shared her thoughts on this with me:

> Now seventy-eight years old, and seeing the dream-like nature of the world, and appreciative of the Zen-like approach of letting go and letting be; I perceive mental conditions associated with aging as possibly being a withdrawal of consciousness from this present dreaming of the world, in preparation for the next state of awareness/existence after the dropping of the body. In other words, they may be quite natural shifts in consciousness.

Chapter 8

The Miracle of Ineffability

What can't be said can't be said. It can't be whistled either.
—Ram Dass

Most researchers into mysticism speak of *ineffability* as one of its foremost characteristics. Zen speaks of the *satori* experience as a "wordless realization." The mystic's way of knowing, like love, cannot be captured by words. Fortunately, in addition to words, the world is also filled with music, math, art, nature, emotions, sensations, and intuition—all of which provide intimations of immortality.

Mystics are contemplatives—spiritual travelers seeking a peaceful state of mind. The world is now and always has been filled with distractions, politics, and controversy. The more we do the inner work, however, the quieter we become, and the less distracted by the world. This often comes with in-depth spiritual study, which, Rumi tells us, does not occur on "speech's playing-field." The ineffable resides, rather, in the miracle of wordless wonder.

Of course, like all of the beautiful poems and books written by mystics, the Course, the Bible, and the Koran are all made up of words. Words, like the body, are tools we use to work our way through the world. When it comes time to lay the body down, however, the Course says we should simply thank it for all the service it has given us and let it go. As we approach the end of the journey, we also find that words begin to outlive their usefulness. Inner knowing surpasses words. "Words will mean little now," the Course teaches us. "We use them but as guides on which we do not now depend. For now, we seek direct experience of truth alone" (W–Part II.In.1:1–3).

Remember that the ego is merely a projector, a judge, an opinion-maker, a name-caller. Mystics, on the other hand, are receptors rather than projectors; they just *see*. They see the insanity of the world and they choose not to be caught up in it. They refuse to look out upon the world in fear. They refuse to recognize enemies. They harbor no thoughts of attack or defense. If thoughts like these arise in you, look at them carefully and let them go. Anita Moorjani, in describing her near-death experience, talked about speaking with her father telepathically. Words, spoken or written, are *things* that can, at best, only point to the truth. Truth surpasses all words. The Course asks us to unite with the truth (the love) we find in one another.

Beyond Words

As long as we are in this world of form and duality working with our physical bodies, we work with words. We must simply do the best we can, knowing that words, at best, can only point us to the truth. "Nor is there any need for us to try to speak of what must forever lie beyond words," the Course observes. "We need remember only that whoever attains the real world, beyond which learning cannot go, will go beyond it, but in a different way. Where learning ends there God begins, for learning ends before Him Who is complete where He begins, and where there is no end" (T–18.IX.11:2–4).

This expresses the central tenet of *apophatic* mysticism. The term "apophatic" comes from the Greek *apophasis*, meaning "negation." Apophatic mysticism is thus grounded in the conviction that it is easier to say what God is *not*, than what God *is*. Speaking of Allah, Islamic mystic Ibn Arabi, a central spiritual teacher in medieval Sufism, writes: "He is not accompanied by thingness, nor do we ascribe it to Him. The negation of thingness from Him is one of His essential attributes." Apophatic mysticism is also clearly seen in the classical *Tao Te Ching*, which begins: "Even the finest teaching is not the Tao itself. Even the finest name is insufficient to define it. Without words, the Tao is experienced, and without a name, it is known." What this brand of mysticism calls for, then, is an emptying out of our insane thinking to make room for God. After all, as English Taoist philosopher Wei Wu Wei points out: "Rationality can take you only so far."

In a similar manner, the anonymous mystical work *The Cloud of Unknowing*, written in the latter part of the 14th century, emphasizes the importance of a contemplative inner life. In order to see clearly, it claims, we must transcend the world. Contemplation, the main tool of the mystic, is a form of inner turning that lifts us up beyond the world. Mystics know that the answers to life do not reside in the world. Therefore, they turn ever more inward. Teresa of Avila gives the first Devotion of the Heart as mental prayers or contemplation, which she describes as the withdrawal of the soul from without. "When peace comes at last to those who wrestle with temptation and fight against the giving in to sin; when the light comes at last into the mind given to contemplation; or when the goal is finally achieved by anyone, it always comes with just one happy realization; *I need do nothing"* (T–18.VII.5:7).

Panning for Gold

If you don't wash out the stone and sand, how can you pick out the gold? Carefully seek the heart of heaven with firm determination and you will see the original thing! (Qiu Chuji)

I enjoy reading 20th-century Indian teacher Ramesh Belsekar because his teaching is so simple and clear. According to Ramesh, who was influenced by the teachings of Ramana Maharshi and Wei Wu Wei, analyzing and conceptualizing are a waste of time because enlightenment can come only to an empty mind. Our task, he says, is to "wake up." Upon awakening, we see—we always have been and we always will be. "What is absent in enlightenment," he claims, "is duality—'me' as a separate entity and 'you' as another separate entity." This message is essentially the same as that of the Course—that we have already achieved (already are) what we are trying to realize, or "wake up to." According to Ramesh, words are a distraction to enlightenment. To be enlightened, we must be free of concepts.

Contemplation is observation of inner thoughts without condemnation. It calls upon us to look deep within, to be reflective, and to refrain from projection so that we find, like a miner with a lamp, where the gold is hidden in the dark. From this perspective, we can also see the slag, the dross—the unwanted portion. That is, we know what is not worthwhile as well as that which is. As the *Tao Te Ching* puts it: "Muddy water let stand will clear."

There is a type of thinking that is not thinking. Rather, it is a cleansing, a reducing down and a filtering out—a dropping or releasing—of the unessential. To get to God, to get to the gold, to become receptive, *all* projections must be laid aside. It does not matter how absurd, ridiculous, or far-fetched someone's ideas may be—that person needs my love, not my judgment.

According to Ramana Maharshi, in rapture or ecstasy, the purified mind can be so absorbed that it can be complete. Go deeply enough and you'll find rapture and ecstasy. Rapture means "being carried away." Ecstasy means "standing outside oneself." To say something is "breathtaking" also means that it is "thought-taking." There are no words to describe the mystical experience; yet it provokes a profound deep inner knowing. As the Buddhist *Lankavatara Sutra* teaches us: "Words and sentences are produced by the law of causation and are mutually conditioning. They cannot express highest Reality."

Twice Removed

God does not understand words, for they were made by separated minds to keep them in the illusion of separation. Words can be helpful, particularly for the beginner, in helping concentration and facilitating the exclusion, or at least the control, of extraneous thoughts. Let us not forget, however, that words are but symbols of symbols. They are thus twice removed from reality. (M–21.1:7–19)

Indeed, the word "mystic" is related to the word "mute." Both are derived from the Greek root *mustes*, meaning "close-mouthed." Words create distinctions and, thus, duality. Naming something sets it apart and separates it, as it distinguishes the thing named from other things. Once we know that a chair is a "chair," we will never again look at a chair and not think "chair," as something separate from furniture. We don't consciously think about this; it just appears in its immediacy. Whether written or spoken, words are "physical" things, involving the duality of subject and object. A written word is visible and a spoken word is a series of sound vibrations. But both are physical in nature.

Rod Chelberg, a friend mine who is a medical doctor, described his experience of having a stroke like this:

> When I had my stroke, I could not speak for a while. I saw things and recognized them, but I could not name them or speak about what they were. I looked at the office, chairs, and people but they made no sense to me. What I saw lost all reality for me and I was just observing. I was disconnected from the reality of the ego and I had no fear, only confusion. I did not know what things were for or what they were. It seems that if we cannot name something,

then it loses its meaning and reality for us. Objects lose their value as separate entities. When we take the names away from objects, their reality is lost and, for a moment, we have no ego because the ego needs to name things in order to create this world. There is no value in this world until I choose to give a name to something. Once named, the object has value and meaning—but only to the ego.

Who Wants to Know?

I had a similar experience after viral encephalitis put me in a coma for several days. I awoke by myself late at night in a hospital bed with only a small red light glowing over my head. The first thing I did was to raise my right hand and bring it around in front of my face. I said: "That is a hand." It really was profound. I wondered how I knew what the name of this object was. How did I even know what language was? How did I know anything at all? Then a voice from somewhere deep inside said: "Who wants to know?" Who was asking the question? That was the most fascinating question of all.

Giving value to any "thing" of the world—an object, a place, a person—can turn that "thing" into a block to higher awareness. Pseudo-Dionysius, a theologian, philosopher, and Christian mystic of the 5th century, used the analogy of a sculptor cutting away that which is superfluous to get to the identity buried beneath the surface reality. He sounds like the *Tao Te Ching* when he writes: "That One which is beyond all thought is inconceivable by all thought." Menachem Nachum Twersky, an 18th-century Ukrainian Hasidic scholar, reflects the teaching of the Course when he says: "Mind comes from this sublime and completely unified source above; it is divided only as it enters into the universe of distinctions."

Try to define love. You cannot do it. You can write beautiful poetry about it, but that does not define it. Socrates said that, while he could not show us the "good," he might be able to show us what "a child of the good" looks like, so we could have some idea about what the parent—the thing itself—looks like. Still, the picture is not the thing itself. American mystic Robert Adams, speaking of his mystical experience, said: "I'm trying my best to speak intelligently and trying to use words to explain what happened, but you can't." Rumi points out that the here-and-now can be described only by words that lose their meaning and are "swept out the window" in the face of mystical experience.

Thirteenth-century Italian theologian Thomas Aquinas is regarded as the Father of the Catholic Church; his *Summa Theologica* is, perhaps, the greatest of all medieval theological treatises. Before Thomas, only Saint Augustine played such a significant a role in formulating Catholic doctrine. Aquinas had a mystical vision two years before his death, after which he said: "All that I have written is so much straw." Then he ceased writing altogether. After this experience, all he could say was: "God is that He is."

Speechless

We say "God is," and then we cease to speak, for in that knowledge words are meaningless. There are no lips to speak them, and no part of mind sufficiently distinct to feel that it is now aware of something not itself. It has united with its Source. And like its Source Itself, it merely is. (W–Part I.169.5:4–7)

~~~~~~

We say "God is" and then we cease to speak because, in the face of God, nothing can be said. Words are completely inadequate. Angela of Foligno, a 13th-century Italian Franciscan who gained so much respect that she became known as Mistress of Theologians, wrote: "The beholding, whereby the soul can behold no other thing, is so profound that it grieves me that I can say nothing of it. It is not a thing which can be touched or imagined for it is ineffable." In the same way, American spiritual teacher Myrtle Fillmore—who, along with her husband, Charles, founded the Unity Church movement—decided that by changing her mind, she could cure herself of tuberculosis, which she did! Myrtle writes: "I have come so close to breaking right through into the wonderful things of the kingdom; and at times I seem most bursting with beautiful, powerful realities that I would have humanity see and realize. But these great impressions and surges of power don't seem to put themselves into words and I can but radiate them."

Mysticism is about healing the mind. A sick mind cannot find its way Home because it is lost and lacking in clarity and purpose. The main thing is that, by removing the blocks to an awareness of love's presence, we can let love shine through. We don't have to figure everything out. What is important is the love. And love can find a way.

The Decision-Maker

The power to decide is *our last remaining freedom* as prisoners of the world. We need to be decision-makers in this world because it is a divided world. There is no decision-making in Heaven because there is no division—no right and no wrong. The choice is easy when the results are clearly seen. Therefore, mystics learn how to decide in favor of what they call right-mindedness. And right-mindedness leads to One-mindedness. Here is a simple diagram showing how this process works.

Spirit/Heaven/Mind

decision-maker

ego/body/mind

At any given moment, we (the decision-makers) are free to choose between ego/body/mind (separation and conflict) or Spirit/Heaven/Mind (Oneness and peace). As we'll discuss in chapter 14, the body is the ego's chosen home. The body is obtrusive and sometimes so dominant that we can't help but think we are bodies and nothing more. Fortunately, everyone also has a mind. And within every mind, there is a spark of divine light that can, given the opportunity, bring us back to life again. "In many only the spark remains," the Course observes, "for the Great Rays are obscured. Yet God has kept the spark alive so that the Rays can never be completely forgotten" (T–10.IV.8:1–2).

Behavioral Science

Behave as though the self does not exist. (Buddha)

Sometimes the opportunity for awakening comes crashing and burning all around us. It can also come slowly and gently. The good news is that "love waits on welcome, not on time." "There is a way of finding certainty right here and now," the Course assures us. "Refuse to be a part of fearful dreams whatever form they take, for you will lose identity in them" (T–28.IV.2:1–2).

Mystics struggle to awaken from dreaming. The proof that we are not yet fully awake is the presence of guilt and fearful, ego-driven dreams. Mystics are simply those who are developing an ever-deeper trust in God. "The first change, before dreams disappear," the Course explains, "is that your dreams of fear are changed to happy dreams" (T–18.II.6:3).

> Think like Him [the Holy Spirit] ever so slightly, and the little spark becomes a blazing light that fills your mind so that He becomes your only Guest. Whenever you ask the ego to enter, you lessen His welcome. He will remain, but you have allied yourself against Him. Whatever journey you choose to take, He will go with you, waiting. (T–11.II.5:4–7)

Vision, Revelation, and Wisdom

Objective understanding of the world of form, whether from perception or reasoning, is simply not enough. It cannot bring us to be truly awake unless we use the mind to go *beyond* the mind. The intellect, in and of itself, is never enough. The intellectual alone is dry and barren. According to many mystics, simply "looking" (perception) is judging and must, therefore, be abandoned, remembering always that "the memory of God comes to the quiet mind" (T–23.I.1:1).

The ego limits perception to the bodies of those around us and to the things of the world. When we first meet people we haven't seen for a while, we often ask them how they are, and then give them some "positive" opinion of how we think they look. They may then return the sentiments. This, of course, is not true vision. It's the ego talking. But, as the Course tells us: "The universe of love does not stop because you do not see it, nor have your closed eyes lost the ability to see" (T–11.I.5:10).

Wrong Way

Reason will tell you that the only way to escape from misery is to recognize it *and go the other way.* (T–22.II.4:1)

Vision is the direct perception of essence that enables us to see God in everything. Once we are ready and willing to know God, we will. God is ready now and, if we are ready now, we can see as God does—which means loving everything we see. There is nothing partial about knowledge. Knowledge is whole. It has no separate parts and no degrees. Although perception of form gives the appearance of separation, you/I/

we are not bodies and we are not separate from each other or from God.

The truth of our identity is not grasped by the reasoning mind alone. Based on information, facts, and associations gathered from the world of form, intellectual knowledge is complex, specialized, and changeable. Wisdom, however, is knowledge of reality as "simple," all-pervasive, and immutable. Wisdom is not emotional or intellectual. It is a permanent inner knowing, a form of "mystical illumination," a deep and profound insight into essence. Such experience is not bodily or sensuous. It is inaudible to and unknowable by the intellect—yet it is known without doubt by direct revelation.

For Shankara and Eckhart, the way of salvation is the way of knowledge, or *revelation*. Revelation is an intensely personal experience—a direct contact with God that transcends time and abolishes fear. Inevitably, mystics say that they see something that they did not know before, although they may not be able to tell us in everyday words what it is they know. Yet, they have received unquestionable insights and revelations beyond doubt. "Revelation," the Course tells us, "is literally unspeakable because it is an experience of unspeakable love" (T–1.II.2:7). Pseudo-Dionysius calls it an "unknown knowing."

According to D. T. Suzuki, the man who brought Zen Buddhism to the West, mystical awareness cannot be described, because such experience stands *above* or *outside* words and reason. Suzuki says: "When language is forced to be used for the 'transcendental world,' it becomes warped and assumes all kinds of oxymora, paradoxes, contradictions, absurdities, oddities, ambiguities, and irrationalities."

Another way to say this is that to know Heaven is to know love, and to know love is to know Heaven. Even though we know it, we cannot say what love is. Yet, when love is present, it is present without question. However, before we can know Heaven, before we can know God, we must let go of what we "think" is real—all the stuff on the outside that comprises the ego/body/mind's version of reality. Satori, the spiritual goal of Zen Buddhism, is both a knowing and an intuitive awareness. The goal is the "feeling" of infinite space freed of concepts.

Plato said that our task in life is a matter of "remembering or putting back together again" what the soul already knows. This *re-collection* is not of this world, but of our real Home—a place free from the dreaming of the world. The word I prefer to use here is *re-cognizing*, that is, bringing back into the mind what the mind already knows. In his book *The Seven Storey Mountain*, Thomas Merton writes: "A memory that is not alive to the present does not 'remember' the here and now, does not 'remember' its identity, is not memory at all."

What Mystics Know

- Mystics know how to keep the mind in line with the One Mind.

- Mystics know that "thoughts" affect everything and do not project onto others.

- Mystics have insight into the human comedy that often brings joy and laughter.

- Mystics understand the inner connection of everything and how it all fits together.

- Mystics know there is no such thing as death and that the body is ephemeral.

- Mystics know that consciousness transcends the physical and that the body limits true vision.

- Mystics know how to experience unspeakable love.

My friend Rod Chelberg, the doctor who experienced a mystical awakening after having a stroke, sent me this description of what happened to him in one of his morning meditations:

I walked into the vastness of Heaven. I could see the whole world and the Sonship. I love the feeling of Love flowing through me. My mind is perfectly quiet and I feel the deep peace of Love. There is absolute stillness and quietness in my mind and yet I know everything without speaking. I see everything with perfect clarity. I have infinite mind and no limitations at all when I am deep into this place. Christ visited with me. No words were spoken, only the awareness of Love between us. It was perfect communication.

Chapter 9

The Miracle of Disillusionment

Great doubt results in great enlightenment,
small doubt results in small enlightenment,
no doubt results in no enlightenment.

—Zen Saying

The outside world, as constructed by the ego, is one gigantic multiple personality disorder. Therefore, *disillusionment*, or giving up on the world, is an imperative prelude to mystical awareness. American author Dan Millman, in his book *Way of the Peaceful Warrior*, says that disillusionment is the best thing that can happen to someone, because it reveals what does not have real meaning. It comes down to the realization that love is the only thing that is truly valuable, and that all the rest is merely dust in the wind. Many of the mystics who seem the most authentic come to truth as the result of falling apart, hitting bottom, or "losing everything."

Being caught in our stories in the world, we can't see that it's not real until we question the patterns handed to us through societal standards, religion, politics, the media, our families, and ourselves. "There is no point in lamenting the world," the Course tells us. "There is no point in trying to change the world. It is incapable of change because it is merely an effect. But there is indeed a point in changing your thoughts about the world. Here you are changing the cause. The effect will change automatically" (W–Part I.23.2:2–7).

Eighteenth-century French philosopher Denis Diderot similarly claimed that skepticism was "the first step on the road to philosophy." Seventeenth-century French mathematician and philosopher René Descartes concurred: "If you would be a real seeker after truth, it is necessary that at least once in your life you doubt, as far as possible, all things."

Why are we living in these bodies, in this world, at this time? Is there some "purpose" to all of this or is it all a mishmash of mindless accidents? Every mystical tradition I know sees this world as a school—a place where we learn to forgive ourselves for what we think of as our sins. Our bodies, time, words, and the world we inhabit are thus all just learning devices.

Life is, of course, filled with meaning. We did not come here without a purpose. Indeed, living out that purpose leads us to our greatest happiness. The first step for every generation is the questioning of the nature of reality as handed down through the ages. Mark Twain rightly advised us not to take ourselves or the society of which we are a part too seriously. American author H. L. Mencken, known as the Sage of Baltimore, said: "Men become civilized, not in proportion to their willingness to believe, but in proportion to their readiness to doubt." A seeker after truth, therefore, inevitably questions ingrained traditions.

Ego Thoughts

All the early workbook lessons in the Course are about watching our thoughts or the process of thinking. We learn, among other things, that nothing we see means anything, that we have given everything we see all the meaning it has, that our thoughts mean nothing, that our minds are preoccupied with past thoughts, which are merely images we have made.

Clear Reflection

Earth can reflect Heaven or hell; God or the ego. You need but leave the mirror clean and clear of all the images of hidden darkness you have drawn upon it. God will shine upon it of Himself. Only the clear reflection of Himself can be perceived upon it. (T–14.IX.5:4–7)

Lesson 10 of the Course tells us that our thoughts mean nothing because they are not our real thoughts. Our real thoughts are of a much deeper nature, having nothing to do with the surface realities and the soap opera stories that tie our minds into knots, inevitably blocking true perception. Thoughts of peace are examples of our *real* thoughts. In Lesson 45, we read: *"God is the Mind in which I think."* Our real thoughts are those we think in alignment with the Mind of God. All else is illusion. Albert Einstein hinted at this truth in a letter to the Royal Society of London in which he says

"Anyone, who finds a thought which brings him closer to Nature's eternal secrets partakes of a great grace."

The thoughts of the ego are not loving; therefore, they are not real. Much of our thinking is projective and often condemnatory. For this reason, it is a good idea not to get involved in political squabbles and ideological differences, because these are but "surface" realities. As Einstein said: "Politics is for the present. I'm interested in eternity." In Lesson 47 of the Course, we are asked to: "Let go all the trivial things that churn and bubble on the surface of your mind, and reach down and below them to the Kingdom of Heaven" (W–47.7:3). What is called for is thus a complete "reversal in thinking." We must first put a stop to projective thinking, which is in alignment with the ego. This opens the door to a new way of thinking in which forgiveness shines on everything.

Mysticism entails reaching back to Heaven through our polluted thoughts to the thoughts of God and to a remembrance of Heaven. How do we reach back to Heaven? First, we must begin to distinguish between our ego's "reactionary" thoughts and our real thoughts. For example, if you ever say that you don't like someone, you can be sure it's because of your "surface reading" of them. There is depth in every soul and, if we are willing to look more deeply, we can see it.

Someone who is "thin skinned" is easily insulted and unable to deal with criticism. In such an individual, the ego is so dominant they cannot know the unfathomable truth buried deep within. They cannot know that God is the only Mind in which we can think and be whole and happy. The Course helps us remove the blocks to an awareness of love's presence. The ego lives on the surface, caught in "make believe." So it is that *the thoughts we think we think are not our real thoughts,* because they come from the ego. But "you" are not an ego.

Real Thoughts

As we can begin to see, there are many reasons to dislodge our ego thoughts so that we can experience our real thoughts. In a mystical experience, these surface thoughts are relinquished because we are "forced" to let go. This may happen in a near-death experience, during meditation, or by going through a "process" like that of the Course. And there are, as we have seen, other ways as well. Sometimes this experience happens for no readily explainable reason. Thoreau found such thoughts in solitude, writing: "I never found a companion so companionable as solitude."

Now You See It . . .

The world is an illusion. Those who choose to come to it are seeking for a place where they can be illusions, and avoid their own reality. Yet when they find their own reality is even here, then they step back and let it lead the way. What other choice is really theirs to make? To let illusions walk ahead of truth is madness. But to let illusion sink behind the truth and let the truth stand forth as what it is, is merely sanity. (W–155.2:1–6)

Thinking that we know is a major obstacle to the awareness of love's presence. First, we must be done with our dreaming of the world. Power plays, rules, laws, dogma, creeds, doctrine, canons, and systems of belief all stand as blocks to an awareness of love's presence. Skeptics question traditional, commonly accepted ideas and social norms that serve a ritualistic and/or habituated pattern. Healthy skepticism is essential in the face of the incredulous. All mythologies are just that—mythologies. Our stories are not realities.

Mark Twain was the archetype of a modern skeptic. As he got older, he became progressively disenchanted with "the damned human race." "Civilization," he claimed, "is a limitless multiplication of unnecessary necessities." Though Twain's profound skepticism kept him from higher mysticism, he could see the divine within the ordinary. "A soap bubble," he wrote, "is the most beautiful thing and the most exquisite in nature." In his longing to be free of the illusions of society, he echoes the conclusions of thinkers like Eckhart, Descartes, and Thoreau.

Friedrich Nietzsche carried this scepticism even further when he wrote: "The experience of consciousness free of concepts is freedom." Like earlier mystics, Nietzsche recognized the importance of emptying the mind of all concepts and beliefs. Sometimes it's important to completely clean out the house to let God come in. Nietzsche's honesty and open-mindedness were remarkable and always evolving. Every time he suffered through a psychological crisis, his philosophy went deeper. "What was needed," he said, "was a will to truth, love, and that which was eternal."

True mystics question the nature of reality presented by parents and society. They are out to find a better way.

Though he did not think of himself as a mystic, Nietzsche brought philosophy closer to the truth and, thus, closer to mysticism. "Do not allow yourselves to be deceived," he said. "Great minds are skeptical." Our task, Castaneda tells us, is to *see* rather than to *perceive*. Don Juan instructed Castaneda in the art of "stopping the world," the first step in learning to *see* without judgment. J. G. Krishnamurti expressed it thus: "The highest form of human intelligence is being able to observe without evaluating."

Vicki Poppe, a serious long-term student of the Course from Massachusetts, gives this description of a mystical experience. She had been part of a spiritual community in Wisconsin during the 1990s, but had felt uncomfortable there. Describing a reunion visit in 2016, she writes:

> I was back in Wisconsin and had a delightful time, everything was sparkling, the trees, the river, the stars and most especially the people, it was clearly beautiful in every way possible. The fact is that, twenty-five years ago, I had lived in this same place for three years and found it to be dreary, suffocating, and boring at best. I laughed and realized how judgment had literally clouded my view and how, this time, I was witnessing what had been there all along! I don't know when the healing happened. It was all in the most ordinary ways of daily prayer and living with a simple thought of God. I thank the Holy Spirit for this surprise correction and healing through Grace. The real world *is* just an unclouded thought away!

Mystics do not project onto the world; they give the world the freedom to be what it is. Mysticism is *seeing* without projection, contamination, or corruption. It is seeing without ego-involvement. It is the seeing of the pure of heart. Our perception of the world changes when we stop our inner dialogue—when there is no longer any questioner. Then we see with wonder and with awe. As long as we cling to our inner dialogues and the ego's version of reality, we remain blind. "Don't seek the truth," says Zen Buddhism. "Simply cease to cherish opinions." "Those who remember always that they know nothing, and who have become willing to learn everything, will learn it," the Course promises. "But whenever they trust themselves, they will not learn. They have destroyed their motivation for learning by thinking they already know" (T–14.XI.12:1–3).

Who Cares?

Every month, a young disciple faithfully sent his master an account of his progress toward enlightenment. In the first month, he wrote: "I feel an expansion of consciousness and experience my Oneness with the universe." The master glanced at the note and threw it away. The following month, the disciple reported: "I have finally discovered that the Divine is present in all things." The master seemed disappointed. The third month, the disciple exclaimed: "The mystery of the One has been revealed to my wondering gaze." The master shook his head and threw the letter away. The next letter said: "No one is born, no one lives, and no one dies, for the ego is not." The master threw his hands up in utter despair. A month passed by, then two, then five—and finally a whole year without another letter. The master reminded his disciple of his duty to report on his spiritual progress. The disciple wrote back: "Who cares?" And the master smiled.

Seeing Is Believing

Seventeenth-century German mystic Jacob Boehme experienced a religious epiphany when a ray of sunlight reflecting in a pewter dish catapulted him into an ecstatic vision of God. Boehme writes: "If men would as fervently seek after love and righteousness as they do after opinions, there would be no strife on earth, and we should be as children of one father, and should need no law or ordinance." Likes and dislikes are the ways we "make things up." They are the ways in which we cement the world together. All opinions are ego-invested. Thoreau says: "We must look a long time before we can see." We can only see when, in our seeing, we do not add anything to the picture.

"Look at a cup, for example," the Course instructs us:

Do you see a cup, or are you merely reviewing your past experiences of picking up a cup, being thirsty, drinking from a cup, feeling the rim of the cup against your lips, having breakfast, and so on? Are not your aesthetic reactions to the cup, too, based on past experiences? How else would you know whether or not this kind of cup will break if you drop it? What do you know about this cup except what you learned in the past? You would have no idea what this cup is, except for your past learning. Do you, then, really see it? (W–P.I.7.3:1–7)

To have mystical awareness, something must happen first. First, *we have to stop thinking!* Twentieth-century English mystic Douglas Harding described this experience in his book *On Having No Head: Zen and the Rediscovery of the Obvious*:

What happened was something absurdly simple and unspectacular: I stopped thinking. A peculiar quiet, an odd kind of alert limpness or numbness, came over me. Reason and imagination and all mental chatter died down. For once, words really failed me. Past and future dropped away. I forgot who and what I was, my name, manhood, animal-hood, all that could be called mine. It was as if I had been born that instant, brand new, mindless, inno-cent of all memories. There existed only the Now, that present moment and what was clearly given in it. To look was enough.

The ordinary mind, busily engaged as it is with thoughts, opinions, and judgments, simply cannot see anything but the mind's own projections. But, as William Blake pointed out: "If the door of perception were cleansed, everything would appear as it is, infinite." To be truly aware, we must stop all ego machinations and maneuvering. Blindness is based on prejudice and fear. Spirit sees through eyes of love, free of contamination. As Aldous Huxley expressed it: "If you could get out of your not-self's light, you could be illumined. If you could stop anxiously cogitating, you could give yourself a chance to be cogitated." The Course tells us that, when we attempt to interpret error, we give it power. "Having done this," it says, "you will overlook truth" (T–12.I.1:8).

Be Still

Simply do this: Be still, and lay aside all thoughts of what you are and what God is; all concepts you have learned about the world; all images you hold about yourself. Empty your mind of everything it thinks is either true or false, or good or bad, of every thought it judges worthy, and all the ideas of which it is ashamed. Hold onto nothing. Do not bring with you one thought the past has taught, nor one belief you ever learned before from anything. Forget this world, forget this course, and come with wholly empty hands unto your God. (W–Part I.189.7:1–5)

Imagine what it would be like if we loved everything our eyes fell upon. Instead, we judge things almost instantly. To see what is true is to be deceived no longer by the ego. American-born spiritual teacher Gangaji, dedicated to sharing the mystical path through direct self-inquiry, asks us to: "Stop all your doing. Stop all your beliefs, all your searching, all your excuses, and see for yourself what already is always here. Don't move. Be still." The purpose of meditation is to be free of the thoughts—the illusions—we normally take to be ourselves. The idea is to quiet the mind and disconnect from the ego, or at least to slow the pace of internal chatter. If we're lucky—and diligent—we will be able to stop the self-talk. If we can disengage from the constant inner babble and projection of beliefs and prejudices, then we can really begin to see.

Various experiences can bring on a dropping, or temporary stopping, of the inner chatter of the mind and provide an opportunity for pure seeing. Meditation, which we will look at more closely in chapter 12, is one of them. But God is often found in becoming aware of—in *seeing*—the smallest of things. Fourteenth-century English nun Julian of Norwich saw God and the whole of the Universe while looking at an acorn. She writes: "In this Little Thing, I saw three properties. The first is that God made it. The second is that God loveth it, the third, that God keepeth it." Perhaps the best-remembered verse of William Blake is this: "To see a world in a grain of sand and heaven in a wild flower, hold infinity in the palm of your hand and eternity in an hour."

We are sometimes shaken out of the busyness of the ego mind by life-events like crash-and-burn scenarios of despair, a divorce or bankruptcy, the loss of a loved one, or the prospect of our own death. Mystical experiences like these can also come to us in solitary moments like running, skiing, skating, bicycling, listening to music, creative work, and focused relaxation. The following is from the *Kena Upanishad*, which scholars believe was composed around the middle of the first millennium BCE:

What cannot be spoken with words, but that whereby words are spoken: know that alone to be Brahman, the Spirit; and not what people here adore. What cannot be thought with the mind, but that whereby the mind can think: know that alone to be Brahman, the Spirit; and not what people here adore. What cannot be seen with the eye, but that whereby the eye can see: know that alone to be Brahman, the Spirit; and not what people here adore. What cannot be heard with the ear, but that whereby the ear can hear: know that alone to be Brahman, the Spirit; and not what people here adore. What cannot be indrawn with breath, but that whereby breath is indrawn: know that alone to be Brahman, the Spirit; and not what people here adore.

Chapter 10

The Miracle of Surrender

*When you have become willing to hide nothing, you
will not only be willing to enter into communion but
will also understand peace and joy.*

T–1.IV.1:5

Holy Instants are clear windows into the Divine. Although
most profound, however, they are still "instants." They often
do not last. The following story tells of a mystical awakening
experienced by a young Chinese girl. What makes this story
unique is that this experience did have a lasting transformative effect. The wisdom that percolates forth from Zhao's
experience is amazing. It's hard to believe that she was only
nineteen when she wrote this description and only fourteen
when the experience occurred. Zhao's experience was truly
life-transforming, and her challenge since has been to integrate its lessons into her everyday life. First, I give you the story
in Zhao's own words. Then we will look at it more closely.

Zhao's Story

My story started as far back as I can remember. I had difficulties identifying with this body since I was a child. Eating,

sleeping, and walking were very hard to understand for me. It took me a long time to adjust myself to this world—to live like a human being. I was unhappy with my life. I saw everything distorted, ugly, and meaningless. I knew there was something missing and that I must find it. My home had a rich library which contained many philosophical and Buddhist books. These texts provided me the chance to read and explore. I filled dozens of notebooks, analyzing every thought to see what was inside. When I dug into any of them, they disappeared, became unreal, were empty.

At the age of fourteen, after seven years of intensive reading and reflection to find the answers and failing, I decided to commit suicide. I said to myself: "Since there is no meaning to life or to the world, then there is no difference between being alive or dead." Then, suddenly, the whole world disappeared. My self disappeared. I felt I had melted into God, the supreme good, the most beautiful, peaceful, joyful state I never imagined. I realized that I had been looking for answers in the material world, looking for the answers in a wrong place. The truth is not in the material, it is here—present. I was putting blocks between Heaven and me. This is the answer I had always been looking for; this was the supreme good.

Over the next three days, I started seeing everything as the absolute presence of God—even dung, even people arguing and hurting each other. I began to see everything turned into God's shining presence. Three days later, I came back to earth. My human body could not stay in that rarified state for a long time; it burns up everything, including the body, but the undisturbed Peace stays.

At first, I was not willing to use the word "enlighten-ment" to describe what I had experienced. For a long time, I was not willing to say who is enlightened or not. Most people do not believe that a young person can have an awakening experience. When I tried to relate my own experience, they turned away or said that I was arrogant to say such a thing. But I knew what I had experienced was eternal Oneness, no matter what others wanted to call it. In the end, words are just words. The only test comes from your own heart.

Immediately after my awakening experience, I wrote: "I am God, I am who I am." I wrote the words spontaneously, shocking myself with my arrogance. But I could not help myself. Three days later, I began writing: "Nothingness com-pletely, Nothingness completely," again and again. It was as if I could not control my hands, as if something were leaking through me. I realized that God was the only thing I can never get rid of. Even when I am not aware of its presence, it is still here. God did not hide himself from me. I had been holding concepts which didn't allow me to experience God's presence.

I realized that concepts are the ego's clothes. When all concepts die, the ego dies and that is the true death—the death's death, which is even deeper than our bodies' death. That is why even the concept of God can be dangerous. That is the only thing that does not change. It is your truth.

Let your heart be empty and humble, to see God's pres-ence. I can tell you a truth; God himself does not know his name is God. That is why you can call it anything you like, but all the experiences of God are absolutely the same. God itself is being experienced by itself. There is no God but God. I am speechless now. I see everything so perfect as the presence of God. I am speechless. I see everyone is already enlightened. I have nothing more to say or do.

Enlightenment is a constant state, not an instant experience. The finite experience is just an encouragement that keeps us striving for it. To remain there we must be constantly willing to surrender. Say this to God: "I will what you will." The question you must ask is whether you are living out God absolutely right now, right here without any compromise. After an awakening experience, you must bring this attitude to the world until you forgive all that is unforgiven.

The Course says that the meaning of our earthly lives is removing the blocks we set to the awareness of love's presence. It is like peeling an onion one layer at a time. When you peel the final layer, it disappears. Every time you peel another layer through forgiveness, it is a Holy Instant that lifts you closer to God. Keep peeling until you see God's face.

Thoughts on Zhao

Now let's look at Zhao's story a little more closely to see how it contains many of the elements of mysticism we have identified so far. She speaks of her difficulty feeling at one with her body. This is a central tenet of the Course, in which we find the sentence: "I am not a body" no fewer than forty-six times. I experienced a similar disconnection to my body after awakening from my encephalitis-induced coma.

Next, Zhao describes how she wrote to explore her every thought and "to see what was inside" herself. We have seen that looking inside is an essential discipline required of all mystics. We must never be afraid to look inside and to be honest with ourselves, because that is the only way the "junk" of the ego world can be cleansed from our minds.

This is the reason I know I'm not yet enlightened. The deeper I dig, the more work I know I must do.

The next part of Zhao's description reveals the deepest part of the mystical experience, the crash-and-burn occurrence that leads to enlightenment. Zhao tells us that she decided to commit suicide, concluding that "since there is no meaning to life or to the world, then there is no difference between being alive or dead." And it is at this precise moment that "the whole world disappeared." Zhao entered an awakened state that was "the most beautiful, peaceful, joyful state I never imagined." This sentence expresses the high point of the mystical experience—when the ego self disappears, even if only for a brief time. The unreality of our dreamlike lives must disappear for truth to dawn upon our minds. Only then can we melt back into God.

At this point, Zhao begins to feel the aftereffects of her experience, "seeing everything as the absolute presence of God." This shows us that Zhao's experience is something more than a Holy Instant, because it stayed with her for three days. It's this "lasting" quality that makes her experience so transformative.

Lesson 29 from the Course teaches that God is in everything we see. Zhao saw God everywhere—even in dung and in people arguing—because when God is in our vision, all that we see is beautiful. What a difference there is when we see the world through eyes of love (the vision of Oneness) instead of fear (the projection of separation). The fearful are always ready to attack. To loving eyes, what the ego sees as ugly, Spirit sees as beautiful because everything is filled with love. Seeing with love means seeing without judgment. Everything is beautiful—even dung and people arguing—because it's all part of the process of life itself. Only a mind that has stopped judgment can see it. Krishnamurti tells us that the highest form of human intelligence is being able to observe "without evaluating." Everything is a matter of choice. Will we be host to God or hostage to the ego? Does ego win again, or are we willing to turn everything around and follow the guidance of God?

Three days later, Zhao tells us, she came back to earth, explaining that her human body could not stay in that state for a long time, but that "the undisturbed Peace" remained. Here, Zhao echoes the Course yet again, where we read:

> Sometimes a teacher of God may have a brief experience of direct union with God. In this world, it is almost impossible that this endure. It can, perhaps, be won after much devotion and dedication, and then be maintained for much of the time on earth. But this is so rare that it cannot be considered a realistic goal. All worldly states must be illusory. If God were reached directly in sustained awareness, the body would not be long maintained. (M–26.3:1–4, 7–8)

Zhao's observation that "concepts are the ego's clothes" is among the most brilliant in her description. It reminds me of Greek mystic Gregory of Nyssa, who said: "Concepts create idols. Only wonder comprehends anything. People kill one another over idols. Wonder makes us fall to our knees." Søren Kierkegaard gave a similar warning: "Once you label me, you negate me." Describing concepts as clothes, which are concrete and visible, is a symbolic way of talking about concepts as illusory. To find God, all man-made accoutrements—concepts, doctrine, traditions, laws—must be discarded. Ram Dass tells us the same thing in a more humorous vein: "In most of our human relationships, we spend much of our time reassuring one another that our costumes of identity are on straight." These "costumes of identity" are divisive forms of separation that take us away from, rather than closer to, each other and the truth of Oneness.

Painted Idols

Concepts are learned. They are not natural. Apart from learning they do not exist. They are not given, so they must be made. Not one of them is true, and many come from feverish imaginations, hot with hatred and distortions born of fear. What is a concept but a thought to which its maker gives a meaning of his own? Concepts maintain the world. But they can not be used to demonstrate the world is real. For all of them are made within the world, born in its shadow, growing in its ways and finally "maturing" in its thought. They are ideas of idols, painted with the brushes of the world, which cannot make a single picture representing truth. (T–31.V.7:1–10)

Zhao observes that people often do not believe a young person can have an awakening experience, but tells us that she was eager to share her newfound knowledge. However, she concludes: "I am speechless now. I see everything so perfect as the presence of God. I am speechless. I see everyone is already enlightened. I have nothing more to say or do." Zhao has had an awakening experience, but that does not mean that she is enlightened. She had an opportunity to experience nothingness and see into eternity. Although the memory of such an experience can never be lost, there remains the necessity of living in the world and dealing with the vicissitudes of everyday circumstances. Fortunately, she continues to study the Course, and she has a great thirst to read all things spiritual.

Zhao's experience occurred when she was at the point of greatest despair, the point at which she had decided to commit suicide. At the top of the list of stimulations for a mystical breakthrough given in chapter 4 is despair and depression. Obviously, despair and depression are not mystical states. They can, however, lead you to one. When you go to the bottom of the pit, you have no choice but to let go and let God.

Chapter 11

The Miracle of Suffering

Sometimes the emergence of the mystical consciousness is gradual, unmarked by any definite crisis. The self slides gently, almost imperceptibly, from the old universe to the new. The records of mysticism, however, suggest that this is exceptional: that travail is the normal accompaniment of birth.
—Evelyn Underhill, *Mysticism*

"Suffering," says Dalai Lama Tenzin Gyatso, "is the first step in enlightenment." Indeed, the most common path to enlightenment is slow and gradual and often takes place through suffering. American author Jack Kornfield writes: "The most frequent entryway to the sacred is our own suffering and dissatisfaction." Surviving near death is almost always enlightening. As Jung expressed it: "It is a fearful thing to fall into the hands of the living God. The experience of the self is always a defeat for the ego."

One of the best-known stories of depression followed by a crash-and-burn experience that resulted in mystical awareness is the story of Bill Wilson, co-founder of Alcoholics Anonymous. Wilson struggled with alcoholism. One night, while lying in bed filled with despair, he cried out: "I'll do anything! Anything at all! If there be a God, let Him show Himself!" A bright light appeared, and feelings of ecstasy and serenity came over him. He never drank again. This led to the program for spiritual growth known as The Twelve Steps. As Joseph Campbell expressed it: "It is by going down into the abyss that we recover the treasures of life. When you stumble, there lies your treasure." "Only conscious suffering," says Gurdjieff, "makes any sense."

The Fastest Horse

Suffering is the fastest horse that carries you to perfection. (Meister Eckhart)

No one consciously chooses to crash and burn. The greater the narcissism, the greater the selfishness, the greater the ego, the greater the unconsciousness, and the greater the potential tragedy that comes with a lack of awareness. The bigger the ego, the harder the fall. But no one in their right mind would choose to crash and burn as a preface to awakening. It is rather an *unconscious* way of forcing ourselves to wake up. Crashing and burning may *seem* to come from the outside—since the ego often does not understand how it created what it perceives—but they are still a consequence of the ego mind. To awaken, we must willingly choose to consider the abyss of darkness hiding deep within.

Suffering often brings disillusionment, which, as we have seen, can be an important step along the road to enlightenment.

Although it may not seem like it at the time, being disillusioned is one of the best things that can happen to you. When you crash and burn, you find what is valuable and what is not. "Yours is the way of pain, of which God knows nothing," the Course instructs. "That way is hard indeed, and very lonely. Fear and grief are your guests, and they go with you and abide with you on the way. But the dark journey is not the way of God's Son" (T–11.III.4:2–5).

Implosion

The ego has a tenacious hold on the psyche, and it will not let go easily. The ego thought system, however, has a built-in "implosion" mechanism. It will eventually collapse, simply because all false systems fail. Communism collapsed because it was an "untrue" system. The denial of individual freedom and the use of totalitarian power were an affront to the human spirit. Any philosophical system not grounded in love simply isn't based on truth and will not prevail. Ultimately, when all else fails, we are given an opportunity to let go and wake up as the ego implodes. Bruno Borchert, in his book *Mysticism: Its History and Challenge,* describes the dark night of the soul like this:

> It is an emptiness that often takes the form of a deep depression. The feelings are numb and there is no light anywhere. According to St. John of the Cross, whoever will hold out—so that the depression does not lead to suicide, but to the loss of the greedy self—will arrive at a "new comprehension of God in God." The "I" then experiences its deepest ground;

not from the vantage point of the "I" itself, but from the other side of the ground—which is God.

To get out of the quagmire of despair and depression, you must first admit that you are not happy. For despair and depression to lead to awakening, you must go all the way with the experience. You can't merely be on your way to bottoming out; you can't be in a state of high nervous anxiety. You've got to hit bottom. Only when all ego strategies fail in the face of overwhelming misfortunes will you have a chance to see the light. Osho says: "If I were to make a religion, this would be a basic thing in it, that anybody who becomes enlightened first will have to go through a nervous breakdown, only then will we have a breakthrough."

The mystical experience occurs when we let go of our attempts to control. Crashing and burning stop the wandering mind and force us into the present. Once we surrender to what is, once we turn everything over to a power higher than the ego mind, something remarkable happens. There comes the experience of grace. Love floods in when we stop choosing the ego. Then, despite the seeming severity of our situation, we are okay. Everything is taken care of, even if we don't understand how it's happening. We can then *rest* in the arms of God, rather than trying to manipulate our experience. The Course describes the transition like this:

> You can temporize and you are capable of enormous procrastination, but you cannot depart entirely from your Creator, Who set the limits on your ability to miscreate. Tolerance for pain may be high, but it is not without limit. Eventually everyone

begins to recognize, however dimly, that there must be a better way. As this recognition becomes more firmly established, it becomes a turning point. This ultimately reawakens spiritual vision, simultaneously weakening the investment in physical sight. (T–2.III.3:3, 5–8)

We usually come to the point of crashing and burning after having first tried many things that proved unsatisfactory. Pick an illusion: politics, fame, power, authority, drugs, alcohol, or wealth. One will serve as well (or as poorly) as another. An illusion, is an illusion, is an illusion. And eventually, all illusory paths come to despair and inevitable surrender.

Forward and Back

Some of your greatest advances you have judged as failures, and some of your deepest retreats you have evaluated as success. (T–18.V.1:6)

We handle difficulties more easily when we allow them to transform us. Sometimes, the only way for you to find out what is going on is to have the rug pulled out from under you. Whenever this happens, pay attention. Don't attack anyone and don't play the role of victim. Life has simply given you one of its lessons. You can respond responsibly, or you can project. You can blame others, or you can ask yourself: What lesson does this experience have to teach? How can I be even more aware, so that I keep this same sort of thing from happening again?

The Wanting Creature

When we hit bottom and give up, we begin to see how we were blinded by our own projections and desires. Buddha said that the loss of desire is the key to enlightenment. Of course, every "body" has basic needs for food, clothing, and shelter. But many of the things we think we need may not really be necessary. So the first question to ask is: What is the wanting creature? What is it that needs? And what if there were no "wanting creature"—no ego? What would you have then? Ramana Maharshi asks us to pay attention to how and where our thoughts arise. When asked a spiritual question, he often answered: "Who wants to know?"

Physicist and engineer Lester Levenson gives us a good example of an awakening "after the crash." Levenson attained a high level of material success as a businessman, but suffered from a number of health problems. After his second heart attack, his doctors told him that, unless he wanted a third and probably fatal heart attack, he needed to change how he lived. This caused Levenson to undertake a serious assessment of his life. He began walking the streets of New York City late at night. Over a three-month period, he succeeded in "walking off" innumerable blocks to an awareness of love's presence—and his heart problems disappeared. He became enormously happy and lived to the age of eighty-four, spending the rest of his life teaching others what he called "The Sedona Method"—a spiritual path that consists of asking a series of questions that prompt an awareness of your true feelings in the moment and lead to the release of the ego self.

Idle Thoughts

There *are* no idle thoughts. All thinking produces form at some level. (T–2.VI.9:13–14)

In his deep, personal evaluation of his true feelings, Lester asked himself what he wanted most. The answer was "happiness." Next, he asked himself what would make him happy. He realized that he was happy when he was receiving love. Then he had a further revelation. It was not when he was the *recipient* of love that he was most happy; he was the happiest of all whenever he *was* loving.

Our greatest happiness comes from sharing, loving, caring, and giving. We automatically feel good when we do something that is helpful to others. This is especially true when we feel no need to be recognized for what we have done. Charity that wishes to publicize itself ceases to be charity. Applying this principle in his life took Lester to deeper and deeper levels of understanding and to a progressive opening into expanded awareness. Lester's discovery is not new. A 1999 study by social psychologists concluded that the happiest people spend their days giving their love away.

Another story of "hitting bottom" leading to "waking up" is that of teacher and author Byron Katie. Katie became severely depressed and, for over a decade, lived with paranoia, rage, and self-loathing, with thoughts of suicide. One morning in a mental-health treatment facility, she experienced a life-changing spiritual awakening that she calls "waking up to reality." She wrote: "I discovered that when I believed my thoughts, I suffered, but that when I didn't believe them, I didn't suffer, and that this is true for every human being. Freedom is as simple as that. I found that suffering is optional. I found a joy within me that has never disappeared, not for a single moment. That joy is in everyone, always."

Yunmen Wenyan, founder of one of the five major schools of Chan (Chinese Zen), writes: "The time will come when your mind will suddenly come to a stop like an old rat who finds himself in a cul-de-sac." Eckhart Tolle describes this kind of experience in his book *The Power of Now:*

> I cannot live with myself any longer. This was the thought that kept repeating itself in my mind. Then suddenly I became aware of what a peculiar thought it was. Am I one or two? If I cannot live with myself, there must be two of me, the "I" and the "self" that "I" cannot live with. "Maybe," I thought, "only one of them is real." I was so stunned by this strange realization that my mind stopped.

What is so wonderful about hitting bottom is that it enables us to move beyond the evaluating mind that gets us stuck in analysis, a major block in the route to mystical awareness. Bernadette Roberts writes: "The only way out is to be submissive, to accept our helplessness and to recognize the peace of soul—the way it can be found—is our greatest ally." If we truly mean that we need help and we are willing to surrender our own attempts to figure things out, a miraculous thing happens. It's called grace. God steps in. God can't help us when we're trying to control things. We have free will. We can muck things up as much as we want to. Or, we can follow God's lead and enjoy life. The truth is that nothing feels better than the sense that you are leading a guided life.

Oswald Chambers, a well-known Scottish minister, lecturer, and author, realized that, after years of trying, no matter what he did, he couldn't force himself to be holy. He then had a mystical breakthrough, which he described in his book *My Utmost for His Highest* as a "radiant, unspeakable emancipation." Chambers writes: "When you are in the dark, listen, and God will give you a very precious message."

Spanish mystic Saint John of the Cross, along with his teacher Teresa of Avila, was known for a deep love for God. He was among the first to subject mystical experiences to what he called "intelligence"—what we today would call psychological investigation. Suffering, he said, is "epistemology." In other words, we learn through suffering. In his most famous work, he wrote: "In the dark night of the soul, bright flows the river of God."

Prophecy or Paranoia?

Mystical experience is the mirror image of paranoia: it sees the universe as a conspiracy organized for my benefit. (Andrew Weil)

Hitting the bottom is not fun, however. It can awaken us, but the price is high. We can go through repeated episodes of loss and despair before truly surrendering—after which a spiritual path or discipline becomes necessary. We fall into great loss and despair when the strategies of the ego lead us nowhere. This does not happen through what seems to be conscious choice, however. After all, no one wants to hit bottom. But it is inevitable that we will encounter difficulties with personal interactions, finances, health, and ongoing relationship issues. Still, there is nothing that says we must crash and burn. We can, with some facility, simply go through a gradual awakening process. Nevertheless, it is true that the darkest moment can reveal the light.

Hubris and Nemesis

Hubris means "excessive arrogance" that creates an image of ourselves that is not real; *nemesis* is "the one thing we cannot overcome." Hubris is always a preface to nemesis, because hubris makes us blind to the needs of others, and in that blindness lies the ego's demise. The ego (which does not exist) thinks it is possible to think a thought outside the Mind of God. But thinking a thought outside of the Mind of God implies separation. Separation can be said to come from arrogance, from a belief by the ego that it actually exists outside of God. The Course takes this a step further: "To accept yourself as God created you cannot be arrogance because it is the denial of arrogance. To accept your littleness is arrogant, because it means that you believe your evaluation of yourself is truer than God's" (T–9.VIII.10:8–9).

How did we get into this predicament of separateness? Where does it come from? "'No man cometh unto the Father but by me' does not mean that I am in any way separate or different from you except in time, and time does not really exist," the Course explains. "The statement is more meaningful in terms of a vertical rather than a horizontal axis" (T–1.II.4:1–2). God did not reject Adam and Eve, and he did not force us out of the Garden of Eden (T–3.I.3:9). We left on our own. We said: "Thank you very much, God, but I would rather do it myself." The theme song of the ego is surely Sinatra's "I'll do it my way." We cannot, however, make it on our own. We can't live without God because *God is Life.*

God is life and God is reality. While we cannot live without God, we can, of course, "try" to live in our own artificial, made-up, dreamlike world. Since God is not only life but reality as well, when we try living without God, we are not fully alive. Some dreams are hellish; some dreams are enjoyable. But they are still all dreams. We read in the Course: "Only after a deep sleep fell upon Adam could he experience nightmares" (T–2:I.4:5). And the worst nightmare of all is that we are alone with no recourse to help.

Simply put, we created this insane dreamworld of separation when, in our own arrogance, we rejected God. In rejecting God, we rejected life. To try to live without God is to create an impermanent fantasy world that is not real life. It is sleeping and dreaming. To find our way Home, we must first awaken from the dream of separation by reversing the thinking of the ego mind. We must change perception and move from selfishness to selflessness, from individuality (separateness) to wholeness (Oneness), from exclusivity (specialness) to inclusivity (Unity). Truth takes no part in all the mad projections of this world. "Arrogance is the denial of love," we learn in the Course, "because love shares and arrogance withholds" (T–10.V.14:1).

Another way to think of arrogance or hubris is as pride. As the saying goes: "Pride cometh before the fall." Pride looks down on others and, when we look down from a great height, we can get dizzy and fall. Adam's selfishness was symbolically "the fall of humankind" into sin and separation. Yet this fallen state does not really exist. We can only dream of separation. We cannot, in fact, be separated from God.

The house of pride is a lonely place where Heaven is shut out. "The Voice of the Holy Spirit does not command, because It is incapable of arrogance," the Course explains.

> It does not demand, because It does not seek control.
> It does not overcome, because It does not attack.
> It merely reminds. It is compelling only because of what It reminds you *of*. It brings to your mind the other way, remaining quiet even in the midst of the turmoil you may make. The Voice for God is always quiet, because It speaks of peace. (T–5.II.7:1–7)

Pride is considered the most serious of the seven deadly sins, as it is the source and ground of the other six. Being prideful, we think we have the right to be greedy, lustful, gluttonous, wrathful, envious, and slothful. Dante spoke of pride as a "perverted love of self." Along with pride come aggression, attack, and a horror of justified injustices. But attack thoughts never serve us, as the more we attack, the more we hurt others and ourselves. Therefore, mystics are enjoined to give up unkind and aggressive thoughts.

For mystics, One-mindedness is the goal. Right-mindedness is the part of our separated mind that contains the Holy Spirit, and right-mindedness must be achieved before One-mindedness can be restored. One-mindedness is eternally whole and cannot be split. The more we choose for the right mind, the more we progressively move toward the one Mind. One-mindedness (our natural home) is the Mind of God— unified Mind. *Ultimately* (which means "now"), only One-mindedness exists. *Ultimately,* only Heaven exists. *Ultimately,* there is nothing outside of Heaven. Only within an illusory dream world can we "think" (hallucinate) that it is possible to live outside of the Mind of God.

We are all the One Child of God. We always have been and always will be. Since God is life, we cannot live without God. If we try to live without God, we are living in a dream world of our own making; and such a world is not reality—it is dreaming. Mystics seek to awaken to an awareness of an identity that is not a separate, broken off, lonely, isolated, egoistic individual. Egos simply do not exist, now or ever, because fantasy is not reality.

Chapter 12

The Miracle of Silence

The pure truth of Atman [Self], which is buried under
Maya [illusion] and the effects of Maya, can be reached by
meditation, contemplation, and other spiritual disciplines
such as a knower of Brahman may prescribe.
—Shankara

In the last chapter, we examined suffering as a path to Oneness. The next most common way of coming to a mystical state is through the exact opposite of the chaos that comes with suffering—meditation, contemplation, and prayer, all of which rely on being quiet and listening. The purpose of meditation is to find freedom from the "self-talk" that keeps us focused on the world. Meditation occurs in a state of non-doing, in simply disconnecting from ego and entering a condition of watchfulness free from ego gratification. Meditation entails watching out for sabotaging thoughts and slowly dismissing each one, coming to silence, and being receptive to guidance.

The intention of meditation and contemplation is liberation. The mind can truly rest only when it is not narcissistically engaged in the ego thought system. "You can speak from the spirit or from the ego, as you choose," the Course says:

If you speak from spirit, you have chosen to "Be still and know that I am God." These words are inspired because they reflect knowledge. If you speak from the ego you are disclaiming knowledge instead of affirming it, and are thus dis-spiriting yourself. (T–4.In.2:1–4)

If we cannot stop the ego mind, we can at least get to a neutral place of detached objectivity. We can be careful and aware when using words like "upset" or "disappointed." What is it that is upset? What is it that is disappointed? Only an ego can be upset. Only an ego can be disappointed. We can observe the mind and thoughts without attachment. When we stop judging the world—when we stop "making up the world"—then we can see more clearly. Meditation and contemplation are means of sharpening and freeing the mind from the ego thought system so this can occur.

The ego is always ready to attack and to defend. But attack and defense are unknown in Heaven. "Be still and know" is thus central to understanding reality. Each of the world's religious faiths has a monastic branch whose purpose is to step away from the world. Moving into a "cloistered" situation and being still makes room for contemplation. Many of our most devoted mystics have been monks and nuns who stepped away from the world and moved into presence—into an inner knowing of reality/God. Heraclites tells us: "When one's mind becomes stilled, intelligence is experienced separate from appearances."

The final stage reached by a teacher of God—by someone who lives from knowledge of God—is complete open-mindedness. We want to see everything as God does. With new awareness, we can let go, be cleansed, and relinquish the ego thought system and its projected illusions.

Conversing with God

To be contemplative is not to be silent, but to be in silent dialogue with God. The more awake we are to divine reality, the more we actively engage in such dialogue. Yet this conversation is not what we commonly think of as dialogue. Rather than chattering back and forth, contemplative dialogue is a focusing of thoughts. It involves deliberate attention and a conscious stilling of the ego mind so that deeper thoughts can arise.

Contemplation is not a complete stopping of the mind. It is rather a quieting of the mind. Contemplation simply sees what is. It is *loving sight*. Scholars of all sorts—mathematicians, artists, writers, musicians, anyone who can focus attention away from themselves to enlarge their awareness—engage in contemplation. Through it, artists become great artists. Through it, Einstein became a famous mathematician and a great mystic. According to Evelyn Underhill, all artists are, of necessity, contemplative. She calls it being "innocent of eye." In her book *Mysticism*, she describes three forms of contemplation:

1. *Contemplation of the natural world of becoming:* witnessing the natural world in whatever form presents itself to the eye, be it an ant or the Alps.

2. *Contemplation of the metaphysical world of being:* witnessing without the bodily senses, being engaged in awareness, without evaluation.

3. *Contemplation of divine reality:* a combination of
   the first two that entails the dying away of the
   will so that only absolute love is experienced.

Wisdom Seeds

Thirteenth-century Buddhist Master Dogen taught
a variety of Zen called *zazen*—a practice in which
the meditator sits "in a state of brightly alert attention," free of thoughts, directed to no object, and
attached to no particular content. This state of
mind is "present everywhere." There is nothing
it does not contain. "However," said Dogen, "only
those who have planted wisdom seeds will be able
to continuously see it."

If possible, try to have some quiet time every day, or
even several hours every week. Go for a walk in a cemetery
or a park, or find a trail. Ride a motorcycle across the desert. Go for a bike ride, go fishing, play music, paint, write,
read, do some journaling. Just sit. Do not be projective. Listen. Be contented with the world. Thoreau headed for the
woods. Thomas Merton went to a monastery. Refrain from
places that cost a lot of money, where people eat a lot of food
and drink intoxicants. Retreat from the world. Go into the
woods. Visit a yoga studio or Zen center. In the Hindu tradition, the elderly used to become forest dwellers, spending
time in peaceful preparation for the transition from life to

life. The mind must disengage from the ego in order for the mystical to come into view.

Fourteenth-century German mystic Johannes Tauler, following Meister Eckhart, stressed the inner person rather than outer works. His writings were popular in Protestant circles during the Reformation and later in the Romantic Era. He was believed to be part of the community that produced the *Theologia Germanica,* a mystical work that proposed that God and man can be wholly united by following an inner path of perfection. According to Tauler: "Everyone should find some suitable time, day or night, to sink into his depths, each according to his own fashion. Not everyone is able to engage in contemplative prayer."

A friend in his sixties tells a story about taking a walk among the giant Sequoia trees in Washington State with his four-year-old grandson and a puppy. The child was completely lost in play with the puppy, and the puppy was lost in sniffing out all the wonderful smells of the forest. He sat down at the foot of a huge Sequoia tree, laid his back against the trunk, and just watched his grandson and the dog at play. "The moment," he said, "was absolutely perfect." He felt as if he were in Heaven. He had no major cares or concerns, and a deep sense of the interconnectedness of all things came over him. He found himself in a state of bliss. Then his grandson tripped over a root, fell, and started to cry. The world was back, and he was back in it.

More or Less

"Egoless" does not mean "less" than personal; it means "more than personal." (Ken Wilber)

Solitary sports like running, hiking, rock climbing, biking, sailing, flying, soaring, gliding, and fishing provide time for inner reflection and revelation. When I was growing up on the farm in Missouri, while the rest of us went to church on Sunday mornings, my dad went fishing. We had a pond on the back of our farm that he kept stocked with freshwater bass. Dad couldn't say: "You guys go to church. I'm going to go meditate out by the bass pond." He had to have a reason, so he took along a fishing pole. We often had fish dinners on Sunday evenings. Thoreau must have been thinking of someone like my dad when he wrote: "Many men go fishing, all their lives, without realizing—it's not fish they are after."

Contemplation is simply being very aware of our surroundings at all times. And this means our inner surroundings as well. Pay attention to what you are doing and how you are feeling as you perform the many small acts that make up your day. There are many times during our routine and seemingly mundane lives that we can access moments like this—moments of stillness and calm. Artists talk about getting into the flow when they let go, lose track of time, and then enter a deep place of peace called the "zone." Athletes talk about "the runner's high." An international triathlon winner once told me he won a triathlon event when an inner voice told him he did not need to stop and rest as the others were doing. His legs went on automatic pilot and he just kept moving, transcending the pain and finding a place of peace.

In the morning in the shower, when you are alone and no one is likely to walk in, you can close your eyes and imagine yourself being baptized, the water washing more than your body. Your mind is still uncluttered with thoughts of the day and you can feel a growing awakening going on inside. John Lilly once called driving a car "the American mode of meditation," because, although driving initially requires concentration, it rapidly becomes second nature and we do it intuitively. When I was younger, one of my favorite modes of meditation was riding my motorcycle through the open desert in Southern California. There was one spot where a wonderful set of small hills rolled out like a roller coaster. Even now, driving home at night, I sometimes turn off the radio or CD and just listen to the sound of the tires on the pavement. I no longer have a motorcycle.

Creative expression is driven by the same psychological processes as contemplation. Thus mystical awakenings can also occur during moments of profound creativity, when the mind "disengages" and we see the interconnectivity of all things. This vision often happens when two or more fundamentals—like words and musical notes, or shapes and colors—come together in a new and pleasing way. English art critic Cyril Connolly once said: "The reward of art is not fame or success but intoxication." We get lost to find ourselves. According to an article in *Scientific American Mind*, those who throw themselves into "ideas" that are bigger than they are are never bored. People like Thomas Edison, Nikola Tesla, Albert Einstein, and Madame Curie were never bored.

The Power of Prayer

Prayer is the center of all religious life. Devout Muslims pray five times each day. Buddhists, Hindus, Christians, and Jews pray daily. Even atheists pray when they are in trouble. Truly, there are no atheists in foxholes. In fact, "allegiance to the denial of God," the Course observes, "is the ego's religion" (T–10.V.3:1). There is also no one who has not experienced what seems to be failure at prayer. When that happens, we may wonder: "Is God listening? Or, am I just not a good communicator?"

Lost at Sea

Two shipwrecked sailors were adrift on a raft for days. In desperation, one knelt and began to pray. "Oh, Lord, I haven't lived a good life. I've drunk too much. I've lied. I've cheated. I've gambled. I've caroused with women. I've done many bad things. But, Lord, if you'll save me, I promise . . ."

"Don't say another word!" shouted his shipmate. "I think I spotted a ship."

Twentieth-century science historian Jacob Bronowski notes in his book *The Ascent of Man* that success in science does not come until science asks the right question. The answer is always there; but first, we have to ask the right question. Prayer works in much the same way. God cannot answer prayer with an illusion, nor is it possible that God can give you something hurtful. Much of what we call prayer is simply asking God to help us on our own terms. Contemplative prayer, on the other hand, comes not from need, but from love.

For a number of years, I led monthly discussions at a local bookstore that focused on "Spiritual Books." One month, the manager asked me if I would do a session on *The Secret,* a book based on the Law of Attraction. I agreed and the discussion drew a large crowd. Apparently everyone wanted to know "the secret." The book claims that positive thinking can create positive results. Indeed, it can. We may pray for success, work hard, and achieve it. But we have to think about whom we are praying to and what we are praying for. The ego can also answer prayers, but its answers do not always bring us peace. The ego is very subtle. It may persuade us to go into debt to obtain some earthly reward. That idea may be appealing in the short term, but the debt must be paid eventually—and with interest. "The mind is very powerful," the Course reminds us, "and never loses its creative force. It never sleeps. Every instant it is creating" (T–2.VI.9:5–7). For good and for evil.

There are many examples of how "positive" thinking, or "possibility" thinking, or "prosperity" thinking can keep us focused on getting what we want in the world. Many popular speakers espouse this philosophy, and it is easy to see why they have achieved success. Much power is gained through training and exercising the mind. There are plenty of audio and YouTube productions designed to pump up the mind. But what mind are we pumping up? True happiness lies only in the expansion of peace and thus the creation of Heaven.

Our task is not to affirm the affirmative. Our task is to negate the negative, thereby finding freedom from the ego.

Real success means removing the blocks to an awareness of love's presence. The question is: "To whom do I give my mind?" You can run needles through your body and not hurt yourself. You can walk on hot coals without getting burned. You can endure long periods without sleep. You can lose a lot of weight. You can make a lot of money and amass great wealth and power. *The Guinness Book of World Records* is filled with amazing examples of mind over matter. But these are not miracles and they do not bring us closer to God. They may, on the other hand, be helpful if they bring us to a better understanding of the power of the mind.

These events may also be more "thaumaturgy" than truly miraculous. Thaumaturgy is defined as "the working of wonders or miracles"; but it is also magic. It works on a different level from the truly miraculous. Magic may work with illusion, but God cannot answer prayer with an illusion. God can give only "good" gifts to his children.

The ego can dress itself up with many different chains. I knew a man who chained himself to a luxury car for seven years by committing to $800-per-month car payments. His wife was very angry and might have agreed with the Course when it says: "Escape today the chains you place upon your mind when you perceive salvation here. For what you value you make part of you as you perceive yourself. All things you seek to make your value greater in your sight limit you further, hide your worth from you, and add another bar across the door that leads to true awareness of your Self" (W–128.3:1–3).

Mystics do not confuse form and content. How we stand, sit, or kneel (form) when we pray does not matter, and words are but symbols of symbols. Quieting the mind, looking out the window watching birds at the bird feeder, watching a water fountain, or reverently humming a chant are as much prayers as any said in words. It's the prayer of the heart that blesses the world it sees. It's content that matters. As Bunyan wrote in *The Pilgrim's Progress:* "In prayer, it is better to have a heart without words than words without heart."

Alphabetical Prayers

A grandfather passed his granddaughter's bedroom and overheard her repeating the alphabet. He asked her: "What on earth are you up to?"

"I'm saying my prayers," she explained, "but I don't remember the words, so I'm just saying all the letters. I'll let God put it together for me."

What we ask for is what we receive. So what are you asking for and whom are you asking? Before we choose to do anything, it's best to ask if the choice is in accord with Spirit. If you feel no fear, it's the right answer and the pathway will be clear. We get the wrong answer by making up our mind first, and then telling the Holy Spirit how things should work out. In this case, we have not really asked at all. If your mind is already made up, what good does it do to ask?

What is the difference between the voice of God and the voice of the ego? You can tell by looking at the results. If you do not like the results, one of three things happened: you asked the wrong question; you asked the wrong teacher; or you asked the wrong teacher the wrong question.

Once we abandon our own terms, the right question and the right answer will appear. American Indian poet James Dillet Freeman writes: "Sometimes the answer to prayer is not that it changes life, but it changes you." When the answer to prayer is right—we know; there is no question. We do not have to solve problems on our own. We can ask for help from the ego or from Spirit. Whichever one we choose will give us an answer. When the ego answers our prayers, we are left wanting. When God answers our prayers, we find peace.

Contemplative Prayer

Contemplative prayer is a state of communion and a direct awareness of God. Such communion is the natural state of those who *know* the Divine, and they can live in peace. It is non-thinking meditation. As we move beyond thinking, we *feel* God as a living presence, as an awareness that occurs when we stop incessant thinking. Contemplative prayer is prayer of the heart because, although the heart center is not a place of words, words work in their own small way. Chants and mantras used in different spiritual traditions to "quiet" or "still" the mind consist of one heart-centered thought, phrase, or word that is repeated many times.

Contemplative prayer is an experience of God as the ground of our being. While words may be used to focus the mind, it becomes less and less a matter of saying anything and increasingly a matter of abiding in quietude. It is observing without judgment, interpretation, or analysis. It is acceptance of a movement toward the Divine, a deepening of spiritual life, and a freeing of ourselves from the fetters of the world.

Prayer Is...

- An offering

- A letting go

- A stepping aside

- A giving up of ourselves

- A means of communication

- A time of listening, loving, and surrendering

Contemplative prayer is something we do all the time, something that becomes a part of us. It is an experience of God at the center of our being. Communion comes simply by letting God be God. Such prayer is not supplication or entreaty. It's not magic or wishful thinking. It's not wanting in times of scarcity and lack, nor telling God what we need. And it doesn't really matter if our prayers are answered. Nineteenth-century poet and novelist Jean Ingelow said: "I have lived to thank God that all my prayers have not been answered."

Contemplative prayer is trusting. It is a way of living. It is something we do every minute of every day. It is the opening of the mind, the heart, and the whole being to God. At the core of contemplative prayer, there is silence. It is spoken silently, deeply within, where there is an opening of the heart and a simple receptivity—a knowing. "Prayer is a way offered by the Holy Spirit to reach God," the Course tells us.

"It is not merely a question or an entreaty. It cannot succeed until you realize that it asks for nothing" (S–I.1:1–3).

The first course in my training for the ministry was Beginning Preaching. Yet Jesus never taught his disciples to preach—only to pray. When it came to preaching, he told them to open their mouths and follow inner guidance. When the disciples asked Jesus to teach them to pray, he said: "When you pray, pray thus. Our Father which art in Heaven, Hallowed be thy name, Thy Kingdom come, Thy will be done." There is no greater prayer than *Thy will be done.*

Chapter 13

The Miracle of Work

The spiritual life is not a special career, involving abstraction
from the world of things. It is a part of every man's life; and
until he has realized it, he is not a complete human being, has
not entered into possession of all his powers.
—Evelyn Underhill, *Practical Mysticism*

Erik Erickson, a German-born American developmental psychologist, describes eight stages that we all go through in the process of maturation. Six of Erikson's eight stages occur in the formative years from infancy through young adulthood; the eighth, which he calls the "mature years," applies specifically to older people. The seventh stage, from young adulthood to the mature years, is the longest and constitutes most of our working years. During this stage, says Erikson, we need to be "generative." We need to work, to produce, to create—to be responsible, constructive, contributing participants in this world. If we cannot be generative, we are often frustrated and despairing.

The business of the mystic is the discovery of true knowledge, ultimately found, not in the world, but in the innermost core of our being. While that process of discovery is often called the mystic's "work," it is truly a blessed journey. Sometimes, we may be forced inward by hardship, as was the inspirational American author and lecturer Helen Keller. Unable to hear, see, or speak, she "had" to go within, and there she found God. Having done so, she could say: "I thank God for my handicaps, for through them, I have found myself, my work, and my God." Luke tells us that Jesus, at the age of twelve, asked his parents: "Do you not know that I must be about my Father's business?" (Luke 2:29). Thus, while contemplation implies an inner journey and nonattachment, as David Hawkins tells us, this "does not preclude activity." American psychotherapist Thomas Moore agrees, saying: "You don't become a mystic by wishing it so. There's work to do. You need some quiet time, some contemplation, some meditation, some deprivation, and some deep prayer."

The Alchemy of Work

Given sufficient practice, we can achieve a contemplative state and maintain it while performing everyday tasks. We can even achieve an undercurrent of awareness in everything from taking a shower to eating, to sculpting, to reading, to working at a computer. Something underneath our activities is continuously flowing. Jesus asks: "With what can we compare the Kingdom of God? . . . It is like a grain of mustard seed, which, when sown upon the ground, is the smallest of all the seeds on earth, yet when it is sown it grows up and becomes the greatest of the shrubs, and puts forth large branches, so that the birds of the air can make nests in its shade" (Matthew 13:31–35).

The parable of the mustard seed describes a process by which a mystic may become more aware. There is something deep inside us that produces transformation. The farmer may not know how it happens—we may not know how it happens—nonetheless, the inner working of the seed produces transformation. The alchemists were after gold, but the gold they sought was merely the outward symbol of a transformation that had to occur within them. One ancient alchemical text enjoins the seeker to "forbear who believes that Alchemy is concerned solely with the mundane, mineral, and metallic nature of things. Alchemy is but a symbol used to reveal by analogy the process of achieving spiritualization."

Work speaks in quiet ways. It is a blessing and never a curse. We are always working our way Home—even when we play. Rumi tells us that the desire for work "was put in our hearts." Mark Twain said that he never worked a day in his life. He was always at play. If it had been work, he said, he would not have done it.

Mystics love doing whatever they do. As they become involved in their work, they develop "mastery." Mystics know that, although they may not yet be fully realized Masters, they can find confidence in knowing that their feet are on the path and they are headed Home. As we develop mastery, we find ourselves being transported, promoted, advanced, or "fired" into a yet deeper dimension of work. In the workaday world, we celebrate Fridays and bemoan Mondays because the "nine-to-five" grind can be burdensome and grievous to many. But that's not true for those who love what they do and do what they love. Vietnamese Buddhist Thich Nhat Hanh tells us: "There are two ways to wash dishes. The first is to wash dishes in order to have clean dishes; the second is to wash dishes in order to wash dishes."

Karma Yoga (the way of action) and Bhakti Yoga (the way of love) call upon us to work with devotion through self-less service. When we work with dedication, whether peeling potatoes, sweeping the floor, or cleaning up another's mess, it is not a curse or a chore, but an act of love. Selfless service promotes awareness and develops wisdom, patience, and forbearance. Twentieth-century Indian guru Swami Ramdas lived on charity, but he never accepted money. His practice was to view the world as forms of Ram (God). Therefore, he saw everything that might befall him as the Will of God. "Whatever act you do is worship," he said, "when it is done with the thought of God." Mysticism is the acknowledgment that we are all One. Consequently, whatever good works we do are done for ourselves.

Work is rewarding when we are *engrossed*, *immersed*, or *wrapped up* in it. Then there is only the love of doing what we are doing. Devotion is a way of being with ourselves and with God. Any work done with devotion facilitates awakening. When we move deeply into work and creative endeavors, we set aside the ego. Musicians do not think about where their fingers go. When they start thinking about which finger goes where, they are apt to make mistakes.

Medieval mystics felt that work done with the hands provided knowledge inaccessible to the leisured class. When the Church descended into the Dark Ages and mystical studies were forced underground, they were conducted secretively within the various trades, or guilds. When a corrupt and authoritative Church was unable to offer spiritual solace, people found comfort and mystical insight in the practice of their crafts and trades—blacksmithing, silversmithing, carpentry, masonry, medicine, leatherworking, music, and more.

Freemasonry was one outgrowth of this deep esoteric inner working that was not allowed within the Church. The word "mason," now used to describe the esoteric fraternity, comes from the French word *mason* meaning, "one who works with bricks and mortar." Carl Jung and Winston Churchill both laid bricks to invigorate and center themselves.

On Vacation

When our avocation is our vocation, we are always on vacation. (Jon)

Work is something we do with our heads, our hearts, and our hands. Although fewer people dig, drill, carve, chisel, mold, assemble, forge, cut, weave, sculpt, sew, paint, or saw today, we use our hands to touch computer keys and buttons on our cell phones. The most respected of ancient occupations were actually those in which people did *fine work* with their hands. Thus in art and music, as well as in the trades, people were making inroads into the soul—without the Church. Hermes Trismegistus, legendary Neoplatonist and alchemist, writes: "The work is with you and in you in such a way that once you find it in yourself, where it always is, you have it always, wherever you may be, on land or sea."

The alchemists' symbol is the athanor, the furnace. A furnace is where things are transformed through fire, or heat. Alchemy involves turning things over, buffing them, burnishing them, rubbing and polishing them, improving, changing, and perfecting them until they are fully realized. The book is written, the house built, the concert performed, the painting completed, the Self realized. Fire is the most ancient alchemical catalyst. Human consciousness developed around campfires. Staring into a fire for hours on end leads to meditation. The earliest mystics used fire in their crafts. They were potters, smiths, cooks, and bakers. And like the process of self-realization, the working of pottery, glass-blowing, and forging and molding bronze and other metals all involve a number of stages.

Thich Nhat Hanh describes the symbiotic process of self-realization thus: "Without a rose we cannot have garbage. Without garbage we cannot have a rose." Contemplation calls upon us to "turn things over" until the cooking is done. Through the process of rot or decay and putrefaction, we recycle our lives and turn base things into gold. "For the earth brings forth fruit of herself; first the blade, then the ear, after that the full corn in the ear" (Mark 4:28). We place little "gems" into the soil, water them, and then watch as they come forth from the dark earth, turning into fruit and flowers in the light of the sun. Then we take raw food matter and combine it with other foods. We mix, beat, heat, and cool them until we have turned them into what nourishes the body.

Likewise, when we write, we take an idea, jot it down, work it over, add to it, and work it over again. Then we set it aside, go away, and return to the work with a fresh perspective. Then we edit, cut out the chaff, leave the gold, bring in new ideas, sift through, synthesize—feed again, sift through again—until it's finally done. This process of keeping a spiritual diary deepens the writer. Thoreau and Kierkegaard both took journal writing seriously. Kierkegaard said his journal was his "most trusted confidant." Japanese Buddhist Dainin Katagiri, who emphasized the need to return to our original, enlightened state, claimed: "If you commit to it, writing can take you as deep as Zen."

Such inner work is an ongoing process. It involves the discovery and unfolding of an insight that is progressively wonderful and fulfilling. Gandhi found alchemy in the act of spinning. Your alchemy may be music—or you may knit, or quilt, or sail, or sculpt, or work with wood. Through this work, the wood speaks to the carpenter, the garden converses with the gardener, and the piano plays with the pianist.

Loving what we do and hearing the call of destiny in it, understanding God's plan and throwing ourselves into it, help us discover greater and greater depths of creativity and increase our fulfillment. While insight can be gained instantaneously—in a lightning flash of intuition or insight—for the majority of us trekking through the world of illusion, spiritual maturing takes time. It's the "cooking," the gestation, the seed growing secretly that deepens character. There are many ways of serving God, and no one way is holier than another. But the way we approach the work is holy—or not. Whatever you are doing—cleaning the house or writing a book, washing dishes or playing a musical instrument— when we do it in service and with devotion, we find out more about God.

Commitment

Buddhism emphasizes right livelihood, which involves the integration of survival with doing what you are supposed to be doing. Right livelihood requires commitment to something you are happy doing for a lifetime. How long a project takes doesn't matter. Aging works in your favor when it comes to right livelihood. The more you do our work, the better you get at what you do, the more you develop character and creativity. I once watched a documentary on people in their nineties who were healthy, active, and seemed determined to live past 100. All of them were working!

We've all seen bumper stickers that say: "I'd rather be flying," or "dancing," or "sailing," or whatever. What we *should* be doing is what we would *rather* be doing. People get paid for flying, and dancing, and sailing. Focus on what calls to your soul. As Joseph Campbell said: "Follow your bliss." When you integrate who you are with what you do and what you do with who you are, you cannot be other than happy. To the ego, work is a curse. To the mystic, work is nothing less than a happy means of returning Home. Work is central to who you *already* are. It is grease on the hinge that opens the door. Any work can be creative. The more creative it is, the more we enjoy it. The more we enjoy our work, the more we feel we are doing what we are supposed to.

Self-Made Man

The self you made is not the Son of God. Therefore, this self does not exist at all. And anything it seems to do and think means nothing. It is neither bad nor good. It is unreal, and nothing more than that. (W–93.5:1–5)

Contemporary mystic Barbara Marx Hubbard describes what she calls "vocational arousal" as "your own deep genius turning on." It is your unique life purpose, activating you. Work to be *who you are.* Don't worry about money. Remember what Mark Twain said—if it had been work, he wouldn't have done it.

Hinduism divides life into three stages: in the first, you study; in the second, you become a householder; in the third, you become a *sannyasi* (a renunciate). According to Hindu texts, when your children are grown and your hair is turning gray, it is time to head for the forest, where you can go ever deeper into a contemplative life. Today, this practice is not actively pursued as it once was, but the ideal is still there in our concept of "retirement." To become a *sannyasi* is to become totally devoted to God, renouncing all fears and all desires. The sole aim is to attain *moksha,* or liberation— release from the circle of birth and death. Thoreau writes:

> The choice of how to make one's living is crucial, for the work we do makes us what we become; The blacksmith pounds the anvil—but the anvil also pounds the blacksmith. The clamshell turns golden in the brown depths of the ocean, and in a more subtle way is one's mind colored by the course of one's life. When a man chooses his labor, he chooses his future self.

Pearl S. Buck, author of the Pulitzer Prize-winning *The Good Earth,* agrees. The secret of joy in work, she said, is contained in one word—excellence. To know how to do something well is to enjoy it. Artists do not retire; musicians do not retire; writers do not retire. Whatever you're doing, love yourself for doing it.

PART III

The Miracle of Mysticism

Mysticism is very far away in space and
time and very near if we can see it.
—Jon Mundy

Chapter 14

The End of the Body

Appetites are getting mechanisms, representing the ego's need to confirm itself. This is as true of body appetites as it is of the so-called higher ego needs. Body appetites are not physical in origin.

T–4.II.7:5–7

Metaphysics asks: What is real? What does it mean "to be"? Is any "thing" real? What is man's place in the Universe? Is my subjective experience real? Can anything be known purely objectively? Does the world exist outside of my mind? What is the nature of the events that occur in our lives? Are all events meaningful or is it all happenstance?

The thread that runs through all these questions is *illusion,* which is the ground of all our subjective experience. There are four elements—integrally tied together—that make up this vast illusion that we call "reality." They are: the body, time, the world, and the ego, or what we call individuality. For mystics, none of these are real. Life is a school, and the unwinding of the seeming reality of these four things serves to bring them back to God.

The Ego's Chosen Home

Mystics sometimes have a hard time knowing how to deal with the body. Our appetite for food, sex, and pleasures of all sorts imprisons us in a place the Course calls "the ego's chosen home." The body can do only what the mind asks it to do. Thought always comes first. According to Ramana Maharshi, a man drinks because he hates the idea of being bound by the incapacity to drink as much as he wishes. Having free will does not mean we can abuse freedom. Drinking too much does not bring us liberty; rather it enslaves us. It is the mind, not the body, that decides to have another drink, light a cigarette, take an extra helping of food, or call someone else an idiot.

Some early Christian mystics sought to punish the body through mortification of the flesh—by wearing hair shirts, sitting outdoors in inclement weather, flagellating themselves with whips, or fasting to the point of death. All these attempts to either punish or escape the body, ironically, made the body all the more real. At the other extreme were the freethinking libertines who, while saying that the body was inconsequential, thought they could do anything they wanted with it. They engaged in bodily excesses of all sorts—sex, eating, drinking—that, again, made the body seem all the more real. Fourteenth-century German mystic Heinrich Seuse, a follower of Eckhart, is a good example of this. He endured fasting, sleep deprivation, extreme cold, iron chains, self-flagellation, and a nail-studded coat (ouch!). He rubbed salt and vinegar into his wounds. Eventually, he was healed of this obsession when he said the Holy Spirit told him that God wanted him to stop hurting his body. Seuse suffered persecution by the Church until his death. Five hundred years after he died, the Church made him a saint.

We all have an ambivalent relationship with our bodies. Sometimes we love them; sometimes we hate them; and all the while we wonder how we got into them. Plato called the body a "tomb." Seneca said it was an inn in which we stay only briefly. Palladas, a fourth-century Greek philosopher, called it an affliction of the soul, a burden, a chain, and a tormenting punishment. Mahatma Gandhi called it a prison. "Yet is the *body* prisoner, and not the mind," the Course likewise claims. "The body thinks no thoughts. It has no power to learn, to pardon, nor enslave. It gives no orders that the mind need serve, nor sets conditions that it must obey" (T–3. III.4:1–4).

You are not a body. The body is a limit imposed on the universal communication. The body is a tool we can use to "reduce down" our thinking. While the body appears outside of us, it seems to surround us, as part of our "identity." It is "the central figure in the dreaming of the world." It is a "tiny fence" around a little part of a glorious and complete idea in the Mind of God. Philo of Alexandria, who lived during the first century, described the body as a tomb. Eleventh-century Islamic scholar al-Ghazali likened it to a camel carrying its burdens through the world. According to the Course, the body is a thought of separation projected by the mind into form. It is our error of identifying with the body that results in a split mind—and, therefore, bewilderment. On the one hand, while we intuit the illusory nature of the body—with all its pleasures, its aches and pains—we experience overwhelming affirmation every day that we *are* bodies.

The Ego and the Body

The ego has three primary uses for the body: attack, pleasure, and pride. It is easy to remember them by the acronym APP.

We are very good at attack—with our tongues, with the written word, with fists and guns. Of course, the idea that we can get what we want by attack is insane. Physical attack emanates from the lowest form of thinking. Do we really want to hurt? "No one attacks without intent to hurt," the Course tells us. "This can have no exception" (W–170.1:1–2).

When we attack, we feel guilty afterward. Then we try to escape the guilt by projecting it. By projecting guilt, we hold on to it. "Projection will always hurt you," the Course maintains. "It reinforces your belief in your own split mind, and its only purpose is to keep the separation going. It is solely a device of the ego to make you feel different from your brothers and separated from them" (T–6.II.3:1–3).

The attraction of guilt within leads to seeing guilt in others. From this perspective, we "love" to find problems in the world. By finding guilt in others, we hope to demonstrate our own innocence. Of course, this ploy never works. But now we run into a paradox and a problem. When we attack, we inevitably create more guilt. Not wanting to look at how much we are attacking, we bury the source of our guilt ever more deeply—which is why we must look honestly at it. The ego's game is one of seesaw. By putting someone else down, we rise—or so the ego thinks. "Name calling" and any other form of attack never get anyone anything but pain. "You who think you hate your body deceive yourself," the Course teaches us. "You hate your mind, for guilt has entered into it, and it would remain separate from your brother's, which it cannot do" (T–18.VI.2:7–8). Looking at the guilt within isn't easy, but with the aid of the Holy Spirit, we can learn how to forgive ourselves and the resulting freedom we gain is well worth the effort.

Who Do You Love?

It is the nature of love to look upon only the truth, for there it sees itself, with which it would unite in holy union and completion. As love must look past fear, so must fear see love not. (T–19.IV.A.10:2–3)

The second way in which the ego uses the body is for pleasure. There is nothing wrong with pleasure. The difficulty with pleasurable activities is that their resulting gratification is temporary and they must be repeated over and over to maintain the experience. We can juxtapose *pleasure*, which is of the body and temporal, with *joy*, which is of the mind and eternal. "Joy is an ongoing process, not in time but in eternity" (T–6.V.1:6). Since pleasure must be repeated to maintain the experience, it can lead to addiction. Overindulgence never makes us happy; we feel guilty when we get caught in overeating, drinking too much, taking drugs, or being judgmental.

It is really very simple: the more we eat, the more we want to eat. The less we eat, the less we need to eat. As with everything, it is a choice. Those who achieve freedom from addiction say that, once they were clearly beyond the addiction, they could no longer understand why such a hurtful habit once seemed so important. "You do not ask too much of life, but far too little," the Course points out. "When you let your mind be drawn to bodily concerns, to things you buy, to eminence as valued by the world, you ask for sorrow, not for happiness" (W–133.2:1–2).

After attack (A) and pleasure (P) comes pride (P), the third letter of our acronym. Pride is a close cousin to power. Pick up a magazine. Flip through the pages and look at the ads. Most of them are about something to make the body look better (clothes, jewelry), smell better (perfume, cosmetics), or feel better (alcohol, sweets). And then there are the endless ads for drugs. At the heart of the ego's thought system is the belief that, if I am sinful, if I am guilty, if I am a separate body, then I must be separate from God. While this may bring a sense of pride or power, it can never bring us peace. As we get deeper into metaphysics, we learn that "no thing" exists outside of the Mind of God. We cannot exist outside of God's love, which is why the body, the world, and time are all illusions. Mystics learn to be comfortable in the body, in the world, and in time. Peace is a state of mind—the mind at rest in God.

Regardless of the condition or location of the body, the mind can be at peace. Seeking pleasure through the body makes it seem real—which also means making the ego seem real. The only real and lasting joy comes in doing God's will. Choosing the peace and love of God is *our only true pleasure*. "In the holy instant there are no bodies, and you experience only the attraction of God" (T–15.IX.7:3). In fact, there is no ego, and yet it seems very real. Seeing without the ego— seeing through the eyes of love—is always an experience of grace. The ego's world is limited, lonely, and destined to end. But Spirit can't end because, being eternal—it never started!

Bodily pleasures are not sinful. Since every "thing" is temporal, our enjoyment of "things" is also temporal. Lasting satisfaction is only found in the eternal. Joy comes in fulfilling God's plan for salvation. Aligning our mind with God's is our greatest joy. First-century Jewish philosopher and mystic Philo of Alexandria argued that the unitive reality experienced in the contemplative state was ever-one, unmoving, and unchanging. At the same time, it was also manifest in the world of form. The intuitive, direct experiencing and knowing of mysticism are thus more revelatory than philosophical speculation. It is possible, he said, "to actually 'see' God." Philo reflects the basic story of mysticism when he writes:

> All whom Moses calls wise are sojourners. Their souls are colonists leaving heaven for a new home. Their way is to visit earthly nature as men who travel abroad to see and learn. So, when they have stayed awhile in their bodies and beheld through them all that sense and mortality have to show, they may make their way back to the place from which they first set out. To them the heavenly region where their citizenship lies is their native land; the earthly region in which they became sojourners is a foreign country.

Spirit and the Body

Everything the ego uses, Spirit can use as well—but only for good. The acronym—LCFH—indicates learning, communication, forgiveness, and healing.

In the hands of Spirit, the body becomes a *learning device*. We learn through the body, through time, through miracles, and through Holy Instants. "Only the mind can create because spirit has already been created, and the body is a learning device for the mind," the Course points out. "Learning devices are not lessons in themselves. Their purpose is merely to facilitate learning. The worst a faulty use of a learning device can do is to fail to facilitate learning" (T–2. IV.3:1–4).

Second Time Around

The First Coming of Christ is merely another name for the creation, for Christ is the Son of God. The Second Coming of Christ means nothing more than the end of the ego's rule and the healing of the mind. (T–4.IV.10:1–2)

If the body is a learning device, then the world is our school. The way we learn in school is through *communication*. The primary function of the body is to give and receive information—in a word, communication. We learn through talking and listening, through reading and writing, and through trying to understand. We are all *always* teaching and learning. And the question is not: What would you like to teach? The question is: What would God have you learn?

Our primary learning is one of *forgiveness*—that is, learning to let other people be who they are without trying to judge or fix them. That does not mean that we allow others to rape, murder, and steal. Ultimately, we must let go of all that hurts and all things that bring us pain, realizing that only an ego can be disheartened or disillusioned. Only an ego can experience guilt; only an ego can be arrogant; only an ego can live in fear and doubt. Forgiveness simply means "letting go" of everything that hurts, everything that brings us pain. And all this letting go means holding on to nothing.

Forgiveness leads us to *healing*. The body and time are learning devices. But miracles are also learning devices. When we forgive, when we really let something go, we are healed. Then we come to understand why forgiveness is a miracle. The process of learning to forgive occurs through learning and communication; the result is forgiveness and a healing of our minds—and thus also of all our relationships.

The Attraction of God

So you have two choices. We can let the ego use our body; or we can let Spirit use it. We can feed the ravenous ego, or nourish Spirit. When we free ourselves from the ego, we become more aware of the presence of Spirit. There is an ongoing attraction, or "pull," toward God. When we regularly and consistently raise our spiritual awareness, Spirit develops a natural thirst for—an addiction to—God. As we get a positive addiction going, smaller wants and needs seem less attractive.

Moving deeper into the contemplative mind means becoming more aware. There is only one God, one Universe, and one fundamental power that deserves our attention. When we study the lives of the mystics, when we look at the early Church Fathers and Mothers, we find individuals who were so overcome by the attraction of God that they stepped away from "the world" in order to seek only God. Indian teacher Maharaja Nisargadatta said that our true nature is "perpetually free, peaceful awareness." This awareness exists prior to mind, memory, and body. The idea that we *are* the body keeps us from living what he called our "original essence."

The notions of "good" and "bad" appear as the mind judges the functions of the body. The body can be a helpful tool for communication and learning. As the central figure in the ego's dream of the world, it can also be an object of separation. It is depressing to be *only* a body. Spirit, not the body, is reality. Japanese Zen Master D. T. Suzuki says: "Because you think you have a body or mind, you have lonely feelings, but when you realize that everything is just a flashing into the vast universe, you become very strong, and your existence becomes very meaningful."

Chapter 15

The End of Time

The world of time is where all things end.
W–129.2:6

Yogi Berra, the famous Yankee baseball catcher known for his tendency for malapropism (seemingly unintentional witticisms), was once asked what time it was by pitcher Tom Seaver. He responded: "You mean now?" Good question.

Before the "big bang," there was no time. Heaven is not in time. There is no time in eternity. Simone Weil, an early 20th-century French philosopher, understood this when she said: "To always be relevant, we have to talk about things which are eternal." Universally, mystics say the same thing—that time is a dream. We have fallen asleep. We are dreaming the world. Mohammad, speaking of the mind and the body, said: "Men are asleep. In dying they awaken." Although the loss of the body is an aid in awakening us to the remembrance of Self, however, it is the loss of the ego that truly awakens us from the dream. According to the Course, God knows that sleep is withdrawing; waking is joining, and one day everyone will awaken. "What is the *ego*?" it asks, "but a dream of what you really are. . . . Where is the ego? In an evil dream that but seemed real while you were dreaming it" (C–2.1:4; C–2.6.12–13).

Holy Instants happen "outside of time." Ordinary projective human things happen sequentially, one after another, in time. It is the cyclical nature of time—of minutes, of hours, of days, weeks, months, years, centuries, and millennia—that structures our perception of time. Twelfth-century Spanish mystic Moses Maimonides, one of the foremost intellectual figures of medieval Judaism, said that the idea of God creating the world at some point in time can only be a projection from our time-bound circumstances. Therefore, Einstein tells us that the distinction between past, present, and future is only "a stubbornly persistent illusion." Time is a boundary, and there are no boundaries in eternity. The ego's story is based on what has happened in the past. That is why Workbook Lesson 7 of the Course says: "I see only the past."

Time and Relativity

According to Einstein, time is relative. It can speed up; it can slow down. But what if it stopped? What if we could "freeze" a moment? Time is measurable, which is what proves that it exists. A Holy Instant, on the other hand, is a moment frozen in eternity. It is an intuition. It is a kind of seeing. It is a mystical experience. Whenever time stops, we gain a higher, broader perspective. English philosopher and essayist John Fowles, best known for his novel *The French Lieutenant's Woman*, writes: "Time, absolutely, does not exist; it is always relative to some observer or some object." If an astronaut were to leave Earth, travel into deep space, and then return, his childhood friends would be old men and women, while the astronaut would have aged very little. We accept this statement because the scientists tell us it is true, even though we may not understand *why* it is true.

Time makes sense to the human mind because worldly events seem to occur in a logical, linear sequence from the past, through the present, and into the future. Mystical experience, however, enables vertical rather than horizontal sight. "Time is the ego's way of keeping everything from happening at once," the Course maintains. "You can use your body best to help you enlarge your perception so you can achieve real vision, of which the physical eye is incapable" (T–1.VII.2:4). In my own near-death experience, I could see and feel in all dimensions. I also sensed a great synchronicity and familiarity about the experience. It felt as if I were Home, where I had always been. Where we have all always been. Where we all are now—in the center of eternity itself. Nineteenth-century German philosopher Friedrich Wilhelm Joseph von Schelling explains it like this: "God then has no beginning only insofar as there is no beginning of his beginning. The beginning in God is eternal beginning, that is, such a one as was beginning from all eternity, and still is, and also never ceases to be beginning."

No Change

Whatever is true is eternal, and cannot change or be changed. (T–1.V.5:1)

Eternity is a constant—endless, enduring, and everlasting. Time is fleeting—momentary, always passing away. The world and our bodies live in time. Our souls live forever in eternity. Trying to live in two worlds is unnatural and the soul literally longs to go Home. For this reason, mystical awareness is sometimes seen as a "flashback," a "future memory," or a "re-cognition" of what already is.

Guilt and Fear

Guilt is based in the past. Fear is based in the future.

The ego lives in time—in a story, a play, often a drama, sometimes a nightmare. We easily become preoccupied with thoughts of the past—of lost loves and unfulfilled ambitions—and with feelings of nostalgia, regret, and remorse. Being preoccupied with thoughts of the past, we are unable to see things as they are now. Without a past, there can be no guilt. Remorse, penitence, and contrition are all experienced in relationship to the past. The older you are, the more past you have, the more you can look back. You say: "If only . . . if only . . . if only I had made different choices, I would have a different present." But you didn't make different choices, so you are living the present you chose. The younger you are, the more you "project" the future.

John Lennon once famously said: "Life is what happens while we are making other plans." Every painful lesson we learn is a part of the curriculum. Forgiveness of ourselves lies in the recognition that we can never have a different past. The past is also "not here now," and "now" is the only time we have. "Fear is not of the present," the Course tells us, "but only of the past and future, which do not exist" (T–15.I.8:2).

There is no fear in a Holy Instant. How could there be? Fear can only be of an imagined future. "If only" generates our guilt about the past; "what if" generates our fear about the future. "What if I get sick?" "What if I do not have enough money?" "What if there is nobody to take care of me?" Living in the past and projecting the future, you cannot be fully present. You cannot focus on what is "here now." This is the end of time and this is eternity.

Living Hell

> The belief in hell is inescapable to those who identify with the ego. Their nightmares and their fears are all associated with it. The ego teaches that hell is in the future, for this is what all its teaching is directed to. Hell is its goal. (T–15.I.4:1–4)

There is no past and there is no future, simply because, without an ego, there is no story. Rumi teaches us that the past and the future "veil God from our sight," and counsels us to burn them up. The mystical moment, on the other hand, is effervescent, vivacious, vivid, and enthralling. The ego lives in time—rehearsing the past through guilt and projecting the future through fear. But mystics live in the ever-present presence.

The Ever-Present Presence

Judgment rests on the past. In fact, judgment is impossible without the past. The more we move into the present moment, the more irrelevant time becomes. What happened in the past—whatever guilt or blame we place upon ourselves or others—is not here now. Fears of the future are also meaningless in the ever-present moment. In an emergency, our awareness is heightened and all we perceive is the moment. What is happening is happening in the present moment and requires our full attention.

Most of us don't want to experience Heaven now, afraid that it may mean the loss of our individuality. Heaven is immediately available, but the ego tells us to wait and enjoy our independence a little longer. Time is a great illusion that lives in the past and the future, but never quite here. There are times, however, when we are so "in the now" that we forget about time. This usually happens to children when they are engrossed in play. I once asked a young man who had had several mystical experiences how far he had gone. He answered: "Where?" Good answer. My question implied that there was a height to which he could ascend or a depth he could attain. But these are spatial and temporal limitations. Space and time are ego projections, and the mystic is timeless.

The center of a hurricane is a point of stillness. Around this point, there is an immense amount of chaos. In the center, however, everything stops and there is complete silence. The mystic is simply someone who steps out of the center and comes into time, but never loses awareness of the center. No one ever forgets eternity. In fact, it haunts us, calling to us to return to Heaven where only God is. From this position—at the center—we can have a dispassionate, objective view of the world. The world is crazy. It always has been. Throughout it all, however, mystics remain unbiased, impartial, and calm. They see the chaos and quite simply choose not to participate in it. They learn that only infinite patience produces immediate effects. "This is the way in which time is exchanged for eternity," the Course teaches. "Infinite patience calls upon infinite love, and by producing results *now* it renders time unnecessary" (T–5.VI.12:2–3).

At the Center

By recognizing spirit, miracles adjust the levels of perception and show them in proper alignment. This places spirit at the center, where it can communicate directly. (T–1.I:30)

Eternity is timeless. Love is timeless. God is timeless. We are timeless. Coming into time, we get caught in time. We get caught in our stories, and we lose sight of eternity. The ego analyzes; Spirit accepts. Aldous Huxley describes an experience he had under the influence of mescaline in *The Doors of Perception*. Space, time, and distance, he said, ceased to exist. He looked at his watch and saw it as though it existed in another Universe. He was living then in what he called "the perpetual present." The Course calls it "Present Memory." Present memory is where God is. It is where love is. There is no guilt because there is no past. There is no fear because there is no future. There is simply an awareness that the will of God is One.

"God and the soul," Eckhart tells us, "are not in space-time. They belong to the realms that are intrinsically or essentially real." Time ends, he explains, "where there is no before or after." We perceive "only a shadow of the real, living in a world created and sustained by our own cognition." The ego lives in time. The soul lives in eternity. The ego also "knows" (is afraid) that it will disappear. The soul, knowing that it is eternal, has nothing to fear. When we don't have to live up to an image or be caught up in a personal drama, we experience eternity. Mystics know through existential experience that it is possible to be so alive in the moment that the past and future lose significance. From this point of view, time is no longer a prison. The past is not a place of guilt; the future is not a place of fear. Sin, guilt, and fear lock us in time. But there is no sin, guilt, or fear in eternity, because there is no time. Time and eternity are both in your mind and will conflict until you perceive time solely as a means to regain eternity.

Every age, every culture, develops its own *zeitgeist*—its own morality, its own cultural climate. It's not that one is right and one is wrong. They are just different. Over time, all societies mature and what may have been a sin in one culture—homosexuality, for example—is not seen as a sin in another. Thoreau observed: "Every generation laughs at the old fashions, but follows religiously the new." What if we could jump into the future and look back to now? From that perspective, our present interpretation of reality might seem immature. But in fact, at any given moment, we can choose to see outside of time. In any Holy Instant, we can transcend a limited view. We can let go of the dramas, drop our personal histories, and, in complete freedom, step out of time. According to the Course, "only revelation transcends time" (T–2.V.10:5).

We can imagine a future existence without a body, but we cannot imagine any such existence without the mind. The mind is the determiner of everything. Heaven is here because there is no other place; Heaven is now because there is no other time. Franklin Merrell-Wolff's study of Kant convinced him that "awareness transcends the intellect" and that we can achieve a realization of "Nothingness" that is identical with our own Self. According to Wolff, to realize timelessness is to attain nirvana. Time moves. Eternity stands still, and in that stillness the mystic finds pure presence. As the Course expresses it: "Being . . . is a state in which the mind is in communication with everything that is real" (T–4.VII.4:3–4).

"The present is not a fleeting moment," Wei Wu Wei teaches. "It is the only eternity. In time 'lies' samsara. In the present 'lies' nirvana." *Samsara* means "suffering or sorrow"; *nirvana* means "enlightenment." Time is linear, moving from the past through the present into the future. But the mystical relationship with the infinite is vertical rather than horizontal. Our relationship with God is straight up and down. It is here now, in the pivotal center—the only place it can be. Paul Brunton, author of the best-selling book *A Search in Secret India,* once asked Ramana Maharshi: "Will the Maharshi express an opinion about the future of the world?" Maharshi asked him why he troubled himself about the future, when he didn't even know about the present. "Take care of the present," he advised, "and the future will then take care of itself."

Chapter 16

The End of the World

Here is the paradox that underlies the making of the world.
This world is not the Will of God, and so it is not real.

W–166.3:1–2

We began our last chapter with a quote from Yogi Berra. Let's do so again. "If the world were perfect," said Yogi, "it wouldn't be." Yogi got it right. The world is not perfect. Heaven is perfect. Therefore, Heaven is the only eternal reality. Everything else is fleeting—temporal and impermanent. Ken Wapnick called it "a maladaptive solution to a non-existent problem."

The Course describes the world in a number of ways. It is "totally insane and leads to nothing" (T–14.I.3:8). It is "an uncertain place, in which you walk in danger and uncertainty" (T–30.VII.7:2). It is ruled by "the belief that love is impossible" (T–8.IV.3:11). It is "meaningless in itself" (W–12.1:4). It is "nothing in itself" (W–132.4:1). We live in a material world, inside bodies, subject to the passage of time, and destined for eventual death. We don't necessarily have to deny the "seeming" reality of the world, time, and the body. Our task is to awaken from the dream of the world as it appears to us rather than to attack the figures that populate it. Yet the thing we call "the ego" has no more permanence or reality than last night's dream. We have split minds. Part of our attention is given to God, but a greater part is given to the dream of the ego self.

Saint Augustine expressed it very simply when he said: "Only eternity is real." How simple is the truth? Everything else is fleeting, complex, and constantly changing. The perceived world is part of our attempt to maintain ego identification. "You see the world that you have made, but you do not see yourself as the image maker," the Course points out. "You cannot be saved from the world, but you can escape from its cause. This is what salvation means, for where is the world you see when its cause is gone?" (W–23.4:1–3). Jesus asked: "What does it benefit a man to gain the whole world and lose his own soul?" (Luke 9:25). We cannot lose our souls, but we can get lost in a dreamworld in which the ego seems very real. The more caught up we are in "the dreaming of the world," the more we lose an awareness of our souls.

Bengali poet and mystic Rabindranath Tagore, the first non-European to win a Nobel Prize in literature, tells us that we are the "determiners" of the world we see. The body, time, the world, and the ego are all temporal. Perception and projection define the world and thus give it "reality." But the world we see does not even exist, says Ramana Maharshi. If the mind is eternal and substance and form are temporal or ever-changing, then there is no world because *we're always making up the world*. What we call civilization is based on a colossal number of dreams we all share. Simply put, there is no world because it is a thought apart from God.

Dreaming the World

The world we make up is a dream—sometimes a nightmare, sometimes very ordinary. Even if we dream a happy dream, we are still dreaming. According to Wei Wu Wei, perceiving is impersonal, but *the interpretation* that follows perception is contaminated by the prejudices of the observer. "All 'things' and all sentiments are interpretations only, and interpretations cannot be real in any sense," he maintains. The result is that we all have an oneiric, dreamlike understanding of reality. Many native cultures, like the Australian Aborigines and the native tribes of Venezuela, see the world as a dream.

Our families, social institutions, technology, and the omnipresent media create and Madison Avenue sustains an illusory world often built around what is "in fashion." We make up our own reality in much the same way. In this process, we're all at the mercy of the culture into which we are born. We become domesticated in much the same way that our pets are trained, through a system of reward and punishment. Thomas Carlyle, a 19th-century Scottish author and historian, became frustrated by the profound level of indoctrination he perceived in the Church. Like many mystics, however, he did not lose his faith in Christ. He lost his faith in tradition, dogma, and politics. "Popular opinion," he maintained, "is the greatest lie in the world," concluding: "Silence is as deep as Eternity. Speech is as shallow as Time."

Another Scotsman, psychiatrist R. D. Laing, also questioned the nature of reality as given to us by "the world." According to Laing, much of what we call insanity is really an inability to adjust to an insane world. Some simply find it difficult to adjust to the conflicting and contradictory expectations of parents, society, religion, and more. Unable to cope with "the world," they *check out* mentally. "The real world is all that the Holy Spirit has saved for you out of what you have made," we learn in the Course, "and to perceive only this is salvation, because it is the recognition that reality is only what is true" (T–11.VII.4:9).

The world of Spirit, said Gurdjieff, is governed by cosmic laws, not egoistic laws. The world of social and political trends is contaminated by hubris, arrogance, and a multitude of ego needs. In such a world, the archaic law of "an eye for an eye and a tooth for a tooth" still rules. Man is caught, said Gurdjieff, in a fearful dream and thus prone to psychosis and mindless fits of rage, exemplified in our never-ending desire to go to war. From the mystic's point of view, our job is one of loving the world, rather than looking to condemn it or seeking to transform it.

Peace on Earth

Do you not think the world needs peace as much as you do? Do you not want to give it to the world as much as you want to receive it? For unless you do, you will not receive it. If you want to have it of me, you must give it. (T–8.IV.4:1–4)

In the first chapter of his book *The Four Agreements*, contemporary Mexican author Don Miguel Ruiz says that all of what we hear and see is a dream within a dream. "Dreaming is the main function of the mind," says Ruiz, and we are constantly dreaming. Our nighttime dreams and our daytime dreams take a different form—that is all. What Ruiz calls dreaming, Eckhart Tolle calls "compulsive thinking" and Freudians call "unconscious thinking." The Course calls dreams "perceptual temper tantrums, in which you literally scream, 'I want it thus!' And thus, it seems to be" (T–18. II.4:1). Society, then, is "the dreaming of the planet"—a collection of billions of small dreams carried out according to a wide variety of cultural values and mores. Everywhere, games are played out in politics, religion, and business.

According to Ruiz, we see what we want to see; we hear what we want to hear; and our belief systems are mirrors in which we perceive what we project. In solitude, we have our dreams to ourselves; in society, we dream our dreams in concert. In this way, the world is built through our words and our thoughts. We use language to think and to understand what is going on in ourselves and the world around us. American author Michael Talbot, in *Mysticism and the New Physics,* says: "Reality is a semantic creation largely constructed by cultural beliefs. What we believe to be true becomes true. What we call this reality is learned."

Somerset Maugham wound themes of Eastern mysticism and enlightenment into his last novel, *The Razor's Edge.* According to Maugham: "Man always sacrifices truth to vanity, comfort, and advantage." We live, he claimed, "not by truth but by make-believe." What is right and what is wrong are all simply different interpretations, and we kill each other over our interpretations. "The individual has always had to struggle to keep from being overwhelmed by the tribe," Nietzsche agreed. "If you try it, you will be lonely often, and sometimes frightened. But no price is too high to pay for the privilege of owning yourself." Irish playwright, novelist, and poet Oscar Wilde, a contemporary of Nietzsche, puts the same thought in his characteristically witty way when he points out that the terror of society, which he calls "the basis of morals," and the terror of God, which he calls "the secret of religion," are the two things that govern us.

Someone once sent me the following poem in an email:

I WAS DRUGGED

I had a drug problem when I was young.
I was drugged to church on Sundays.
I was drugged to church for weddings and funerals.
I was drugged to family reunions.
I was drugged to the bus stop to go to school.
I was drugged by my ears when I was disrespectful.
I was drugged to the woodshed and whipped
when I disobeyed my parents.

Well said.

Remember the lines from the movie and play *South Pacific*: "You have to be taught to hate and fear. You have to be carefully taught." From the time that we can understand words, we are told what the world is. This teaching is persistent until we perceive the world as prescribed. After a while, we no longer have to be trained about what to believe, what to think, or what to do. We want to please others, and we act appropriately. Domestication is so strong that we even punish ourselves if we think our actions are inappropriate or if we "get out of line." Mystics, on the other hand, "see" the world differently. Carmelite priest and mystical researcher Bruno Borchert writes: "The mystic has the most disturbing awareness that something is not quite right. The social order, with its world of thought, sentiments, speech, and religion and its entire cultural network, determines our thoughts and actions to such an extent that it is hard to see or accept any alternative."

Worlds within Worlds

We can speak of different worlds—the world of the Babylonians, the world of the Spanish conquistadors, the world of Napoleonic France, or the world of Nazi Germany—as though they represent certain states of mind or attitudes that existed once upon a time, but exist no more. But this is not the entire story. Castaneda asked his teacher Don Juan: "Are you trying to show me the real world?" Don Juan replied: "No, I'm not trying to show you the real world; I'm trying to show you that the world you see is just a view." Sixteenth-century Dominican friar and cosmological theorist Giordano Bruno even claimed that there was an infinite Universe containing an infinite number of worlds inhabited by an infinite number of intelligent beings.

Nineteenth-century Lebanese monk and mystic Saint Sharbel lived as a hermit and so had a different view of the world. He writes: "If a man's choices depend on his passions, or on propaganda, or on current conventions, they are not free choices. It is not the exercise of choice that makes man free, but the determination to choose the Truth." There is great wisdom in taking a break from the world—from television, the Internet, and newspapers. Jesus suggested we be still, quiet the busy ego mind (compulsive thinking), and wait! The Course tells us: "The memory of God comes to the quiet mind" (T–23.I.1:1). It's in the quiet, peaceful mind that we connect to God. We can't see beyond this world until we stop making it up.

Mystics are not "at war" with the world. They are, rather, "lovers" of whatever presents itself—nature, music, or other souls. If you embrace mysticism, you are not required to "hate" the world. To hate the world is just to make it more real in a negative way. Your task as a mystic is to change your vision so that you see all things with love and compassion—what Buddhists call "loving-kindness." In my own Holy Hell experience, I fell into a vast ocean of Mind and lost contact with everything "outside." There was nothing left with which I could identify as a person living in a world filled with anxieties and fears, regrets and nostalgia, remorse, or thoughts of sin, guilt, and fear.

In this experience, I saw a zigzagging line that delineated a new Universe. The world disappeared through that line, and there appeared in its place a multidimensional, multi-colored grid that is impossible to describe, because it was truly of another dimension. The ancient Hawaiians called this grid *Ke Akua*, a divine source through which everything is connected. The Navaho describe it as a web; Tibetans call it a net. Modern cosmologists and astrophysicists call it the quantum hologram. Whatever you call it, I experienced this grid as more "real" than this world. It exists in a place I've been before, and to which we are all now returning. I was not losing reality. I was finding it.

Universe of Universes

There is a very interesting thought that appears only once in the Course: "The Creator of life, the Source of everything that lives, the Father of the universe and of the universe of universes, and of everything that lies even beyond them would you remember" (T–19.IV.D.1:4). This is the only time the phrase "the universe of universes" appears in the Course.

~~~~~~

Doesn't your childhood seem like a dream to you—something that happened once upon a time, in a land far, far away? If you have lived long enough to have gone through major moves and transitions, doesn't it seem as if you've lived other lives that you now remember as dreams? We usually forget our nighttime dreams, even those that are vivid and seemingly real. We forget those dreams because *they were only dreams*. Likewise, the day and the moment we are living in right now will soon be a memory, very much like a dream. As time goes by, we will forget more and more of what now *seems* real.

In his *Meditations*, Marcus Aurelius tells us: "Life is a fearful dream." The so-called "real world" is a place of separation, sadness, sin, sickness, and suffering. It is a realm of illusion, where the ego and the body are made to seem real and God is nearly forgotten.

In God's creation, however, there is no suffering, pain, loss, separation, or death, because God's creation is love itself—an eternal, changeless reality we call Heaven. Nothing in this world is eternal. In the world of form, illusions hold sway and Heaven seems like a fantasy. For mystics, however, it's the other way around. Heaven is reality, and this world is a dream. To be free of the world, we must forgive the world for all the things *we think* it has done to us. This means forgiving ourselves for the insanity we have created—the insanity that keeps us from love. In a sense, we are all prodigal sons and daughters who have split ourselves off from our Source. At any instant, that Source is ready to provide us with guidance that will help us return to the eternal reality of God's love. It does not matter what we have done or what we think we have done. God is always ready to welcome us Home with open arms.

The body is temporal and will die. But the Kingdom of Heaven is eternally alive. "It is hard to understand what 'The Kingdom of Heaven is within you' really means," the Course explains. "The word 'within' is unnecessary. The Kingdom of Heaven *is* you" (T–4.III.1:1–4). We cannot, however, see the Kingdom of Heaven when we look for the inside on the outside. We've got it flipped around the wrong way and, for this reason, the Course says we must reverse our thinking. As C. S. Lewis writes: "If I find in myself a desire which no experience in this world can satisfy, the most probable explanation is that I was made for another world."

We are indeed made for another world because we are "of" another world. Heaven is not something we have to hope for or work to earn. It is not something that is going to happen *someday*. Heaven is *now* simply because there is no other time. When we are living in a drama, we know it; we can feel something "artificial," something that is not quite right. When we come to see that Heaven is within, we can see the craziness around us and not go crazy. We can see the hatred and not hate. We can see the misery and not be miserable. When we are unaware of Heaven within, it is easy to go crazy, to get angry, or to sink into misery. To come to Heaven is to come to ourselves. German physicist Max Planck affirms the teaching of the mystics when he says: "There is no material world as we know it. All that we perceive to be matter is held together by a force, and this force is intelligence. As a man who has devoted my entire life to studying the substance of which the world is made, I can firmly state that mind is the matrix of all matter."

Mind as the Matrix of Matter

That there is no "real" world as we perceive it with our senses is corroborated on a deeper level by the insights of subatomic physics. The photons that comprise light have been observed to consist of waves and particles—but not of both at the same time. Instead, the observer's *intent* determines which one is seen (wave or particle), which is another way of saying that the observer's perception literally creates reality. With this comes the further realization that every "thing" we see is a projection from our minds. Although we do not literally "make up other people," we do "make up" our interpretation of everyone we see.

There is something holding the Universe together, and it's not gravity. Gravity works within our own and other planetary and galactic systems, but it is not a sufficient force to explain why the Universe is not literally flying apart. *Something* is keeping everything together. The physical Universe, made up of what we call "atoms," makes up only 4 percent of the Universe as a whole. Another 23 percent is made up of what is called "dark matter." Although dark matter is not observable, scientists know that galaxies, clusters of galaxies, and the Universe itself contain far more matter than just that which interacts with electromagnetic radiation and can, therefore, be detected. The remaining 73 percent is made up of what cosmologists call "dark energy." No one is quite sure what dark energy is, as we do not have any means of measuring it. There is, however, some force acting in opposition to gravity that holds everything together, even though the Universe is expanding. Why don't we call this thing that has no form, no dimension, and cannot be measured Mind, or Love, or God? Like Mind, like God, Love has no form, no dimension, and it cannot be measured.

The main question is not: How do things work in the world of physics? The main question is: How do things work on the level of mind? In his book *Reality Is Not What It Seems*, Italian physicist Carlo Rovelli points out that the more science discovers about matter, the more we realize how much we do not know. The difference between physics and metaphysics is that, in physics, we are forever looking for deeper answers to deeper questions. In metaphysics, we find those answers—that is, we can come to know the Mind of God—because we have forever been a part of it. Who runs this "mind machine" anyway? Is it all a matter of behavioral conditioning, fantasy, and ego control? Or is there a higher, brighter, more brilliant way of seeing, free from all external restraints? Mystics claim that this way of seeing is found, paradoxically, by turning everything over to God.

Nothing matters except what we make "matter" by bringing it into form physically or mentally through imagination. When distinctions created by imagination are taken to be real— especially the distinctions between "subject" and "object," "I" and "other," "self" and "world," "we" and "they"—we lose sight of reality's wholeness and fall into an illusion of separation. Mystics reach for a higher point of view wherein there is no separation and time gracefully stops, as does the world. From this perspective, there is no judgment and thus there are no problems. Mystics can continue to act in the world, but need not "worry" about the world, simply because they know it is ephemeral, while Spirit is eternal. When we experience the unbounded vastness of Spirit, Heaven comes into view. We can then "reflect" Heaven here and now.

This world of time and space is often depressing, making us feel alone, isolated, cut off, and separate. This illusory world is a place of duality where we witness and experience war, sickness, depression, poverty, and powerlessness. We can easily get caught in judgment and condemnation of this world. It is, however, much more fun to reflect Heaven here. "You cannot stop with the idea the world is worthless," the Course teaches, "for unless you see that there is something else to hope for, you will only be depressed. Our emphasis is not on giving up the world, but on exchanging it for what is far more satisfying, filled with joy, and capable of offering you peace" (W–129.1:2–3).

Reading the World Right

It's important not to blame our difficulties on the world. After all, it is we who create the world we see. The world is what it is. Your ego can be insulted. In the truth of who you are, however, *you* cannot be insulted. Once you see this, you can be content regardless of what comes your way. Let the world be what it is. Simply love it, and it will change by being loved. The Course puts it like this:

> Healing is the gift of those who are prepared to learn there is no world, and can accept the lesson now. Their readiness will bring the lesson to them in some form which they can understand and

recognize. Some see it suddenly on point of death, and rise to teach it. Others find it in experience that is not of this world, which shows them that the world does not exist because what they behold must be the truth, and yet it clearly contradicts the world. (W–132.7:1–4)

As we have seen in the previous chapters, from the perspective of the mystics, who we are—ultimately, and therefore in truth—has nothing to do with the existence of what we call an ego, or a body, or space, or time. The body is merely a temporal dream that exists only for a moment in space and time. No dream has any *form,* being strictly the composition of an "unconscious mind." According to the Course: *"At no single instant does the body exist at all"* (T–18.VII.3:1).

Clearly Invisible

When you made visible what is not true, what "is" true became invisible to you. Yet it cannot be invisible in itself, for the Holy Spirit sees it with perfect clarity. It is invisible to you because you are looking at something else. Yet it is no more up to you to decide what is visible and what is invisible, than it is up to you to decide what reality is. What can be seen is what the Holy Spirit sees. The definition of reality is God's, not yours. He created it, and He knows what it is. You who knew have forgotten, and unless He had given you a way to remember you would have condemned yourself to oblivion. (T–12.VIII.3:1–8)

There are many things that are invisible, yet we know they exist. Love is invisible; thought is invisible; learning is invisible; God and the Holy Spirit are invisible. Light is composed of photons, so it is reasonable to assume that photons have mass. The scientists tell us, however, that photons of light are massless—they have energy and momentum, but no mass. When we talk about them, we are talking about "some thing" that seems to have form because we can only talk about it from a position of our being "in relationship" to it. In a similar way, the mind is naturally abstract (T–4. VIII.1:2). And, by definition, that which is abstract is apart from "concrete" realities. The Course tells us that divine abstraction takes joy in sharing (T–4.VII.5:4). Furthermore:

> Creation and communication are synonymous. God created every mind by communicating His Mind to it thus, establishing it forever as a channel for the reception of His Mind and Will. Since only beings of a like order can truly communicate, His creations naturally communicate with Him and like Him. This communication is perfectly abstract, since its quality is universal in application and not subject to any judgment, any exception or any alteration. God created you by this and for this. (T–4.VII.3:6–10)

Like photons of light, Mind (as something separate from the brain) has energy and movement, but no mass. In the same way, Spirit has no mass. An "idea" has no mass. In a similar way, there is, in fact, no such thing as a rainbow, except insofar as someone's eyes perceive light traveling through droplets of water hanging in the air. According to modern physics, there is an invisible energy field (the Higgs field) that exists throughout the Universe. The existence of this field was proven after forty years of research, when particles of light passed through the Large Hadron Collider in Switzerland were *given* mass. Just as any object moving through molasses must slow down, the light photons colliding with each other in the Hadron Collider became slower as they collided. Prophetically, mystic Ralph Waldo Emerson expressed this same truth over a century before when he described the world as nothing "but thickened light."

Since the world is a place reliant on perceptions of time, we can, in fact, think of every "thing" as "thickened light." The Course thus teaches: "Life and death, light and darkness, knowledge and perception, are irreconcilable" (T–3.VII.6:6). Astrophysicist Neil deGrasse Tyson observes that the only thing that can travel faster than the speed of light is something that does not have mass. What does not have mass? The abstract does not have mass. Mind does not have mass. Love does not have mass. God does not have mass. And yet we "know" that there is thought, and there is love, and there is God.

Chapter 17

The End of the Ego

You who identify with your ego cannot believe God loves you. You do not love what you made, and what you made does not love you. Being made out of the denial of the Father, the ego has no allegiance to its maker. You cannot conceive of the real relationship that exists between God and His creations because of your hatred for the self you made.

T–4.III.4:1–4

And now comes the biggest news of all. There never was a fall from grace. Since there is no world, and there is no time, and there is no you and no me in the "individualistic" sense, how can there be separation between you and Spirit?

The ego is a tyrant. We have willingly let this tyrant into our house and it is making a mess of things. But, in the end, all tyrants die. Alexander the Great, Genghis Khan, Napoleon, Hitler, Mussolini—all gone. And the ego will eventually go the way of all tyrants, the Course assures us:

> Whatever is true is eternal, and cannot change or be changed. Spirit is therefore unalterable because it is already perfect, but the mind can elect what it chooses to serve. The only limit put on its choice is that it cannot serve two masters. If it elects to

do so, the mind can become the medium by which spirit creates along the line of its own creation. If it does not freely elect to do so, it retains its creative potential but places itself under tyrannous rather than Authoritative control. As a result it imprisons, because such are the dictates of tyrants. To change your mind means to place it at the disposal of "true" Authority. (T–1.V.5:1–7)

The goal of the ego is power, and tyrants go to any length to gain and hold power. Spirit, on the other hand, is free and under "Authoritative control." Authoritative control means following the guidance of a higher power. Nothing feels better than *leading a guided life* free of chaos. The ego is chaotic; God is in control. Which path would you rather follow? Is the way not clearly marked? Will you choose a path of chaos, or will you maintain control by following the guidance of God?

The Tyrant Within

This is your chosen self, the one you made as a replacement for reality. This is the self you savagely defend against all reason, every evidence, and all the witnesses with proof to show this is not you. You heed them not. You go on your appointed way, with eyes cast down lest you might catch a glimpse of truth, and be released from self-deception and set free. (W–166.7:1–4)

Wouldn't it be nice to be free of this insane thing we call an ego that rattles around inside our minds, telling us all sorts of unpleasant things? The Course asks us not to underestimate the power of the ego's belief in separation (T–5.V.2:10). Dig deep and you'll see that all guilt comes from separating ourselves from God, and this we do by separating ourselves from each other. Guilt is a trap that imprisons us in time. The ego is a mind locked into itself, believing in its self-made reality and ever fearful of death and annihilation. The ego is like a straightjacket that keeps us confined in a little prison of our own making.

The ego is never happy. It is always hungry and in search of more power, more wealth, more control, or perhaps more sleep, more unconsciousness, less awareness. Central to the mystical teaching of every religion is an awareness that only God "is" and that you are one Self, united with your Creator. The truth is that we cannot and do not live outside of the Mind of God—nor do we want to. The goal of mystic experience is to reunite with God. Trying to live outside of the Mind of God creates great misery. Only by recognizing ourselves and each other as children of God can we know our one, true identity.

How simple is salvation? We are saved by a simple acceptance of truth. In time, there are two selves and thus, a divided world. But the Gospels teach us: "No one can serve two masters. Either you will hate the one and love the other, or you will be devoted to the one and despise the other" (Matthew 6:24). Mystics, knowing this, seek freedom from all self-imposed illusions. "A concept of the self is made by you," according to the Course. "It bears no likeness to yourself at all. It is an idol, made to take the place of your reality as Son of God" (T–31.V.1:5–7, 2:1–2).

The self-made man or woman is a fictional character and, like all imaginary characters, is not part of reality. The self-made man, the actor on the stage, is always performing, always playing a part to maintain his self-made identity. This self wears a mask, dissembles, and overtly enjoys creating a show—sometimes a very great show. But every play must end. Inevitably, every book must have a last page. While no "body" lasts, however, Spirit is eternal. "The Holy Spirit knows the truth about you," we learn in the Course. "The image you made does not. Yet, despite its obvious and complete ignorance, this image assumes it knows *all* things because you have given that belief to it" (M–29.4:6).

Good News

The good news is that the light of Self never goes out completely. There is nothing like being a know-it-all, and the ego loves to assume that role. The ego can take over and rule the self, giving the impression that there is no real Self at all. But, although the ego may be in control, there is always some "suspicion" hidden somewhere deep inside that the self-created self is not real. Despite what the ego may tell you, the Course says: "You are not special. If you think you are, and would defend your specialness against the truth of what you really are, how can you know the truth?" (T–24.II.4:1–2).

Nothing is more blinding than self-absorbed narcissism and grandiosity. Self-absorption keeps love away. We may think that we are special because of our DNA, our heritage, our jobs, or our money. But as the Course assures us: "Specialness is a false impression we hold about ourselves and a lack of faith in everyone except ourselves" (T–24.VI.1:1). There is nothing wrong with being handsome, beautiful, youthful, and rich; but neither youth or age, nor attractiveness or position, nor power or money makes anyone special. Spiritual seekers who think that they have achieved something others have not engage in as much grandiosity as any materialist. But the Course tells us: "It is easy to distinguish grandeur from grandiosity, because love is returned and pride is not. Pride will not produce miracles . . . because pride is not shared" (T–9.VIII.8:1–2, 4). Fortunately, God has no favorite children.

Stories and dramas that separate us from others simply keep us from awakening. One Chinese Chan master says: "He who is in the habit of looking down upon others has not got rid of the erroneous idea of a self." No one is better than or worse than any other. All are equal in God's eyes. Judgment and love are opposites. Being *better than* or *less than* implies separation.

We Are So There!

Seventeenth-century German priest and poet Angelus Silesius once said: "God, whose love is everywhere, can't come to visit unless you're not there." But we are so there! We are so into our heads and into thinking that we completely shut God out. The self-talk going on within our minds can be so dominant that we do not—indeed, we *cannot*—hear the voice of God. Ram Dass asks: "Are you genuinely seeking greater truth, or playing the game of recognition and success?"

> Let me remember that my self is nothing but my Self is All. (W-358.1:7)

Mystics live each minute in the immediacy of life in all its pristine purity. They have no need to "fix" anything. Bangladeshi mystic Anandamayi Ma said that she was completely empty, with no sense of "I am." She often objectified her body by describing her actions in the third person: "she was nobody," "this body did this," or "this body went there." Anandamayi described four stages in her spiritual evolution:

- Her mind was "dried" of desire and passion so it could catch the fire of spiritual knowledge; she found "things" less attractive and her body became less obsessed with the need for pleasure.

- Her body became still and her mind was drawn inward.

- Her personal identity was absorbed by an individual deity (God) and she was able to function in the world, even though a distinction between form and formlessness still remained.

- She experienced a melting away of all duality, and her mind was free from the movement of thought with consistent, full consciousness, even in dreams.

When Indian mystic Paramahansa Yogananda met Anandamayi, he asked her about her life. She answered:

Father, there is little to tell. My consciousness has never associated itself with this body. Before I came on this earth, "I was the same." As a little girl, "I was the same." I grew into womanhood; I was still "the same." And, in front of you now, "I am the same." Ever afterward, though the dance of creation changes around me in the hall of eternity, "I shall be the same."

Anandamayi described experiencing a great void and a deep peaceful emptiness. We may think of the void as a farewell to all that is human—the cessation of the ego and an absence of self. In the Bible, God says to Moses: "Tell them, 'I am that I am.'" Anandamayi writes: "So long as the sense of 'me' and 'mine' remains, there is bound to be sorrow and want in life. God is one's very own Self, the breath of one's breath, the life of one's life, the Atman."

Differences just don't make any difference. Black, white, brown, and yellow are only differences on the outside. The ego is shallow in its belief in an outside world, when all the while the ego itself is nothing more than a shadow that disappears when the light has come. The more well-defined our position, the less freedom we have. Titles are divisive. Thoreau once said that he would rather sit on a pumpkin and have it all to himself than to sit on a throne with all the problems of the world at his feet. Everything we perceive as the outside world is a part of ego identification. When we drop our personal histories, we gain a taste of eternity, freedom, and happiness.

I Am Not

The gross body which is composed of the seven humors, *I am not.*

The five sense organs which apprehend their respective objects, *I am not.*

Even the mind which thinks, *I am not.* (Ramana Maharshi)

We are not our bodies, our occupations, our religion, our city, our state, or our nation. We are not our race, our clan, or our family. All thinking that is of the ego—we are not. Insane we are not. Paranoid we are not. Our only real thoughts are those we think with God. This is not arrogance. It is perfect sanity. The good news is that it only takes an instant. And how long is an instant? "As long as it takes to reestablish perfect sanity, perfect peace, and perfect love for everyone, for God and for yourself" (T–15.I.14:14–15).

Matter Doesn't Matter

The essence of a mystical experience is awareness without an object. Is the mind a "thing"? Is love a "thing"? Everyone attests to the reality of love, yet love is beyond description—even poetry doesn't do it justice. Poetry can point the way, but even poetry talks "about" love. David Hawkins maintains: "To truly 'know' is to 'be,' at which point one does not know; instead one 'is.'" How simple is all reality? No one is special, different, or better than anyone else. There are no degrees; there is no hierarchy. Our bodies come through different terrains of biology, time, geography, and social circumstances, but none of these circumstances make us special. In fact, the closer we are to "nothing," the better for our sanity. "Of yourself you can do nothing, because of yourself you *are* nothing" (T–8.IV.7:3).

The Self is beyond selfishness. The Self is spaceless, timeless, infinite, and empty. "The Soul," said Emerson, "is tied to no individual, no culture, no tradition, but rises fresh in every soul. The soul bows to nothing in the world of time, place, and history. We all must be and can only be a light unto ourselves." Eckhart used the words "desert" and "barren" to describe his experience of illumination. Teresa of Avila spoke of the "still wilderness" or the "lonely desert" of the journey. This is the true country of the soul, a space free from desiring, where the ego does not reign. In his book *Silence of the Heart,* Robert Adams describes it as "pure awareness," as being "aware of the whole universe." Tibetan Buddhist Lama Yeshe says simply: "Emptiness is the ultimate nature of everything that exists."

Having no wants or desires, not needing or judging, we find peace, expansion, and freedom from boundaries. Nothingness is full, whole, and infinite. It is everything, and it is everywhere. Being nobody is refreshing. You don't have to *do* anything. You don't have to *be* anybody. Being anonymous is liberating. Being anonymous is just being. There is no need to be attached to any outcome. Whatever happens is okay. If you don't make any appointments, you can't be disappointed. According to the *Tao Te Ching,* if someone thinks they have knowledge of the Tao that makes them special, they are not in tune with the Tao. A little knowledge is a dangerous thing if we think it makes us wise. The person who values power least makes the best ruler.

Blame Game

If your brothers are part of you and you blame them for your deprivation, you are blaming yourself. And you cannot blame yourself without blaming them. That is why blame must be undone, not seen elsewhere. Lay it to yourself and you cannot know yourself, for only the ego blames at all. Self-blame is therefore ego identification, and as much an ego defense as blaming others. "You cannot enter God's Presence if you attack His Son." When His Son lifts his voice in praise of his Creator, he will hear the Voice for his Father. Yet the Creator cannot be praised without His Son, for Their glory is shared and They are glorified together. (T–11.IV.5:1–8)

We destroy our motivation for learning by thinking that we already know. The following four sentences by Ralph Waldo Emerson are almost a perfect description of a mystical experience:

"Standing on the bare ground, —my head bathed by the blithe air and uplifted into infinite space, —all mean egotism vanishes. I become a transparent eyeball; I am nothing. I see all; the currents of the Universal Being circulate through me. I am part and parcel of God."

How did Emerson see all? First, he had to get to "I am nothing." Once he got to nothing, he became a "seer."

To see into eternity, we must let go of our stories and our everyday dramas. Although they may seem real, they are nothing more than dreaming. Holding on to specialness and individuality makes us separate. Self-inquiry leads to the realization that *there is no inquirer and nothing to attain.* Who are we beneath, below, or prior to the pseudo-self? If we succeed in finding release from the prison of individuality, what then? Once the illusion of self-importance is dropped, mystics describe a new awareness of a supreme identity with the All, with universal Spirit. What we find is the soul, the Self, unhampered by the ego. We *are* eternity. We *are* love. We *are* all these wonderful things and more.

Your true Self is pure witness. It exists prior to time. It is not born. It does not die. Hindu poet Lalleshwari writes: "When the mirror of my mind became clear I saw that God is not other than me, and this non-dual knowledge completely destroyed all thought of 'you' and 'I.' I came to know that this entire world is not different from God."

The made-up self disappears simply because it is an illusion. How can fantasy be reality? "Fantasy is a distorted form of vision," the Course says. "Fantasies of any kind are distortions, because they always involve twisting perception into unreality" (T–1.VII.3:1). The self-made self cannot die because it was never alive. It can only disappear back into the nothingness from which it came. Just like last night's dream, it disappears when morning comes; the "Son" arises and the light grows bright and clear. The self-made self is, as Shakespeare said in *Macbeth*: "a walking shadow; a poor player, that struts and frets its hour upon the stage, and then is heard no more—a tale told by an idiot, full of sound and fury, signifying nothing" (5, 5:19).

The Course tells us that we must choose between ourselves and the illusion of ourselves that we have created. "There is no point in trying to avoid this one decision. It must be made. Faith and belief can fall to either side, but reason tells you misery lies only on one side and joy upon the other" (T–22.II.6:4–8).

Let It All Go

Your past is what you have taught yourself. Let it all go. Do not attempt to understand any event or anything or anyone in its "light," for the darkness in which you try to see can only obscure. Put no confidence at all in darkness to illuminate your understanding, for if you do you contradict the light, and thereby think you see the darkness. Yet darkness cannot be seen, for it is nothing more than a condition in which seeing becomes impossible. (T–14. XI.3:6–10)

PART IV

Mysticism in a World of Miracles

To the world, generosity means *giving away* in the sense of *giving up*. To the teachers of God, it means giving away in order to keep.

M–4.VIII.4–5

Chapter 18

Mysticism and Mortality

Nothing real can be threatened. Nothing unreal exists.
Herein lies the peace of God.

T–In.2:2–4

Tibetan Lama Sogyal Rinpoche writes: "When we finally know we are dying, and all other sentient beings are dying with us, we start to have a burning, almost heartbreaking sense of the fragility and preciousness of each moment and each being, and from this can grow a deep, clear, limitless compassion for all beings." While it would be wonderful to just "know" the truth, to just "see" the truth, and to just "be" the truth, most often we come to the truth through experience. Sometimes, even when we lead a healthy lifestyle, our health can change suddenly, perhaps due to accident or injury. Perhaps for no clear reason at all, an apparently healthy person must look at death up close and personal. Near-death experiences have a way of stopping us and bringing us very much back to the present, back to the moment, back to now.

Indeed, illness is an important stimulus to mystical experience, according to Hardy's research. Several well-known mystics had visions during times when they were ill and/or dying. Saint Francis of Assisi was struck down by a serious illness and, feeling disgusted by his empty existence, turned to a life of devotion. Suffering from a severe illness and thinking she was about to die, Julian of Norwich experienced a series of visions that were the source of her major work, *Sixteen Revelations of the Divine*. "Truth sees God," she wrote, "and wisdom contemplates God, and from these two comes a third, a holy and wonderful delight in God, who is love." French mathematician Blaise Pascal had an intense mystical vision after prolonged illness and, like Julian of Norwich, was from then on subject to states of rapture.

In his article "Mysticism and Schizophrenia," Ken Wapnick discusses the similarities and differences between mystical and schizophrenic experiences. Both schizophrenics and mystics follow similar paths of development. The essential difference is that mystics follow a structured, controlled, contemplative process, while schizophrenics are "overwhelmed, with no means of dealing with [their] experience and no conviction that [they] will survive it." In his highly acclaimed interview with mythologist Joseph Campbell, Bill Moyers asked him: "How can you tell the difference between someone having a spiritual experience and someone having a psychotic episode?" Campbell answered: "The psychotic is drowning in the water in which the mystic swims."

The Death of the Body

The subject of death is a big one—and one that I have treated at length in my book *Eternal Life and A Course in Miracles*.

From the standpoint of the ego, death is witness to the reality of the body. If the body dies, it must have lived. This means that the body's creator, the ego, must be real. However, there is only Life. The sentences "God is Life" and "God is Love" are tautological, which means that they can be read frontward or backward and still make sense. And by the logical rule of association, if God is Life and God is Love, then Love is Life and Life is Love. So the more we live in love, the more we know of life. The more we know of love, the more we know of God. Essayist Anaïs Nin writes in her diary: "People living deeply have no fear of death."

There are many states of being, or reality, that are not physical. Love does not have a form. Eternity does not have a form. God does not have a form. Truth does not have a form. All there is, is life; and, life is not dependent on form. The body is ephemeral. To say that life is eternal does not mean that we go from one body to another—that would be a continuation of dreaming. Who wants to go from story to story, from drama to drama?

The dissolution of the body is simply the quiet laying down of the body and the transformation from a dream; it is an awakening into life as mind, not body. When the body disappears, then all there is, is Life. God/Life/Mind is all-encompassing. There is no opposite of God. Whatever is all-encompassing cannot have an opposite. As the Course teaches:

> When your body and your ego and your dreams are gone, you will know that you will last forever. Perhaps you think this is accomplished through death, but nothing is accomplished through death, because death is nothing. Everything is accomplished

through life, and life is of the mind and in the mind. The body neither lives nor dies, because it cannot contain you who are life. (T–6.V.A.1:1–4)

Jesus did not resist the crucifixion. He knowingly and willingly went to the cross to show us that, although his body could be killed, he could not. As we saw in chapter 14, the body is the ego's chosen home. It is a limitation in form that imposes a false image of separation. In that sense, it is also a prison. According to the mystics, being one with all, we have nothing to lose, not even our bodies. To lose a body is just to lose a "lifeless" material form. Life does not begin with the birth of a body, and it does not end with the body's death. What we call "death" is no big deal. It is our birth into this world that should give us pause. Omnipotent, omnipresent Spirit cannot be limited to a specific experience in space and time.

Who would want to live forever within the confines of a body? American actor and filmmaker Woody Allen once jokingly said: "I do not want to gain immortality through my work. I want to gain immortality by living forever." The Spirit manifesting as Woody Allen is immortal and *will* therefore live forever, but not in his body and not in his works—and not as Woody Allen. None of these illusory manifestations of time and space are eternal. Nothing physical is immortal. William Penn defined death as "no more than a turning of us over from time to eternity."

A Matter of Timing

Those who die before they die don't die when they die. (Anonymous)

From the mystic's point of view, space and time are a trap. Why not escape? Why not know truth and freedom? I'm not suggesting that we do away with our bodies. The body is a tool, and we've been given this tool to learn the lessons we need to know before we move on. Indeed, Gandhi enjoined us: "Live as if you were to die tomorrow. Learn as if you were to live forever." There is obviously no eternity in any body—the form of "the thing" is never "the thing" itself. Dying is thus, paradoxically, a coming back to life, not a loss of life. It is a rising of consciousness, not a loss of consciousness. It is an awakening from a death.

The illusory world is nothing when considering/remembering the reality of God. To be truly awake is to be free of dreaming. To share in the vision of Christ is to see Christ in everyone. We love all people by letting them be who they are in reality and not worrying about what they seem to be within the dream. Getting on with fulfilling our destiny, we can't help but help others to fulfill theirs.

The body has no place in eternity. It is only a fleeting physical form, not eternal essence. We are the immutable, eternal essence of Spirit, not form. There is nothing to be afraid of, and there is no one we need attack—ever, for any reason. We must speak the truth to enter Heaven. The truth is simple and can be spoken easily. At the gate of Heaven, when asked your identity, say simply that you are a child of God. Then walk through the doors that never are and never were closed. The Dalai Lama tells us: "If you are mindful of death, it will not come as a surprise—you will not be anxious. You will feel that death is merely like changing clothes. Consequently, at that point you will be able to maintain your calmness of mind."

Chapter 19

Mysticism and Monism

The Holy Spirit teaches thus: There is no hell. Hell is only what the ego has made of the present. The belief in hell is what prevents you from understanding the present, because you are afraid of it. The Holy Spirit leads as steadily to Heaven as the ego drives to hell.

T–15.I.7:1–4

We learned in chapter 8 that words create distinctions and that these distinctions result in the perception of duality. On the other hand, all mystical philosophy is monistic, teaching that God alone exists, and that the perceived "outside" world is an illusion or a dream. There is one God, a singular experience of love beyond all names, words, and religions. Love, God, and Heaven are synonyms. As German mystic Johann Fichte said: "Being is absolutely singular, not manifold; there are not several Beings, but one Being only."

When we speak of the universal, we mean that there is no division and, therefore, only Oneness. Both holographic research and DNA research tell us that the whole is in every part and every part is in the whole. Following this same reasoning, only that which we think in alignment with God is true. Everything else is bound or limited by space and time and, therefore, dreamlike and illusory. American mystic Edgar Cayce found the essence of mysticism in knowing the underlying unity of all things that otherwise appear to be distinct. Mysticism, according to Cayce, means going beyond differentiations that distinguish between inner and outer, dark and light, good and bad. "Only in Christ Consciousness do the extremes meet."

If this is true, it is impossible to be separated from God. However, the ego tries to create a world in which God is a "nice idea" perhaps, but not reality. From the viewpoint of the ego, the unity of Heaven seems like a fantasy, and the separation of this world looks like reality. Yet the most common experience for mystics is unity and connectedness—the sense that everything is whole and complete. According to Huang Po, a ninth-century Zen master: "Mind, which is without beginning, is unborn and indestructible. It transcends all limits, measures, traces, and comparisons."

The Greek philosopher Plotinus was the father of Neoplatonism, a philosophy based on a form of idealistic monism that teaches that all is one. Like all mystics, the Neoplatonists saw the soul as eternally real and the body as existing only for a moment in space and time. Plotinus speaks of "another intellect," different from that of reason and "rationality." This intellect—this mind—is not irrational, but rather "trans-rational." Transcendentalists spoke of something similar.

As early as the sixth century BCE, the Greek philosopher Heraclitus was saying that there is one universal soul and that the object of philosophy was to understand how "all things are steered through the All." Since then, philosophers in all cultures have been advancing similar thoughts. The *Lankavatara* Buddhist sutras tell us: "Things are not two but one and all duality is falsely imagined." Meister Eckhart claimed: "If we will see things truly, we are strangers to that which creates distinction." Krishnamurti agreed, observing that consciousness was a phenomenon shared with all humanity. Austrian quantum physicist Erwin Schrödinger declared simply: "The overall number of minds is one." The Course carries on this tradition: "The power of one mind can shine into another, because all the lamps of God were lit by the same spark. It is everywhere and it is eternal" (T–10.IV.7:5–6).

Above the separated ego and intellect is one Mind. Lesson 52 from the Course asks us to say to ourselves: "Would I not rather join the thinking of the universe than to obscure all that is really mine with my pitiful and meaningless *private* thoughts?" Our "pitiful and meaningless private thoughts" are the ego's thoughts of separation—hidden thoughts, guilty thoughts. We seek to hide these thoughts; and yet, they mean nothing in truth, as they are not of God. They fill our consciousness and dominate the mind. They are the creators of the world we see. According to the Heisenberg Uncertainty Principle, it is impossible for the perceiver not to affect the object perceived, and therefore *mind* determines the reality of everything. We are constantly superimposing our interpretations on the world, believing that we see things as they are. For mystics, however, there is only one way to see, and that is "seeing" in alignment with the Mind of God. All else is an illusion.

American writer and philosopher Robert M. Pirsig is best-known for his book *Zen and the Art of Motorcycle Maintenance,* in which he developed the idea of a "Metaphysics of Quality," a view of reality that incorporates Asian philosophy, pragmatism, and American Indian philosophy and reflects the Vedantic concept of *"Tat tvan asi,"* Sanskrit for "Thou art that." "The Metaphysics of Quality," says Pirsig, "is a more accurate way to see reality than the traditional dualistic (subject-object) view. . . . Everything that we think (subjective) and everything we perceive (objects) are undivided." To realize this lack of division, this absolute Oneness, he claimed, was to be enlightened.

The Problem of Evil

Unity minister Eric Butterworth writes: "Evil and evil spirits, devils and devil possession are the outgrowth of man's inadequate consciousness of God." According to the Course, God does not hold our so-called "evil" deeds against us, knowing they are illusory and that, one day, like the prodigal son, every child of God will come Home.

Mystics avoid thinking of evil as a thing in itself—a force that works against God that must be fought. Just as there is no ego, so too there is no evil as "a thing" at war with God and man. Christians, Jews, and philosophers of all cultures have wrestled with the problem of evil since time immemorial. Jewish philosopher Benedict de Spinoza, one of the outstanding rationalists of the 17th century, argued that all reality consists of one substance—God or nature—and that the pure, uncontaminated love of God frees us from desire and brings immortality. Spinoza writes: "If men were born free, they would, so long as they remained free, form no conception of good and evil." The very idea of duality (self and other), he claimed, is the root of all our problems. It is our belief in separation, our projection of ourselves as being separate from or "other than" whatever we perceive, that is literally the root of all evil. Mystics say very simply is that there is no other; there is no outside. There is no difference, no duality, and no separation. Thus, there is no existential evil. "A sense of separation from God is the only lack you really need correct" (T–1.VI.2:1).

Simply Heavenly

Heaven is not a place nor a condition. It is merely an awareness of perfect Oneness, and the knowledge that there is nothing else; nothing outside this Oneness, and nothing else within. (T–18.VI.1:5–6)

In Greek, the word for devil is *diabolos*, which means "slanderer." Paul and the early Gospel writers called the devil Satan, meaning "adversary, accuser, or separator." The difference is significant, because, from the mystic's point of view, there simply cannot be an opposite of God. There can be no external evil agent. According to the Course: "The mind can make the belief in separation very real and very fearful, and this belief *is* the 'devil'" (T–3.VII.5:1). If we believe evil is "out there," then we can justify attacking it. Once we accept duality, we accept good and bad, and the world becomes a battleground between these energies or forces. Conflict is the ultimate result of believing that we are separated from God.

Conflict subtracts; peace brings abundance. In the hell of conflict, everybody loses.

Belief in the devil is just that—a belief. Therefore, we can be free of the devil by seeing it for what it is—a projection of the ego. Joseph Conrad had it right: "The belief in a supernatural source of evil is not necessary; men alone are quite capable of every wickedness." The ego creates the idea of the devil to project the problem of evil "into the world" instead of seeing it in itself. By making the devil seem real, we give its illusions power over us.

The devil exists only insofar as the ego exists. And the ego no more exists than does the devil. The devil is a bad dream and bad dreams are not eternal. As angels are symbolic extensions of the thoughts of God, the devil is a symbolic extension of the thoughts of the ego. Angels are symbols of the light and protection of God that surround us; the devil is a symbol of separation, fear, anger, and aggression. As Dostoyevsky expressed it: "Man has created the devil; he has created him in his own image and likeness."

The word "temptation" comes from the Latin *tenatio* and means "trial" or "test." We experience temptation in our inclination to listen to the prodding of the ego rather than the voice for God. With each temptation comes the opportunity to choose once again. Whenever we are afraid, the ego encourages our fears and tells us to choose in favor of security, status, and possession. "If you cannot hear the Voice for God, it is because you do not choose to listen," the Course observes. "That you *do* listen to the voice of your ego is demonstrated by your attitudes, your feelings, and your behavior" (T–4.IV.1:1–2).

Abraham Maslow describes a "hierarchy of needs" that roughly appproximates the temptations Christ encountered in the Gospels. The first temptation is the need to satisfy immediate needs. Jesus experienced this when he was hungry from his long fast; but he knew, as all mystics know, that it is better to control the appetites than to let them control us. The second is the need to show off. Jesus felt called; he had a mission to fulfill. He could have done something spectacular to convince people of his power, but chose instead the path of humility. The third is the need for power. Jesus could have controlled and manipulated events to enhance his earthly power, but his Kingdom was not of this world. He listened instead to the voice of God.

If Jesus had given in to any of these temptations, there would be no Gospels to inspire us and show us our true nature. Jesus never gave in to the seductions of the ego, and he maintained an awareness of his identity. In most other hero stories, the Hero is seduced by the ego and is then faced with a need to overcome failure. Eventually, the Hero comes to the Self again and finds the way out of darkness.

Jesus went into the desert to encounter the devil. Saint Anthony, Buddha, and Teresa of Avila all recount similar experiences. We go through trials and tribulations, caught up in our complexes, compulsions, and battles for status and control. We often give in and listen, not to the voice of Holy Spirit, but to a voice that calls upon us to show off, forget about God, and build up our own power in a world wherein we judge, condemn, and control. The temptation to engage in separation keeps us in a hell made with our own hands. Fortunately, this state is not eternal and, therefore, not real. Psychiatrist Ernest Jones, friend and biographer of Sigmund

Freud, wrote: "A man's chief enemy is his own unruly nature and the dark forces pent up within him."

Youmeuswe

There is something great that we can see.
It surpasses all definition of "you" and "me." (Jon)

We can look at the selfish, separating ego self and then look beyond it. Mystics look at the ego, not to affirm its reality, but to see beyond illusion. In fact, we cannot let go of the ego until we see its illusory nature. If we try to kill or attack the ego, it grows stronger. But there is nothing to fear. We are, in truth, *one Self, united with our Creator.* That means that we have no enemies, even within ourselves. Nonetheless, during our lives, we will each run into resistance and hostility. One of the most important lessons we can learn is how to disagree with people without attacking them. Thus those we may perceive as our enemies can help us discover our own deeper truth. Edmund Burke said: "Our enemies are those who strengthen our nerves and sharpen our skill." Martin Luther did not want to leave the Church. Once he was excommunicated, however, he had no choice but to continue to deepen his spiritual search on his own. In remaining true to himself in the face of powerful opposition, Luther helped birth the Protestant Reformation. Jesus, Gandhi, Martin Luther King, Jr., Nelson Mandela, and many more like them changed the world by peacefully facing their opponents.

Oceanic Consciousness

Freud coined the term "oceanic" to describe the falling away of the borders of consciousness and the pleasurable experience of Oneness. Melting into Oneness and unity is not an altered state, however. It is simply seeing without contamination. In oceanic consciousness, there are no blocks to awareness. "Oneness is endless, timeless, and within your grasp because your hands are His" (T–24.V.9:4). Fourteenth-century Japanese master Muso Kokushi, an influential garden designer, wrote: "When it's cold, water freezes into ice; when it's warm, ice melts into water. Similarly, when you are confused, essence freezes into mind; when you are enlightened, mind melts into essence."

Seventeenth-century French mystic Madame Guyon was an advocate of quietism, a practice considered heretical by the Catholic Church. Deeply attracted to mysticism, she devoted her entire life to the inner quest. She was known for her imposing appearance and the clarity with which she explained mystical concepts. Her teachings had a tremendous influence on the German philosopher Schopenhauer. Madam Guyon writes:

> The soul which is reduced to the Nothing, ought to dwell therein; without wishing, since she is now but dust, to issue from this state, nor, as before, desiring to live again. She must remain as something which no longer exists in order that the Torrent may drown itself and lose itself in the Sea, never to find itself in its selfhood again; that it may become one and the same thing with the Sea.

Mystics are absorbed in a boundless ocean, a great sense of connectedness with the whole. In Sufism, the whole is likened to the ocean and the part to a drop; when the drop becomes one with the ocean, it sees with the eye of the ocean. When we lose the sense of personal self, we are like a drop of water disappearing into the ocean. Alan Watts tells us: "If you go into a far, far forest and get very quiet, you'll come to understand that you're connected with everything."

Indian scientist and teacher Deepa Kodikal said she discovered, as a child, that she could direct her dreams and achieve a mystical state of absorption. Her mystical experiences (galaxies within galaxies) provide a picture of an infinite colossal tapestry in motion, with different dimensions of time in different spatial dimensions and yet other dimensions not available in ordinary awareness. Her description of her experience is one of the most "cosmological" descriptions I've ever read and one of the closest to my own experience. In her book, *A Journey Within the Self,* she claims: "I felt that I was vast, limitless in size. A feeling of all-pervasiveness swept over me. I was everyone, and everyone was me. There was one continuous principle pervading everything. Everything was one." Later in the book, she writes:

> I began by seeing the universe as one sees the sky from earth. Slowly, my individual identity was broken down and when my limiting individuality was totally demolished, I assumed the universal form. I was everywhere at one time, seeing everything, the micro, the macro, from the closest quarters, from the furthest range. I was omnipresent, all-knowing, and all-enjoying. But I was not the universe. I was

totally free of it, independent of it and uninvolved in it. I spread everywhere, but formlessly and unencumbered by attachments, an eternal witness not bound by the universe. I was pure and intelligent consciousness, seeing all and knowing all but not depending on the universe for sustenance.

Mystics are not in charge of their mystical experiences. They happen to and through them. They are not the authors of them. Teresa of Avila insisted that the special quality of the mystical state is that, although you can prepare for it, you cannot attain it by your own efforts. It comes, at last, by grace. "Grace," the Course says: "is the natural state of every Son of God. When he is not in a state of grace, he is out of his natural environment and does not function well" (T–7. XI.2:1). If you try to control, manipulate, or label a mystical experience, the experience disappears. The best way to sustain mystical awareness is to surrender to it and let it flow, without analyzing what is occurring. Can you remember as a child falling asleep in the back of the car at night and having your parents carry you to bed? Remember the gentle feeling of trusting your body to the arms of your mother or father? Surrender is like that—a willingness to go with the flow, a willingness to be carried Home.

Chapter 20

Mysticism and Synchronicity

Overcome space, and all we have left is here. Overcome time, and all we have left is now. And in the middle of here and now, don't you think that we might see each other once or twice?
—Richard Bach

Synchronicity is the coincidence in time of events or thoughts that are seemingly unrelated. Mysticism reflects a belief that this simultaneity has meaning beyond mere coincidence. From the mystic's perspective, everything—even things that do not make sense or seem significant—reflects a plan. The script is written. Our passage through time and space is not without design. When we come to revelation, we come at last to the knowledge of "what already is."

In *The Celestine Prophecy*, James Redfield lists nine insights that can lead to enlightenment, the first of which is becoming more conscious of coincidence. Coincidence "appears to be" an unplanned alignment of events—things happening in a way that seems planned, even though we did not consciously make the plan. Chinese theories of medicine, philosophy, and architecture are based on a *science* of coincidence.

Chinese texts do not ask what causes something; they ask what *likes to occur with* something. According to Chinese philosophy, certain events "like" to cluster together. Thus there is a pattern to everything, and everything flows naturally from one thing or event to another.

So perhaps it is no accident that Carl Jung's fascination with physics began with a series of dinners with Albert Einstein. Jung was fascinated with the concept of synchronicity, sometimes called serendipity. Joseph Campbell once said: "Unless you allow for serendipity, you will never find your way." Serendipity occurs when we find something we weren't looking for or expecting to find, but discover that it is exactly the right thing. Sometimes to find ourselves, we must get lost. We go on a detour and there discover the very thing we need. Sometimes, at the precise moment you think things cannot or will not change, everything changes. "There are no accidents in salvation," the Course observes. "Those who are to meet will meet, because together they have the potential for a holy relationship. They are ready for each other" (M–3.1:6–8).

Patterned events, synchronicities, are more clearly seen during "crucial" phases in spiritual development. Jung noticed prior to World War II that many of his patients were having horrific dreams of fire, war, destruction, and death—apocalyptic images. He was concerned that his patients were going mad. Then he realized that their dreams portended World War II. In another example, Jung tells how he watched a beetle crawling up the curtain behind a patient, while the patient was describing a dream about an Egyptian scarab. The movie *Crash* is a good example of how synchronistic events occur. People come "crashing" into each other, but there are a host of decisions made by everyone leading up to this moment, and then another host of experiences that result from the crash—all of which lead to the fulfillment of destiny.

The Dalai Lama once said: "When everything is falling apart something else is trying to be born." Accepting responsibility for what is happening helps us through loss. Life then takes an upward turn. We are not driven by external, purposeless events. Everything comes our way as part of our spiritual journey, and no accidents are possible in the Universe, as God created it. Remember Einstein's assurance that God does not play dice with the Universe. In every seeming accident, there is a lesson and we are constantly learning.

The older we get, the more we learn about life beyond this life. One advantage of getting older is that the longer we live, the more we understand why our lives went the way they did. According to an article in *Scientific American Mind*, as we get older, one of two things happens: either we get grumpier, more mean-spirited and projective; or we become more open-minded, laid back, loving, and receptive. Which way do you want to go? Fortunately, most folks choose the more loving response.

Problems are doors that lead us Home. Vaclav Havel, former President of Czechoslovakia, said: "Hope is not the conviction that something will turn out well, but the certainty that things make sense, regardless of how it turns out." We can procrastinate and we can find innumerable excuses for not paying attention. Eventually, however, we must face life straight on and deal with whatever stands in front of us. Eventually, all bills must be paid or forgiven.

Gift in Hand

There is no sickness, no physical loss, no financial difficulty, no interpersonal problem, and no death, no experience, however extraordinary or mundane, that does not come our way holding a gift in its hand. (Vaclav Havel)

In this moment, "right now," we either know the peace of God or we do not. The next moment is the same, as is the next. But we have a choice as to how to view the moment. The power of decision is our "last remaining freedom." By changing our minds about the mind, we change everything. Letting destiny unfold in accordance with God's will is beautiful. Everyone has a mission. Those who find a way to fulfill their destinies tell us that they "knew" there was something they had to do. Destiny "had" to be fulfilled, and the best thing to do was to fulfill it.

Behind everything, there is something analogous to the genetic code of the Universe. There is a "reason" why each of us goes through life the way we do. Computers today are a billion times more powerful than they were twenty-five years ago, and this growth is continuing exponentially. The more their capacity grows, the faster it grows. It's amazing to think how much information can be carried around in our cell phones, and they keep getting smaller. Within all that overwhelming mass of information, there is always an algorithm—always a pattern, always a plan. Jesus tells us in the

Gospels that "even the hairs on your head are numbered" and "not even a sparrow falls to the earth without God's knowledge." God's voice speaks to us every minute of every single day. Radio station WGOD is broadcasting a "program" we can follow and things will work out the way they were intended. His plan is the best plan. Having free will, we go with WEGO and turn off WGOD.

God's Plan for Salvation—GPS

A GPS system tells you where to go—make a left, make a right, mile-by-mile, even foot-by-foot. God also has an amazing plan for salvation—a GPS—designed to direct us back Home. Right now, anyone on Earth can pick up a cell phone and, within seconds, be talking with someone on the other side of the world through microwaves sent through the air. God's got your number, and guidance is being sent to every one of us every moment of every day. For each of us, however, the path is *highly individualized*. What you must go through to get back to God is different from the terrain others must travel. If we're lucky, maybe our paths will cross and we'll enjoy the overlap.

So, what happens if we go through life and decide not to follow God's plan for salvation? What if we ignore the GPS? What if we choose some diversion or some detour? You may think: "This guy is cute, I'll chase after him for a while." Or "I think I'll see if I can make a lot of money." Or "I think I'll have another drink." We have free will and, like the prodigal sons and daughters that we are, we can go off, like Sinatra, and try to "do it our way." If we choose not to follow God's plan, we will still get Home. Taking detours, however, makes the trip longer and harder, and there are often rough places along the way—bumps in the road like divorce or bank-ruptcy. Rather than seeking the entrance to God's Kingdom, we can try building our own kingdom.

God's plan is all laid out for us and, if we choose to follow it, we find that the path is straight and the way is smooth.

Enter in at the straight gate, for wide is the gate, and broad is the way, that leads to destruction and many there be which go there in. Straight is the gate and narrow is the way, which leads to life, and few there are that find it. (Matthew 7:13–14).

Few find the straight path and the narrow gate because we're caught in some diversion, some distraction, some habituated activity. We're off trying to build our own world or we're trapped in a "somebody has done me wrong" song. God's GPS remains operative always and is persistent in its gentle guidance, regardless of the detour we may have cho-sen. God does, indeed, speak to everyone, every moment of every day. The question is, are you paying attention? If you're driving with a GPS system and you decide to turn off the prescribed route for lunch or for gas, the GPS system simply recalculates the way home. Every single moment of every single day, you receive direction from God's GPS. If you choose instead to slip into denial, anger, or projection—if you choose to go off course—God's GPS immediately recal-culates the way back to the main road and you are headed Home once again.

Those who impeccably pursue their destinies are the happiest people, though they may choose to remain single, turn down wealth, or even be crucified. No step that anyone makes along the road, however, is inadvertent. We've already walked this road, so it is a matter of remembering what we already know. We are already Home, resting in the arms of God. The story has been played through; the dream is ended. We have attained entrance to the Kingdom of Heaven. We are already perfect and whole, even while the ego dreams strange dreams. "When experience will come to end your doubting has been set," the Course reminds us. "For we but see the journey from the point at which it ended, looking back on it, imagining we make it once again; reviewing mentally what has gone by" (W–158.4:4).

Chapter 21

Mysticism and Paradox

Salvation is a paradox indeed! What could it be except a happy dream? It asks you but that you forgive all things that no one ever did; to overlook what is not there, and not to look upon the unreal as reality.

T–30.IV.7:1–3

A paradox is something that is contrary to expectations, existing beliefs, or perceived opinions. Paradox is a universal feature of mysticism because the world of perception, the world of the ego mind, is upside down and backward from reality. The rational ego mind works through perception and, thus, duality—subject/object, knower/known, right/wrong. This "level" of thinking, however, has limitations, since perception is inherently—and therefore, inevitably—tainted by the interpretation of the observer. For this reason, the ordinary ego mind must come to a complete halt before there can be a pure, mystical awareness of perfect Oneness. In such "knowing," there are no differences and no perception of forms—and therefore no paradox.

The rational ego mind finds it difficult to handle paradoxical information, in which what may be true at the level of ever-changing form is untrue at the level of absolute reality—the Mind of God. By its nature, the ego is "insane" or "wrong-minded," simply because no one in their right mind would want to live outside of the Mind of God. And so the Course tells us: "It is essential it be kept in mind that all perception still is upside down until its purpose has been understood" (T–27.VII.14.3–8). Until we are enlightened, we are all a bit unbalanced. Perfection seems beyond our reach, and yet, perfection remains the goal. The goal of the mystic is healthy-mindedness; indeed, the goal is enlightenment. We are called upon to remember our identity as children of God and, as children of God, we must be perfect. "God's perfect Son remembers his creation. But in guilt he has forgotten what he really is" (T–31.I.9:6–7).

As Ken Wilber expresses it: "The mystic who tries to speak logically and formally of unity consciousness is doomed to sound very paradoxical or contradictory." The Course asks that you engage in a reversal of thinking. Rather than seeking "reality" in the world, we must realize that, as Jesus says in the gospels: "The Kingdom of Heaven is *inside you.*" It is not in the body. It "is" in the Mind. We must engage in a reversal of thinking to see correctly. As it is, we see everything "through a glass darkly," witnessing our own projection coming back our way. Therefore, to the ego, ". . . it is kind and right and good to point out errors and *correct* them. This makes perfect sense to the ego, which is unaware of what errors are and what correction is. Errors are of the ego, and correction of errors lies in the relinquishment of the ego" (T–9.III.2:1–3).

Man of Action

He who sees inaction in action and action in inaction, he is wise among men; He is a man of established wisdom and a true performer of all actions. (Bhagavad Gita IV.18)

Beyond Reason

Zen *koans* are inherently paradoxical (contrary to expectation), because the goal of Zen, as with all mystical experiences, cannot be described satisfactorily in words. Zen masters seem to be talking in riddles as they point toward the mystical state. Zen speaks of obtaining a state of mind beyond thought and "no-thought." It points to a state in which there is no striving and in which the labeling of things has ceased—a state of mind that is free of judgment, or what we can think of as "pure mind."

Mystics ask us to accept the loving thoughts of others and regard everything that is not love as an appeal for help. If an appeal for help comes your way, your job is to help, not to judge or condemn. It is not to punish, although it may be necessary to restrain those who would hurt others or themselves. All fearful, jealous, anxious thoughts—all guilty, lustful, selfish thoughts—are not real. Nothing that is not loving is real. Therefore 19th-century Indian mystic Ramakrishna says: "A man who has realized God shows certain characteristics. He becomes like a child or a madman, or an inert thing. If you must be mad, why be mad for the things of this world? If you must be mad, be mad for God." As Zorba the Greek says to his wealthy American companion while dancing on the beach in Crete: "There is only one thing wrong with you, boss! You need a little madness!"

Purely Academic

Take paradox from the thinker and you have a professor. (Søren Kierkegaard)

In the words of American poet Emily Dickinson: "Much madness is divinest Sense To a discerning Eye—Much Sense— the starkest Madness." Wallace Black Elk was a Lakota elder, a mystic, and a Heyoka—a man of paradox. He did things in unconventional ways, like riding a horse backward, wearing clothes inside out, or speaking in reverse. Being a nature mystic, he said that the power of sacredness exists in all things. His visionary experiences were recounted in the book *Black Elk Speaks*. He had, he said, an affinity with birds, four-legged animals, the sky, and plants. His life was, as with all native people, completely intermingled with nature.

One of the things that was most lovable about contemporary mystics Gurdjieff and Osho was their ability to see into the incongruity of the ego. Joking and the ensuing laughter are often based on the paradoxical nature of the punchline, which comes out contrary to what is expected. At one moment, both Gurdjieff and Osho could be deeply reverent—for instance, in their appreciation of meditation—and the next moment point to the futility of rituals and dogmatic traditions. They both loved to joke about politics, religion, and the games society plays. Osho said that his most important teachings were his jokes. We all need to see the joke that is ourselves, and we need to laugh at the illogical and absurd.

After the death of William Blake in 1827, William Wordsworth, reflecting the opinions and beliefs of the time, said of Blake's writings: "There was no doubt that this poor man was mad, but there is something in the madness of this man which interests me more than the sanity of Lord Byron and Walter Scott. No one is a great poet, without being at the same time a profound philosopher. For poetry is the blossom and the fragrance of all human knowledge, human thoughts, human passions, emotions, language."

Blake writes:

This life's dim windows of the soul
Distort the heavens from pole to pole
And lead you to believe a lie
When you see with, not through, the eye.

In his book *The Marriage of Heaven and Hell*, Blake notes: "If the doors of perception were cleansed everything would appear to man as it is, infinite: For man has closed himself up, till he sees all things thro' narrow chinks of his cavern." Sometimes we've got to step out of the ordinary egoistic way of thinking. We've got to go beyond orthodoxy and solidified reasoning and move into paradox. We've got to step out of tradition and—dance with Zorba.

Let's Dance!

Upside Down and Inside Out

In his book *The Hidden Stream*, Ronald Knox, a modern theologian and mystery writer, identified seven paradoxes in mysticism:

- Mystics have a sense of being carried away by a force stronger than self.

- Mystics' apprehension of God becomes more direct.

- Mystics make less use of affection in loving God.

- Mystics' wills become more the center of prayer, while their acts become less and less perceptible.

- Mystics pray more, but ask for less.

- Mystics experience less self-consciousness as they enter Self.

Mysticism is filled with paradoxes, after all. What can never be lost can't be found. Mystics use the mind to go beyond the mind. God is the darkness behind the light. God is not material, but is visible in all things. Mystics are in control as they turn control over to God. Mysticism is the doing of undoing, or the undoing of doing. You must close your eyes in order to see.

Mysticism is non-nihilistic negativity. In other words, all there is, is God. Mystics have knowledge without comprehending. Matter does not matter, while consciousness is something—and nothing. Being is being without being. Mystics are loners, yet connected. To die is to awaken, and pure consciousness is not a consciousness of "thingness." Mystics see the static as dynamic, and stillness as dancing. They find silence at the center of a world of flux. The passivity at which mystics aim is a state of intense activity—a "dazzling darkness." For them, pure unity exists without multiplicity.

Mystics cease to be individuals, yet they retain individuality. To say "Of myself I can do nothing" is to gain all power; to find one's Self is to lose one's self. The mystic who reaches nirvana neither exists nor does not exist. Mystics understand that what they seek is seeking them and that the best way to get somewhere is to let go of the need to be anywhere. Mystics enjoy true liberty in proportion to the things they neither possess nor desire, for what do you lose when you lose an illusion?

In the *Isa Upanishad* (stanzas 4 and 5), we read:

That One, though never stirring, is swifter than thought. . . . Though standing still; it overtakes those who are running. . . . It stirs and it stirs not. It is far, and likewise near. It is inside all this, and it is outside all this.

This is the paradox of mysticism.

The Paradox of the Tao

When you look at it you cannot see it;
It is called formless.
When you listen to it you cannot hear it;
It is called soundless.
When you try to seize it, you cannot hold it;
It is called subtle . . .
It is up, but it is not brightened;
It is down, but it is not obscured.
It stretches endlessly, and no name is to be given . . .
It returns to nothingness.
You face it, but you cannot see its front.
You follow it, but you cannot see its back.
(*Tao Te Ching*)

Chapter 22

Mysticism and Art

All artists are of necessity in some measure contemplatives.
—Evelyn Underhill, *Mysticism*

The topic of art and mysticism is so expansive that I can neither do it justice here nor ignore it. According to the survey by Alister Hardy, the fifth, seventh, tenth, and eleventh most common stimulants to mystical experience are related to the arts—literature, drama, film, music, sacred architecture, and the visual arts. Because the mystical is hard to express in words, it lends itself well to expression through pictures and stories. Imagery, poetry, song, and dance all can activate our creative imagination so that we become intuitively aware—in our hearts, in our minds, and in our souls. Great art and architecture have the power to transcend the physical. They can capture our attention, make us gaze in wonder, and leave us captivated and enthralled. Music can convey the sound of the ineffable, while art is a "language" that can make visible what the mystic "sees."

Artistic creation plays a role in enlightenment for both the artist and the observer. During artistic creation, a dance takes place between creator, creation, and created. As separation between the artist and the work of art falls away, the two can unite. As Thomas Merton wrote: "Art enables us to find ourselves and lose ourselves at the same time." Just as, in mystical experience, the seeker becomes one with what is sought, a good actress becomes the character portrayed; a writer becomes the character described; an artist becomes one with the work. Artists often try to express the "is-ness" of nature—the shine on an apple, the luminescence of a pearl earring, a woman's soft skin, an old man's wrinkles, the crack in a window, a raindrop reflecting the sun. In the same way, if you would know Christ, become the Christ; if you would know what reality is, be real.

For many artists, as for many mystics, life is spent in isolation, devotion, and reflection. Some of the most inspired mystical moments occur when we are absorbed in creation. In such moments, something beyond the little self takes over; there is a forgetting of self and a merging with the act of creation. Many impressionists and abstract artists of the late 19th and early 20th centuries were mystics. Their work was a merging of aesthetics and mysticism. The artist as mystic enters nature so that the inner structure of reality—its beauty—is revealed. Beauty is hiding in every form. We know it in the snowflake and the beating of the human heart. The artist and mystic simply draw it out so we can see it better.

One of the best examples we have of a mad, loving, profoundly visionary artist is 19th-century Dutch Post-Impressionist painter Vincent van Gogh. In his younger years, van Gogh was a preacher, but in later life, he found his vision of God in trees, cornfields, and flowers, painting what he saw. In his paintings, we find a union between art and artist, between a visual medium and "seeing." Van Gogh's "madness" only increased the intensity of his art, while his addiction to color made his paintings come vibrantly alive. We can feel the life force flowing in his work.

Mystic Poets

Mystics are often poets. Sometimes, as with Rumi, William Blake, Rabindranath Tagore, or Kahlil Gibran, poetry, art, and mysticism mingle together in one experience. Indeed, poetry is one of the most concise and effective expressions of the mystical experience. The Course itself is a poetic work of art. All the last several chapters of the Course are written in iambic pentameter, and the whole of the Workbook is presented in blank verse.

Although mysticism is ineffable, through poetry it is possible to glimpse into the beyond. Like a finger pointing to the moon, poetical words and images offer us a lofty experience. Poetry combines imagery and feeling. It suggests something beyond the expected, preexisting belief or perception. The Vedas of Hinduism, the world's oldest spiritual literature, are poetry, as are the Song of Solomon and the psalms and proverbs of the Bible. Many of the medieval mystics were poets. Consider the following from Teresa of Avila:

> *God alone is enough,*
> *Let nothing upset you.*
> *Let nothing startle you.*
> *All things pass; God does not change.*
> *Patience wins all it seeks.*
> *Whoever has God lacks nothing:*
> *God alone is enough.*

The Sufi tradition of Islam produced many great mystical poets, including Rumi, Ibn Arabi, Kabir, and Hazrat Inayat Khan. Likewise, Romanticism, which was a response to the rationalism that dominated philosophy at the beginning of the Industrial Revolution, validated the study of the mind and emotions in relation to the sense of beauty. Like mysticism, it placed an emphasis on freedom, intuition, imagination, and self-reliance, and encouraged the development of a personal relationship with God. Romanticism gave birth to Transcendentalism, which is based on a belief in the supremacy of insight and intuition over logic and reason, the essential unity of all creation, and the innate goodness of man.

Blake saw that the Divine in everyone supersedes reason. Attracted to the writings of Swedenborg, Blake, from his early years, experienced visions of angels. Like that of Traherne, his poetry is filled with energy, combined with a childlike simplicity and clarity. "Painting as well as music and poetry," Blake observed, "exists and exults in immortal thoughts." Samuel Taylor Coleridge and his friend William Wordsworth both wrote of a heightened awareness that embraces the world with love. They found profound beauty in the mundane—Spirit in the world around them.

Wordsworth, in describing an early morning ride over Westminster Bridge in London, wrote:

Earth has not anything to show more fair
Dull would he be of soul who could pass by
A sight so touching in its majesty
This City now doth like a garment wear
The beauty of the morning; silent bare
Ships, towers, domes, theatres and temples lie

Open unto the fields, and to the sky
All bright and glittering in the smokeless air.

Alfred Lord Tennyson, another product of the Romantic school, based much of his verse on mythological themes, but, like Coleridge and Wordsworth, found a spiritual truth and beauty in the objects of the everyday world. In one of his most famous works, he writes:

Flower in the crannied wall,
I pluck you out of the crannies;
Hold you here, root and all, in my hand,
Little flower but if I could understand.
What you are, root and all, and all in all,
I should know what God and man is.

In fact, according to Irish poet William Butler Yeats: "Poetry and religion are the same thing." Yeats read extensively on mysticism and was especially influenced by Emanuel Swedenborg. In 1885, Yeats formed the Dublin Hermetic Order, and became a member of the Theosophical Society. Sometimes, what a mystic sees is quite ordinary, quite plain and everyday, and that is what makes it beautiful. Sometimes the mystical dimension is seen in very simple things. Yeats described one such "seeing" experience thus:

My fiftieth year had come and gone. I sat, a solitary man in a crowded London shop, an open book and empty cup on the marble top. While on the shop and street I gazed my body of a sudden blazed; and

twenty minutes it seemed, so great my happiness,
that I was blessed and could bless.

This experience is like the one my friend Jeff Mills had
when he came out of a barbershop and ran into a woman who
looked like his mother. Yeats and Jeff both experienced an
intuition of inexplicable delight in an otherwise quite ordinary occurrence. They shifted from the mundane to another
dimension, where their delight seemed utterly boundless.

Haiku, a form of Japanese poetry, is traditionally a
seventeen-syllable verse form consisting of three metrical
units of five, seven, and five syllables each, although the exact
syllable count may vary. A haiku provides a picture designed
to arouse a distinct emotion and suggest spiritual insight.
Haiku poems and paradoxical questions or statements often
bring insights as nothing else can. They are designed to shift
perception to a deeper understanding, an inner direct knowing that is difficult to express in dualistic language. Here are
a couple of examples:

> *There is one thing not hidden,*
> *The bridge at Seta Bay.*

> HARVEST MOON:
> *Around the point I wander*
> *And the night is gone.*
> *The first soft snow!*
> *Enough to bend the leaves*
> *Of the jonquil low.*

Music and Mathematics

Mathematics and music speak a purer language than the simple use of words, which can easily be contaminated by meaning. Because of this, they are uniquely suited to convey a mystical message. One wonderful example of mathematics melding with mysticism is the story of Indian mathematician and autodidact Srinivasa Ramanujan. Although he had no formal training, he received a Doctorate from Trinity College in England, where he was made a Fellow in 1918. During his very short life, Ramanujan came up with some 3,900 theorems, all of which have been proven correct. When pressed to explain how he derived his theorems, he said that he received visions of scrolls containing complex mathematical formulae unfolding before his eyes. "An equation for me has no meaning," he said, "unless it represents a thought of God."

Those who excel in math often excel in music. Math can, in fact, be written as music, and music can be written as math. The Greek philosopher Pythagoras was the first to realize that music was mathematical. He taught that the beating of the heart and the inhaling and exhaling of the breath are the basis of musical rhythm. "There is," he said, "a sound without and within that is music." Because of the work of Pythagoras, we talk about half, quarter, or whole notes. Pythagoras writes: "There is geometry in the humming of the strings . . . there is music in the harmony of the spheres."

The purpose of music is to inspire us to become more harmonious in our thoughts, words, and deeds. Music makes us dance, spurring an instinctive ritual that brings the body into a celebration of the Divine. Music is a form of breathing that reminds us of the rhythm of creation. "To sing once is to pray twice," St. Augustine said. "Without music, life would be a mistake," claimed Nietzsche. "Music alone," says Evelyn Underhill in *Mysticism*, "shares with great mystical literature the power of waking in us a response to the life-movement of the universe." Tagore claimed that, although God respected him when he worked, God loved him when he sang.

Music is the most sacred of the arts. Its multi-toned sacredness can be heard in the beautiful Kyoto music of Japan, the ringing of Tibetan bells, the Gregorian chant of Christian monks, the Gospel music of rural America, or the beating of a shaman's drum. Spanish mystic Saint John of the Cross sensed the "unheard melodies" of the spheres and enjoined us to spend time under the starry sky, experiencing the "silent music and the euphonic solitude." Music aids in the unfolding of the mystic's soul and the opening of intuitive faculties. I was once surprised when I burst into tears while listening to a Chopin polonaise. Music lovers can tell of many such experiences. Music charges us with enthusiasm and passion, inducing a form of rapture.

Wind Song

The 27th—Up and then with my wife and Deb to the king's house to see Virgin Martyr. That which did please me beyond everything in the whole world was the wind music when the angel comes down, which is so sweet that it ravished me and indeed in a word did wrap up my soul so that it did make me really sick just as I have formerly been when I fell in love with my wife. Neither then nor all the evening going home and at home was I able to think of anything remaining all night transported so that I could not believe that ever any music hath that real command over the soul of a man as this did upon me. (*Samuel Pepys' Diary*)

While mystical awareness often comes upon us when we are alone, mystical experiences can occur when we are singing together as well—in a choir, or as a congregation in a church, or while chanting in groups. The Sikhs place tremendous value in *kirtans*, ecstatic devotional music common in Hinduism and Sufism. Sikhs are encouraged to listen to and/ or sing guru-kirtan as frequently as possible.

Whether through the visual arts, music, math, poetry, or dance, mystics inevitably seek to convey what they see and know through creative expression. Therefore, God is found in the senses, in the intellect, in the heart, in love, in union—in every way known to man and many ways revealed to the contemplative, who becomes ever more fully aware of the Divine within.

Chapter 23

Mysticism and Ecstasy

A lot can be said about what cannot be said.

—Jon

Mysticism is often thought of as seeing visions and hearing voices. Hearing and seeing are certainly primary when it comes to the body, but the soul has many faculties—including reason, intuition, and feelings. Therefore, there are no "unnatural" or "paranormal" powers of perception, and everyone possesses abilities of which they are unaware. In the past 150 years, technology has opened us to an awareness of X-rays, gamma rays, infrared rays, microwaves, holographs, and more. It seems that the more we know, the less we know we know. According to Buckminster Fuller, since the first publication of the chart of the electromagnetic spectrum, we have learned that what we can touch, smell, see, and hear is less than one-millionth of our reality.

The branch of philosophy called "aesthetics" studies sensory values—judgments of sentiment and taste (beautiful vs. ugly) and the science of how things are known. According to Indian aesthetics, a spectator witnesses a dramatic performance or work of art for enjoyment, or *rasa*, a Sanskrit word meaning "taste, essence, nectar, or delight." *Rasa* is what occurs when we experience, or delight in, the essence of art. As we have seen, mystics are often lovers of art and music, and revel in sound, sight, and smell—as in the use of incense. Fourteenth-century English mystic Richard Rolle was one who appreciated the physicality of mysticism—feelings, colors, sounds, heat, etc. While some mystics emphasize the intellect or the mind, others look to the heart.

John Lilly spent much of his life studying interspecies communication, especially the relationship between humans and dolphins. While the average human has a hearing range of .02 to 17 kHz, the range at which dolphins hear best is 40 to 150 kHz, ten times the sensitivity of the human ear. Giraffes, elephants, and whales all converse at frequencies outside the range of the human ear. A dog's brain is one tenth the size of a human brain, but the part of it that controls smell is forty times *larger* than the part that controls smell in the human brain. This provides a wonderful metaphor of mystical experience. For animals, there is a whole world of experience about which we know nothing.

A Matter of Perspective

United States Naval officer and astronaut Edgar "Ed" Mitchell described an experience that occurred when he was returning to Earth from the moon in 1971: "I had completed my major task and was on my way home, observing the heavens and the Earth from this distance. . . . As we were rotated, I saw the Earth, the sun, the moon, and a 360-degree panorama of the heavens. The magnificence of all of this was a trigger in my visioning. In the ancient Sanskrit, it's called *samadhi*. It means that you see things with your senses the way they are—you experience them viscerally and internally as a unity and a oneness accompanied by ecstasy."

How much exists about which our senses tell us nothing? British primatologist and anthropologist Jane Goodall tells of an experience she had in her book *Reason for Hope: A Spiritual Journey:*

Lost in awe at the beauty around me, I must have slipped into a state of heightened awareness. It is hard—impossible really—to put into words the moment of truth that suddenly came upon me then. Even the mystics are unable to describe their brief flashes of spiritual ecstasy. It seemed to me, as I struggled afterward to recall the experience, the self was utterly absent: I and the chimpanzees, the earth and trees and air, seemed to merge, to become one with the spirit power of life itself. The air was filled with a feathered symphony, the evensong of birds. I heard new frequencies in their music and also in singing insects' voices—notes so high and sweet I was amazed. Scents were clear as well, easily identifiable: fermenting, overripe fruit; waterlogged earth; cold, wet bark; the damp odor of chimpanzee hair, and yes, my own too.

The Course talks about Great Rays as extensions of the light of God that transcend the body and our ordinary perception. "In the holy instant, where the Great Rays replace the body in awareness, the recognition of relationships without limits is given you. But in order to see this, it is necessary to give up every use the ego has for the body, and to accept the fact that the ego has no purpose you would share with it" (T–15.IX.3:1–2).

Our powers of communication are thus not limited to the small range of channels recognized by the world of form. God's voice is available to everyone, all the time, but it is not audible. It is much deeper. Emerson writes:

> There is one mind common to all individual men. Every man is an inlet to the same and to all of the same. He that is once admitted to the right of reason is made a freeman of the whole estate. What Plato has thought, he may think; what a saint has felt, he may feel; what at any time has be-fallen any man, he can understand. Who hath access to this universal mind is a party to all that is or can be done, for this is the only and sovereign agent.

Sacred Sight

The fact that the body is involved at all in vision removes the experience from the realm of pure knowledge. Physical perception can, in fact, be an incredible distraction, as it is for babies, as it is for young men and women with the onset of puberty.

While knowing extends into infinity, visions, however holy, do not last. Perceptual images arise as we appreciate nature, art, and music, and when we meditate, or just whenever we allow for "Beingness"—for being quiet and peaceful. Archetypical images, sometimes encountered in dreams, "speak" to us. Helen Schucman was subject to vivid dreams. Visionary experiences often begin in vivid dreams and may occur when we are ill or near death. During these times, amazing doors and windows can open as we accept death's call and the opening of Heaven's doors. "The laws of the universe do not permit contradiction," the Course promises. "What holds for God holds for you. If you believe you are absent from God, you will believe that He is absent from you. Infinity is meaningless without you, and you are meaningless without God" (T–11.I5:2–4).

From a young age, William Blake claimed to see visions. At the age of nine, he reported seeing a tree filled with angels "bespangling every bough—like stars." On another occasion, as he watched haymakers at work, he saw angelic figures walking among them. His wife, Catherine, recalled the time he saw God's head "put to the window." The vision, she reminded her husband, "set you a screaming."

One of the best-known visionary experiences is the story of Saint Paul on the road to Damascus. Paul, then Saul of Tarsus, was engaged in the persecution of Christians. Then, while traveling to Damascus, he was blinded by a brilliant light and heard a voice saying: "Saul, Saul, why do you persecute me?" Saul, who was later called Paul, regained his sight. As with many converts, his visionary experience made him a true believer.

When it comes to ecstatic visions, mysticism and madness may mix. Hallucinations and distressful images sometimes come to people when they are fearful, or near the end of a long fast. Saint Anthony was tempted by the devil in a vision. Certainly, visions can tend toward the psychopathic. We find one of the most glaring examples of this in Vincent van Gogh. On the other hand, visions are also often cathartic. After an unpleasant vision, we often feel better—the way we feel after regurgitating some unpleasant food or after a good confession.

Zhao says of her experience: "Then, suddenly, the whole world disappeared. My self—disappeared. I felt I had melted into God, the supreme good, the most beautiful, peaceful, joyful state I never imagined." Ramakrishna relates a similar experience:

> I felt as if nothing existed. . . . I perceived a boundless ocean of intelligence. Whichever side I turned my eyes, I saw from all quarters huge waves of ocean rushing toward me, and in short falling upon me, engulfing me completely. . . . I lost my ordinary consciousness and fell to the floor of the room, completely lost in the ecstasy of the vision. I was perfectly unconscious as to what had happened outside, and how that day and the next had passed. The one thing which I was internally conscious of was my soul rolling in an ocean of ineffable joy, the like of which I had never experienced before. At the same time, I was also conscious, to the inner core of my being, of the hallowed presence of the Divine Mother. (From Christopher Isherwood's *Ramakrishna and His Disciples*)

The Voice for God

While visions may seem more dramatic than sounds, mystical experiences are more likely to be perceived as auditory than visual. Mystics are "given messages." They "hear" things. The sense of hearing, in fact, develops before vision. In the animal kingdom, many baby animals are born blind. Kittens and puppies can hear their brothers and sisters barking and meowing for days before they slowly open their own eyes and begin to see. And even when their eyes open, they do not yet see color. It is not until around the fifth month that a child's eyes can work together to form a three-dimensional image of the world.

In his 1901 book *Cosmic Consciousness,* Richard Maurice Bucke describes what he called a spiritual evolution going on inside every soul—biologically within the body, and intuitively and morally within the mind. The apprehension of color, he said, came relatively late to humankind. There is no mention of a blue sky in the Bible. The ancient Greeks, Bucke claimed, saw no more than three or four colors—black, white, red, and grey. Homer, for example, describes a "wine-dark sea."

Imagine that we are all two-way radios, able to send and receive. Our tuners are set to WEGO, which is coming in loud and clear, although sometimes broken up by static and not always the bearer of good news. WEGO speaks to us of guilt and reminds us of fear. The ego is projective, seeing and hearing news of its own and others' sin, guilt, and fear. Busily responding to our own dramas, we are not receptive to hearing a more enlightened message. Mystics are simply tuned in to a "higher frequency." They tune in to WGOD. Which station do you want to listen to? Only "you" can change the dial.

Socrates said there was a little spirit that whispered into his ear and told him what *not* to do, and it always led him in the right direction. Every second, we choose which voice we will follow. To hear WGOD ever more clearly, begin by turning down the volume on WEGO. The path of the mystic is always about "undoing" error, or the illusion of separation that blinds us to the truth of unity. It is never about "doing," for truth, or reality, is ever-present. The voice for God is *always* there, and it is *always* soothing, gentle, and compelling.

Mystics tune in to what Native Americans call "The Great Man in the Heart," or what Christians call the "Holy Spirit." They develop an "inner dialogue" with this mentor within. With practice, we learn to differentiate between the anxious voice of the ego and the still, small voice of God. The question is not: "Is there a voice?" The question is: "Why don't I do what I'm being asked to do, so I can hear this voice even better?" Seventeenth-century Carmelite Brother Lawrence, famous for his book *The Practice of the Presence of God*, said that there was not in the world "a life more sweet and delightful, than that of conversation with God." Indeed, a happy life is a guided life.

Sometimes we must be brought to our knees before we can open our eyes and ears. Only then does true guidance come our way. The Holy Spirit is inside, not outside. There is no gain in looking for the answer where it is not. The most common experiences of inner guidance are intuitive, like "feeling" that someone is going to call. God's voice is always comforting and reassuring. The Holy Spirit is identified in the New Testament as the great comforter, healer, teacher, and guide.

Mahatma Gandhi, one of history's best-known mystics, led a simple life, observing silence, chastity, and vegetarianism.

"If we have ears to hear," said Gandhi, "God speaks to us in our own language, whatever that language may be." Helen Schucman tells us that she *heard* the Course. At perhaps the lowest point in my life, after the loss of nearly everything I had, I sat at my desk, leaned over, and cried out: "Help me." And I heard: "Haven't I always taken care of you?" I lifted my head from the desk and looked around. Of course, there was no one there.

As we progressively let go of the ego, we very naturally become more and more aware of inner guidance. The voice is often very simple, clear, and comforting. A man about to undergo an operation heard: "Fear not, I am always with you." A man who had just been fired and asked for help heard: "You just got help." A woman whose husband was having a heart attack heard: "Patience, patience." The Holy Spirit never frightens his children.

On Mount Horeb, after being told to lead the Israelites out of Egypt, Moses asked God: "Whom shall I say has sent me?" And the reply comes: "I am that I am has sent you." Paul on the road to Damascus heard the voice of Jesus speaking to him. Saint Augustine, after questioning who God was, heard a voice say: "I am that I am." Saint Francis of Assisi heard Jesus from the cross enjoining him: "Repair my Church." At first, Saint Francis took these words literally and became a stone mason. Later, he realized that repairing the Church was something much deeper than fixing cracks in a wall. Once, when I was distressed over the actions of someone and wondered whether to intervene, I again said: "Help!" And I heard: "Let me handle this." That was the right answer, and it was a great relief. There was nothing I needed to do except to be unafraid. "If the center of the thought system is true," the Course assures us, "only truth extends from it. But if a lie is at its center, only deception proceeds from it" (T–6.B.1:10–11).

Sometimes the answer to our requests for help is good common sense, and sometimes the answer is "No." God cannot answer prayer with an illusion or with some sort of ego enhancement. "No" simply means: "Don't play host to the ego." "Don't eat too much." "Don't drink too much." "Don't talk so much." "Do not attack." "Do not defend." "Don't make a judgment." "Don't waste your money." "Don't go this way." God, after all, cannot *not* be God.

We can pray to the ego and the ego may answer our prayers, but it will not be an answer of God. What difference will another drink make? It might make a great deal of difference. Free will is one of the characteristics of our divinity, but it can be misused. We are always able to choose. Which voice do you want to hear—the voice for the ego or the voice for God? If the answer you receive leaves you feeling peaceful, it's the right answer. The voice for God sounds like your voice—because it is your voice. It is also the voice we share. Many mystics—from Teresa of Avila, to Jacob Boehme, to Emanuel Swedenborg, to Edgar Cayce, to Helen Schucman—received a direct inner communication. Such revelation often begins in short sentences and aphorisms.

Outside In

Twentieth-century mystical researcher W. T. Stace posited two kinds of mysticism: extroverted and introverted. The introverted experience is received by direct insight or inspiration without stimulation from the outside world. Meditation is introverted.

An extroverted experience, however, is more sensory, intellectual, and emotional. It looks out from and "feels through" the world to a seeing behind the physical. Stace identified an extroverted mystic as someone like Walt Whitman, who *deliberately* looked through the senses to find Oneness in his world. Mystics perceive the same world of trees, hills, and cities that everyone else does. They just see the innate unity shining through. American singer-songwriter John Denver described an experience of exhilaration he had while skiing down a difficult run and feeling totally immersed in the beauty of the green trees, white snow, and blue sky. He had experienced a particularly wonderful morning with his wife, Annie, and, as he began the ski run, the phrase "You fill up my senses . . ." came to him. In the ten minutes it took him to make that ski run, he said , the whole song *Annie* was given to him.

Walt Whitman wanted to live life fully—*out loud*—to taste every moment of it. His poetry is spiritual, but devoid of traditional religion. Many people of his day saw him as an affront to Victorian values, which he was. Much like Mark Twain, Whitman enjoyed his freedom of expression, and the many visions and voices he describes are those of a true mystic. Whitman writes: "I celebrate myself, and sing myself, and what I assume you shall assume, for every atom belonging to me as good belongs to you."

Chapter 24

Mysticism and Nature

*The goal of life is to make your heartbeat match the beat
of the universe, to match your nature with Nature.*

—Joseph Campbell

The third stimulant for mystic awareness according to Hardy
is what we think of as nature. In fact, the experience of being
One with all of life, in which everything blends together,
is the oldest form of mysticism. Even the most primitive of
men, standing looking at a waterfall, a vast expanse of valleys
or mountains or flowers in the spring, must have been in awe
of the interconnectedness of it all and felt wonder at what
they saw. Mark Twain observed: "We have not the reverent
feeling for the rainbow that the savage has, because we know
how it is made. We have lost as much as we gained by prying
into that matter." Friedrich von Schelling summed it up suc-
cinctly: "Nature is visible Spirit and Spirit is invisible Nature."

We are surrounded by nature, which we think of as the
world of plants, trees, animals, flowers, grasses, and more.
But there is also a deeper nature found in the sum total of
forces at work throughout God's Universe. For Immanuel

Kant, two things fill the mind with ever-increasing awe: the starry heaven above and the moral order within. These combined provide a basis for the apprehension of the Divine. Einstein described the human being as "a part of a whole, called by us the 'Universe,' a part limited in time and space. He experiences himself, his thoughts and feelings as something separated from the rest . . . a kind of optical delusion of his consciousness." But this delusion, he warns, is a kind of prison that restricts us to our personal desires and to affection for a few persons nearest to us. "Our task," he tells us, "must be to free ourselves from this prison."

The Course speaks of our "inner nature" and the "nature of reality," telling us that the world and the ego "go against your nature, being out of accord with God's laws" (T–7.XI.1:5). When we read the word "world" here, however, we can think of it as "society" as constructed by ego, not as the natural world itself. Mystics, however, are receptive to everything—another face, a flower, even a parking lot lined with trees.

Nature mysticism originates as an expansion of awareness triggered by the natural world. As a youth, I often rode my horse bareback out to what I called my Heavenly Spot. There, I lay backward over his broad back and looked straight up into the blue sky, trying to see how far I could see. Trying to see into infinity. I could amplify this experience by lying in a ditch so my vision was blocked to the left and right, simply peering into the heavens. Try lying down quietly on the flat earth in an open space and looking straight up. You'll see what I mean.

Flower Power

If we could see the miracle of a single flower clearly,
our whole life would change. (Buddha)

In the changing of the seasons, the rise and fall of ocean waves, and the ceaseless changes of wind and weather, there is ever-changing beauty. Hindus celebrate Shiva as the destroyer who enables change, Vishnu as the preserver of all life, and Brahma as the creator. The *Upanishads* contain our oldest account of the innate order in all things. There, we learn that, while *any place* can be inspirational, *no place* contains "magical" power. Any place can be a breathtaking spark to inspiration—mountains, rivers, lakes, and streams. But our homes, cemeteries, churches, monasteries, mosques, and temples have "meaning" only in the mind. William Blake writes: "The tree that moves some to tears of joy is in the eyes of others a green thing which stands in the way." What we bring to an experience matters much more than where we are. The farm I grew up on, the one-room country schoolhouse I went to, and the country church I attended are sacred to me in a way they could not be for another.

We can appreciate nature as sightseers. Or we can participate in nature more deeply as outdoorsmen, gardeners, or farmers. Some of the best of Christian mystics from the early Middle Ages were nature mystics. Five hundred years before the invention of the printing press, before the refinement of art and music that grew out of the Renaissance, a primary form of connecting with the infinite was found in the most obvious of places—in nature itself. Bernard of Clairvaux said that whatever he knew about God he learned in woods and fields. Nature, he said, was "a book written by God but not to be confused with God." God is the "force," the "energy," the "love," and the "mind" behind everything. Thus, he could say: "I have no other masters than the beeches and the oaks."

Twelfth-century German mystic Hildegard of Bingen was born into a family of nobles who sent her as a tithe to the Church. She was subject to visions and felt commanded by God to "Write what you see." "Glance at the sun," she said. "See the moon and stars. Gaze at the beauty of the green earth. Now Think!" Hildegard writes: "I, the fiery life of divine essence, am aflame beyond the beauty of the meadows, I gleam in the waters, and I burn in the sun, moon, and stars. I awaken everything to life." Saint Francis of Assisi, perhaps the best known of the great Christian mystics, was especially known for his great love of nature and animals. The following is from his Sermon to the Birds:

> My little sisters, the birds, much bounden are ye unto God, your Creator, and always in every place ought ye to praise Him, for that He hath given you liberty to fly about everywhere, and hath also given you double and triple raiment; still more are ye beholden to Him for the element of the air which He hath appointed for you; beyond all this, ye sow not, neither do you reap; and God feedeth you, and giveth you the streams and fountains for your drink; the mountains and valleys for your refuge and the high trees whereon to make your nests; and because

ye know not how to spin or sow, God clotheth you, you and your children; wherefore your Creator loveth you much, seeing that He hath bestowed on you so many benefits; and therefore, my little sisters, study always to give praises unto God.

Nature mysticism brings with it a sense of the unity of all and a cosmological understanding of how things fit together, as seen in the poetry of Rumi, Emily Dickenson, and Wallace Black Elk. Likewise, Thoreau's *Walden* pulls at the heartstrings of every nature mystic: "I am a mystic, a transcendentalist, and a natural philosopher to boot," wrote Thoreau. He withdrew from work, from incessant labor and the machine-like nature of the world. He went alone into the woods to live, he said, "deliberately." There he could spend an entire morning sitting in his doorway looking and *seeing*—finding himself and his spirit within. His was a non-dominating relationship with the woods and animals, the light, water, air, and ice. Sitting alone beside Walden Pond, he saw in that calm, clear lake a depth he could not find in "polite" society.

English priest and poet Gerard Manley Hopkins developed the idea of "inscape" as a way to talk about the "inner universe." Each "thing" is unique and different from every other thing, he said. Still, a "force of being" holds all things together. "Spirit," Hopkins wrote, "is a falcon hovering in the wind. The harvest under the silk-sack clouds, the dare-gale skylark, the moonrise, the starlit night with its circle-citadels, the very air we breathe all speak of God."

American poet Emily Dickinson was a true mystic, an inspired poet, and a very private person who devoted herself to writing. Only ten of her nearly 1,800 poems were published during her lifetime. Emily was deeply touched by the mysticism and the writing of William Blake and her contemporary, Ralph Waldo Emerson. Norman D. Livergood has called her "a mystic of the first order, in the tradition of Rumi." Her world was the world of imagination, not of social norms and mores. "Some keep the Sabbath going to Church," she wrote, "I keep it staying at Home—With a bobolink for a Chorister, And an Orchard, for a Dome."

Richard Jeffries, a contemporary of Whitman and Dickinson, was a nature mystic who, in 1883, wrote a delightful little book titled *The Story of My Heart.* The following is an excerpt that expresses the core of nature mysticism:

> There came to me a delicate, but at the same time a deep, strong, and sensuous enjoyment of the beautiful green earth, the beautiful sky, and sun. I felt them, they gave me inexpressible delight, as if they embraced and poured out their love upon me. It was I who loved them, for my heart was broader than the earth; it is broader now than even then, more thirsty and desirous. After the sensuous enjoyment always come the thought, the desire: that I might be like this; that I might have the inner meaning of the sun, the light, the earth, the trees, and grass, translated into some growth of excellence in myself, both of the body and of mind; greater perfection of physique, greater perfection of mind and soul; that I might be higher in myself.

Austrian esoteric philosopher Rudolf Steiner said that, when it came to developing a love of the mystical, anyone who grew up in nature was especially fortunate. He describes his own childhood in Austria thus:

> The scenes amidst which I passed my childhood were marvelous. The bald rock face of the Schoenberg caught the sun's rays, which when they were projected on the little station on the fine summer days, were the first intimation of the dawn. The gray ridge of Weichsel's mountain made a somber contrast. The green prospects which welcomed the observer on every side made it seem as if the mountains were thrusting upwards of their own volition. The majestic peaks filled the distance, the charm of nature lay all round.

Although Jiddu Krishnamurti is not generally thought of as a nature mystic, there is a strong sense of Earth-based mysticism in this description from his work *The Only Revolution*:

> There was a silence that was really extraordinary. Not the silence between two noises, but the silence that has no reason whatsoever, the silence that must have been at the beginning of the world. It filled the whole valley and the hills. . . . The dew was especially heavy, and as the sun came up over the hill it was sparkling with many colors and with the glow that comes with the sun's first rays.

Sacred Places

Sacred sites are among the most loved and visited places on our planet. The oldest of these seem to draw the greatest attention.

Since prehistoric times, we've made pilgrimages to sites like Stonehenge in Britain and the pyramids in Egypt. Some places—Lourdes in France, for example—are believed to heal the body. When French soldiers under the dispatch of Napoleon came for the first time upon the great temple of Karnak in Egypt, without being given an order to do so, they stopped, formed rank, and to the accompaniment of fife and drums, presented arms. What made them stop and offer their respect?

Still, we must remember that no place is any more sacred than any other place. It is the mind that brings the sacred with it to a site. As the blind poet John Milton expresses it in his work *Paradise Lost:* "The mind is its own place, and it can make a hell out of heaven or a heaven out of hell." The ancient Ganges River is sacred to the people of India. Here people come to die, to turn their lives back over to God. For the native people of Australia, Ayers rock (Uluru to the Aborigines), the world's largest sandstone monolith, is a sacred place bespeaking eternity. For Buddhists, the Bodhi tree (*ficus religiosa*), said to be a descendant of the tree under which Buddha reached enlightenment, is sacred. But it's not necessary to travel to the Grand Canyon, the Galapagos Islands, the Great Barrier Reef, the harbor of Rio de Janeiro, Mount Everest, or Victoria Falls, or any other majestic and moving site to be inspired. My wife and I go each fall into the nearby Catskill Mountains to look at leaves turning color and are, without fail and endlessly, struck by their divine beauty.

For the ancient Greeks, Delphi, the home of the ancient oracle, was sacred. Here the oracle sat on an elevated chair above a fissure in the earth where, scientists now believe, ethylene gasses escaped from below, inducing a hypnotic trancelike state. From a position above the fissure, the oracle answered questions. Delphi was revered throughout the Greek world as the site of the *omphalos*, a stone that looks like a gigantic phallus. The site was thought to be the center, not only of the Earth, but of the whole Universe. For the Incas, the ancient city of Tiwanacu, constructed on the shore of Lake Titicaca in what is now Bolivia, is thought to be the birthplace of mankind. Similarly, according to the Shinto religion, Japan is the center of the world. The Pueblo and Hopi Indians reenact the cycle of what Mircea Eliade called "the eternal return" in underground *kivas* where they perform ceremonies to return people to their origins, pass on ancient knowledge, and perform rites of passage. In these sacred places, people sing, dance, meditate, pray, and listen to the stories of their shamans and elders.

For many people, a pilgrimage to one of these holy spots is both an inner and outer spiritual journey. Thus Muslims, at least once in their lives (if possible), must make the *hajji* (sacred pilgrimage) to the Kaaba and the holy black stone (an ancient meteorite) in Mecca. Many Christians journey as pilgrims to Jerusalem, to the Vatican, or perhaps to one of the great cathedrals like Notre Dame in Paris or Santiago de Compostela in Spain. More than 500,000 people visit the temples of Angkor Wat in Cambodia each year. These ancient temples, built between 800 and 1220 CE, are among humankind's most astonishing architectural achievements. Originally built in honor of the Hindu God Vishnu and then taken over by Buddhists, these temples are now sacred to both faiths. Lhasa, located on the Tibetan Plateau, is home to the palace of the Dalai Lama and is a place sacred to Tibetan Buddhists. The palace is a magnificent complex, some of which dates back to the seventh century.

For you, the grave of your ancestors and other loved ones may be a holy place. Or perhaps the home you lived in as a child. I try to make a pilgrimage each year to the farm where I grew up in Missouri. The best time is always in August, when all the sounds and smells of nature are most alive—the dry earth, the newly mown hay, the katydids, tree frogs, and crickets, and the grave of my parents, grandparents, great-grandparents, and great-great-grandparents. It is all there in the country, on the open plain, near a little one-room country church. This place is sacred to me.

Chapter 25

Mysticism and Enlightenment

Enlightenment is but a recognition, not a change at all.

W–188.1:4

According to Lama Surya Das, an American-born Lama in the Tibetan Buddhist tradition: "Enlightenment is not about becoming divine. It's about becoming more fully human. It is the end of ignorance." In this sense, it is also the end of hiding. Mystics are thus those who open their minds completely unto God.

Following the mystic path involves the integration of experience into an ongoing, deep, contemplative knowing. While it is possible to reach a plateau of peace and maintain a high level of stability, as long as we inhabit a body, there will always also be time, and therefore possible distractions—health, finances, children, mates, and more. French philosopher Jean Paul Sartre once said, somewhat jokingly perhaps, that "Hell is other people." And it is true that relationships are certainly our biggest challenge. Indeed, the path to Heaven outlined by the Course consists in healing *all* our relationships. Until we can see the Christ in everyone, the path to Heaven remains blocked.

Iranian mystic Javad Nurbakhsh believed that all people are equal when seen truly in the spirit of love. He writes: "The capital of the Path is, in truth, nothing other than sincerity. Sincerity has been defined as 'showing yourself as you really are' and 'being inwardly what you show yourself to be.'" According to the Course:

> The habit of engaging with God and His creations is easily made if you actively refuse to let your mind slip away. The problem is not one of concentration; it is the belief that no one, including yourself, is worth consistent effort. Side with me consistently against this deception, and do not permit this shabby belief to pull you back. The disheartened are useless to themselves and to me, but only the ego can *be* disheartened. (T–4.IV.7:1–4)

The vision of truth is thus not self-denial, Underhill tells us in *Mysticism*, but rather self-fulfillment.

Time and the body are deeply connected, simply because time is where our stories play out. All bodies have a beginning and an ending in time, and, in time, temptations arise now and again. The purpose of time is to help us learn how to use it constructively in the healing of all relationships. Sometimes children are difficult. Most addictions are hard to break. But remember: The goal is no unhealed relationships. The goal is truth and integrity, a place free of guilt, shame, and fear. We attain this plateau by realizing that we already have what we need. Continuing to look for the answers to life's problems is like looking for your glasses while they are resting on your nose. The Kingdom of Heaven, truly, is in you. The purpose of Atonement is the complete healing of all relationships. "You taught yourself the most unnatural habit of not communicating with your Creator," the Course points out (T–14.III.18:1).

God knows nothing of our fearful dreams. He knows us as we are—free of sin—and so it is that we are to come to know each other. "In no one instant is depression felt, or pain experienced or loss perceived," the Course maintains. "In no one instant sorrow can be set upon a throne, and worshipped faithfully. In no one instant can one even die. And so each instant given unto God in passing, with the next one given Him already, is a time of your release from sadness, pain and even death itself" (W–P.I.194.3:1–4).

There is a concept in Zen Buddhism known as *kensho*, meaning "seeing into one's true self or nature." It is a state beyond duality, a state of mind free of all judgment, including the "belief" in subject and object. It is a state of bliss, in which inner nature and pure mind are known directly. Transformation comes through the mind, the heart, and the hands. If you learn how to read music, but never play music, you will never *master* music. But this has nothing to do with competition or being able to do things better than others. Creation is the extension of God's being or spirit. God is the cause—the Son is the effect. Being of God, it is the Son's function to continue creation. Creation is healing.

As children of God, it is our function to continue in the process of creation, which is ongoing in Heaven. We are all students here. We are "always" learning our way up to Heaven's door. The mystic journey ends in realization of the Self. Nothing is lost along the way except ignorance, and enlightenment comes with our emergence from spiritual immaturity.

Enlightenment brings "freedom" from ignorance. We are called upon to be mature beings free from ego contamination. We are called upon to return to innocence, where guilt is unknown and only Heaven is. When we are contemplative, we listen to a deeper voice. Bernadette Roberts says it simply: "A mystic is an authentically mature human being."

John White, author of *What Is Enlightenment?*, says: "Enlightenment is realization of the truth of Being." It is a continuous contemplative state where the path, the goal, the journey, and the teaching become One. It is the surrender of duality that entails living wonderfully, delightfully—meaningfully. Wei Wu Wei refers to it as "whole-mind." Enlightenment, which the Course calls open-mindedness, "comes with lack of judgment. As judgment shuts the mind against God's Teacher, so open-mindedness invites Him to come in" (M–4.10.1:2–3).

Enlightenment is also peace of mind. Ramesh Balsekar speaks of it as "an empty mind." An empty mind or a whole mind does not mean a mind with no thoughts, however. It means a mind with no guilt, no fear, no anxiety, no distractions—like a calm body of water reflecting the brilliance of the moon. The enlightened, open mind reflects without attachment. Free of busyness, the mind is undisturbed. Simone Weil tells us: "Attachment is the great fabricator of illusions; Reality can be attained only by someone who is detached."

Quick Quiz

What is the difference between an enlightened person and an unenlightened person?

The difference is that the unenlightened person sees a difference.

~~~~~~

Obsessive-compulsive, neurotic thinking cannot find a home in open-mindedness. An open mind is free, fresh, and creative, while a closed mind is imprisoned by its own thoughts. When the mind is still, the Universe opens up and surrenders its truth. Ramesh Balsekar says that it is impossible for *any* so-called master to ask anyone to do something to achieve or *get* enlightenment, because enlightenment is the *annihilation* of the "one" who "wants" enlightenment. How can anyone achieve what, in truth, already is? It's a paradox, indeed. D. T. Suzuki tells us that we cannot make a date with enlightenment: "Enlightenment is an accident and spiritual practice makes us accident-prone." Even surrendering is not in our control. So long as there is an individual who says, "I surrender," there is an ego. "Spirit," the Course teaches, "is in a state of grace forever. Your reality is only spirit. Therefore, you are in a state of grace forever" (T–1.III.5:4–6).

Spiritual sight, or true vision, brings light. Enlightenment means being free of darkness. Nothing happens in this process other than a shift from darkness to light. The most profound element of enlightenment is simplicity. Awakening simply means waking up; there is nothing we must do. "When peace comes at last to those who wrestle with temptation and fight against the giving in to sin; when the light comes at last into the mind given to contemplation; or when the goal is finally achieved by anyone, it always comes with just one happy realization; 'I need do nothing'" (T–18.VII.5:7).

Stop, Look, and Listen!

Once we achieve freedom from the ego, what then? As long as the body continues in time, there will be another minute. What do we do in the next minute? And the next? Mystics stop, look, and listen. When we are free from the tyranny of the ego and its "special" needs, there is just Beingness, free of unhappy dreams and ego dramas. We embrace the world, knowing it is an illusion. Free of judgment, everything has a fresh, "expectant shine." It's wonderful just "being," which, the Course tells us, is "a state in which the mind is in constant communication with all that there is" (T–4.VII.4:4).

In this state of "beingness," there is no worry about getting ahead in the world. Rather, mystics simply delight in being alive. As my friend John White responds when asked how he is: "I am blessed." Indian teacher Vimala Thakar describes it this way: "As a lover of life, how can I stay out of life?" Alive, alert, and attentive, we are free to enjoy whatever presents itself—nature, relationships, exercise, sexuality, dancing, laughing, playing music, singing, working, eating, reading, or simply whatever is. Mysticism includes both Stoicism—maintaining a will in accordance with nature, having courage and moral strength—and Epicureanism—living modestly, and thus free from disturbance or pain. Thus mystics may live alone or with others with equal composure and equanimity.

An apple eaten in a conscious, contemplative state is as delicious and as satisfying as a multicourse meal. There is no need to avoid, mitigate, dull, or dilute life. Present in each moment, mystics delight in what is. Herman Hesse, in his book *Siddhartha,* follows his contemporary Somerset Maugham, who showed in his book *The Razor's Edge* that one need not withdraw from life to know holiness. It is found simply by living in the world.

According to Franklin Merrell-Wolff, mystics are anything but ascetics. He writes: "He who has realized Spiritual Gold enjoys more, not less." Buddhism speaks of mind-fullness and prayer-fullness. There is no past where sin and guilt may abide. There is no fear of some future punishment. There is no place else to be. There is no place else to go. There is no fearful dreaming. All we need, we have. Present in the moment, we savor the moment, whatever it is. Mysticism simply sharpens our focus as we do whatever needs doing. We are then attentive drivers, good typists, skilled cooks, dishwashers, or cleaners, loving mothers, fathers, brothers, sisters, daughters, and sons, valued employers and employees.

Events occur in the world that elicit a response. We may receive unwanted news. Although mystics know there is no death, because they love deeply, they will naturally mourn the loss of a parent, spouse, child, friend, or pet. As an aspect of spiritual growth, mourning is a sincere response. Overburdening grief, on the other hand, often signals unfinished business. Either way, if loss comes your way, embrace the pain. As Winston Churchill told us: "When going through hell—keep going." Time is a physician; mourning is medicine, and a necessary lesson in your letting go of the world. Though the bodily presence of a love may be gone, eternal love can never be lost.

Mystics are free because they live by one rule, one they gladly choose to follow: Do the will of God, which is your own. There are no laws for mystics, no rules or required ways of believing or behaving. We cannot be required to love. Love, coming from deep inside, must be given freely.

A Rest Most Busy

The contemplative mind is calm, detached and involved, relaxed and alert. Its relations are harmonious. Why wouldn't they be? There is no need for projection, reproof, argument, or reorganization. In the Buddhist *Sutra Nipata,* we read: "When faced with the ups and downs of life, still the mind remains unshaken, not lamenting, not generating defilements, always feeling secure. This is the greatest happiness." Realizing yourself as the Self means being selfless. "Selfishness is of the ego," the Course notes, "but Self-fullness is of spirit because that is how God created it" (T–7.IX.1:4). When there is no ego needing things to happen, when there is no need to change the world, we can love as God does—without condition. The enlightened mind is a place of peace and ordered activity. It is, says English mystic Walter Hilton, a *rest most busy*. Mystics are alive, alert, attentive; yet passive, quiet, and serene.

According to Thich Nhat Hanh, the seven factors of enlightenment are mindfulness, investigation of mental objects, energy, joy, tranquility, concentration, and equanimity. Being mindful, we bring awareness to all activities—working, shopping, washing dishes, making the bed, or exercising. Also, we do "whatever" for the joy of doing it, with whomever, wherever, whenever. One of my favorite mystics is a philosophy professor who windsurfs; another is a musician; two are airline flight attendants; one is a doctor and another a therapist; yet another is an accountant. They are all mystics because they embrace life and others in fullness, loving what they do, doing what they love. Walter Hilton says: "Enlightenment is a symptom of growth, or a living process. Spirit is overcome by a heavenly peace; but it is the peace of ordered activity, not idleness." Seeing the insanity of the world, mystics simply choose not to be part of it.

Coming to awareness of, and identification with, Self is coming Home. It is a returning to awareness of who we already are. Along with the validation of Self, there comes a deep humility that consists of being "empty" and "plain." In humility, we realize our small wonderful part in God's Universe. Nineteenth-century French mystic Thérèse de Lisieux, known as The Little Flower of Jesus, was especially remembered for her spiritual memoir, *L'histoire d'une âme* (*The Story of a Soul*), in which she writes: "I am a very little soul, who can offer only very little things to the Lord." The greater the humility, the greater our serenity.

It is easy to be humble when we know we have everything. "The truly humble," the Course tells us, "have no goal but God because they need no idols, and defense no longer serves a purpose" (S.1.V.2:3). There is nothing we are missing, since all we ever truly need is God. If we are not in a state of grace, we are out of our natural element. Spirit is in a constant state of grace, and our reality is Spirit; therefore, we are in a state of grace forever. The perception of God's grace, coupled with an acute awareness of her own state, formed the heart of 17th-century mystic Madame Guyon's autobiography, in which she writes: "My earnest wish is to paint in true colors the goodness of God to me and the depth of my own ingratitude."

Beyond the Beyond

It [Spirit] is beyond the senses, beyond the understanding, beyond all expression. It is the pure unitary consciousness, wherein awareness of the world and of multiplicity is completely obliterated. It is ineffable peace. It is the Supreme Good. It is One without a second. It is the Self. (Mandukya Upanishad)

Awe and Wonder

Wonder is evoked by the experience of an event inexplicable in the context of worldly laws. Confronted with the Divine, we can only say: Awe, or *Om*, or *Amen*. In awe, we have respect and veneration, honesty and gratitude. In awe, we behold what is and say: "How good it is." "No one," said Charles Spurgeon, a famous London Baptist minister, "has ever been a lukewarm, indifferent, or unhappy mystic." It is an incredible thing to be a human being, and the more awake we are to our reality, the more incredible it becomes. Castaneda's Don Juan says:

> For me the world is weird because it is stupendous, awesome, mysterious, unfathomable. My interest has been to convince you that you must assume responsibility for being here, in this marvelous desert, at this marvelous time. I want to convince you that you must learn to make every act count, since you are going to be here for only a short while; in fact, too short for witnessing all the marvels of it.

Identifying with reality brings freedom from suffering and death. Saint Francis of Assisi embodied joy, as did Mother Teresa, Rumi, Kabir, and Whitman. "Nothing is more exciting than *being,"* the Course promises. "It is okay to have a good time in the universe, salvation is a joyful event. Nothing is more joyful than doing God's Will, since doing God's Will is what we want most. . . . *God's function is yours, and happiness cannot be found apart from Your joint Will"* (T–11.V.12:4).

Some Hindus view the world as a playground. The joyous antics of Hindu gods and goddesses exemplify this attitude. "Joy is an ongoing process," the Course points out, "not in time but in eternity" (T–6.V.1:6). As American actress Katherine Hepburn once said: "I never lose sight of the fact that just being is fun." "Just to be, is a blessing," Rabbi Abraham Joshua Heschel observes. "Just to live, is holy." It is possible in every moment to be "in love" with the Universe. Once we know God as All That Is, we are free. Sorrow has ended, and birth and death are no more. Ernest Holmes writes: "We are born to be happy, to be abundantly supplied with every good thing. To have fun in living, to consciously unite with the Divine Power that is around us and with us, and to grow and expand forever." Responsibility is not a burden. Enlightenment exists in freedom. We are all eternal. God has been, is, and will be taking care of all that is.

Homeland Security

Joy is what happens to us when we allow ourselves to recognize how good things really are. (Marianne Williamson)

Enthusiasm means, literally, the quality of having God within. It comes from the Greek *en*, meaning "in," and *theos*, or God. Therefore, enthusiasm is, literally, being *in God*. Being in God is a blessing. Being ego-bound, however, seems like a curse. Several Protestant sects of the 16th and 17th centuries were called "enthusiastic," meaning that they experienced communion with God in a group setting through an opening up to the Divine within. They regarded creeds and dogma as traps and restraints on the human spirit. They found religion, rather, in the wonder of direct experience and would, perhaps, have felt a kinship with the Course's injunction: "Why wait for Heaven? Those who seek the light are merely covering their eyes. The light is in them now. Enlightenment is but a recognition, not a change at all" (W–P.I.188.1:1–4).

No one can say "I am enlightened," because there is no "I" to be enlightened. Every now and then, nonetheless, someone will claim enlightenment. You may claim you are the Christ—after all, you are—but don't let it go to your head, or ego. Power is an intoxicant and intoxicants can make you feel invincible. History repeatedly shows that power in the hands of the ego can usurp wisdom and derail sanity. Buddhist philosopher Jack Kornfield writes:

> Enlightenment does exist. It is possible to awaken. Unbounded freedom and joy, oneness with the Divine, awakening into a state of timeless grace— these experiences are more common than you know and not far away. There is one further truth, however: They don't last. . . after the honeymoon comes the marriage.

In one of Helen Schucman's dreams, she saw herself entering a cave on a bleak, windswept seacoast. In the cave, she found an old parchment scroll. She picked up the scroll and began to unroll it. In the center of the scroll were the words: "God Is." On either side of these words, she could see the beginning of small letters. Then she heard an inner voice say: "If you unroll the scroll to the left, you will be able to see into the past. If you unroll the scroll to the right, you will see into the future." The letters were beginning to become clearer, and she was tempted to look more closely and turn the scroll to the left or right. She quickly rolled the scroll back up to the middle, however, leaving only the words "God Is" visible. Then she said: "I'm not interested in the past or the future. I'll stop with this." The voice replied, "Thank you. You made it this time."

Helen was given a test, and she passed it. Obsessively digging into the past and projecting into the future are both ploys of the ego that take us away from Home. Since seeing our own egos is difficult, we sometimes need honest critique from family, friends, and coworkers. Listen to them! Freedom from ego requires discrimination, constant vigilance, devotion to truth, and the willingness to choose again—all of which is part of the plan. Bernadette Roberts sums it up this way: "A man without a self is not about to stand up and say, 'I have no sin.' He cannot say this because the truth of the matter is 'he has no I.' When there is no 'who' anymore, the question of who sins or does not sin is a contradiction."

Conclusion
Walking the Mystical Path

It is fair to say that many folks today are abandoning traditional religion in favor of a deeper, more contemplative spiritual life. Mysticism is becoming more mainstream, and religious dogma is less likely to be accepted without question. Whatever the spiritual discipline or path—Sufism, *A Course in Miracles*, *A Course of Love*, Buddhism, Taoism, Gnosticism, yoga, mystical Christianity, the Kabbala, or perhaps your own unique inner path—they all reflect one universal journey that leads to a unitive goal. More and more people are now ready to embark on this journey. They are ready to walk the mystical path.

This can be extremely difficult to do in our often frenetic modern world, however. Invite an enlightened man to take on a $2,500-a-month mortgage, three kids, a dog and cat, a wife who nags, a repetitive boring job and an angry boss, insurance bills, credit card bills, taxes, and more, and see if enlightenment lasts. If you think you are enlightened, try raising a teenager.

Like Helen Schucman, we must withstand continual tests and trials along the way before we arrive at a place where God is all we know, all we see, and all we love. Acceptance and forgiveness can easily be lost in the tangled web of relationships that hamper our progress on our journey. We may think we are beyond judgment and then, unexpectedly, we make a judgment—perhaps not as quickly as previously, but a judgment nonetheless. We may think we have achieved forgiveness, but the ego often slips in the back door when we aren't looking and pulls us back into its world of illusion.

Despite these challenges, the mystical path is a gentle path that can lead you out of the ego world and into Oneness. Ultimately, it is an easy journey because it ends where it begins—in Unity. As we have seen in the foregoing chapters, mysticism is, by its very nature, welcoming and affirming, rewarding and fulfilling. It makes no demands. There are no pledges to sign, no dues to pay. There are no rules or regulations. There are no magical formulas, no mysteries, no secrets, no oaths, no incantations, no rites, no rituals, no dogma, and no creeds. Relax, take a deep breath. Mysticism is free.

When you walk the mystical path, you need not proselitize. Mysticism is not about converting or being in competition with any thought system. It involves no missionary effort and no saving of lost souls, because no one is lost. There are only those who know, and those who are sleeping and will someday awaken. In some ways, we are all like seeds long dormant; when properly nourished, we spring back to life.

Walking the mystical path is simply a matter of "listening to" and following guidance—of seeing the insanity of the world, and then choosing not to play the world's game. When revelation replaces the illusion of a separate ego self, you gain everything and lose nothing, making it easy to share—to live for, and with, God and neighbor. Indeed, it is one of your pleasant obligations on the path to help awaken those who sleep—not by shaking them awake, but by giving a gentle nudge in the right direction. When you walk the mystical path, you identify with the whole of mankind, nature, animals, the Earth, music, the mind, the heart. You are not *against* anything or anyone. You have no agenda, only a sense of purpose. You acknowledge no opposites and no enemies. Since we are all One, there is no need to attack those who see things differently. Mysticism attracts without persuading.

In fact, mystical experience is so simple that it is easily missed, misinterpreted, or misunderstood in today's hectic world. It lies hidden in most "ordinary" experiences and in every part of the whole. It also lies quietly in the heart and naturally finds creative expression in the most ordinary things—in babies, pets, plants, art, music, work, play—indeed, in all of life. Be spontaneous; be humorous; have fun; laugh frequently. Sing and dance and play your way along your journey. In possession of the moment, know that the moment is everything. Be patient and kind, and value your relationships. But always recognize the value of silence and solitude. Remember, no one can be truly alone when the Spirit is always present.

The mystical path leads you to the realization that all there is, is life. Life is eternal and you have nothing to fear. At death, only the illusory shell of your body and your ego self is lost, and in this loss, you find freedom. The prison doors are opened and your ego self loosens its grasp on Spirit—or Spirit loosens its grip on the ego self. This is the message of resurrection—a joyous affirmation of the intrinsic beauty of life and an unequivocal denial of death. As a dewdrop slips from the leaf into the river and the river slips into the ocean, so mystics slip into the All to become the ocean. Having found the last "piece of the puzzle," the whole picture is revealed. What an incredible thing—to be a child of God. What an incredible thing it is to *be!*

Lovingly, Jon

No Place Like Home

There is a place in you where there is perfect peace. There is a place in you where nothing is impossible. There is a place in you where the strength of God abides. . . . And now you have a hint, not more than just the faintest intimation of the state your mind will rest in when the truth has come. (W–P.I.107.3:1; W–49.7:4–6)

Alphabetical Index of Mystics, Masters, Sages, Saints—and Just Regular Folk

A

Adams, John (1735–1826): Founding Father and second President of the United States. A deist. "Religion," he said, "must change and evolve toward perfection."

Adams, Robert (1928–1997): American Vedanta teacher and author of *Silence of the Heart*.

al-Ghazali (1058–1111): Iranian professor of Islamic jurisprudence in Baghdad. He felt that Islamists were merely going through the ritual without engaging in personal transformation.

al-Hallaj (858–922): Sufi mystic who said, "I am the Truth." While some saw what he said as an instance of mystical annihilation of the ego, others saw it as blasphemy and he was executed.

Amritanandamayi, Mata (Amma) (1953–present): Hindu spiritual leader and guru who is revered as a saint by her followers.

Arabi, Iban (1165–1240): Renowned Sufi mystic, poet, and philosopher known as "the great master." He wrote over 300 works, including his magnum opus, the thirty-seven-volume, *Meccan Illuminations*.

Arendt, Hannah (1906–1975): Escapee from Nazi Germany; a philosophy professor at The New School in New York City.

Atterbury, Francis (1663–1732): English man of letters, politician, and bishop.

Assisi, Aegidius (?–1262): Disciple of Saint Francis of Assisi, who called him The Knight of our Round Table.

Assisi, Saint Francis (1081–1126): Italian founder of the Franciscan Order, venerated as one of the most religious figures in history.

Augustine of Hippo (354–430): Bishop of Hippo in North Africa, canonized by the Catholic Church. His *Confessions* is one of the best portrayals of how a divided, besieged soul can be healed through mystical experience.

Aurelius, Marcus (121–180): Roman Emperor from 161 to 180, known as the last of the so-called five good emperors. He was a practitioner of Stoicism and author of *Meditations*.

Avila, Saint Teresa of (1515–1582): Spanish mystic canonized by the Catholic Church. Perhaps the best-known of the female mystics, a Doctor of the Church, and Mother of the Catholic Counter-Reformation.

B

Baba, Meher (1894–1969): Indian guru of Persian descent who spent long periods of fasting in seclusion. From 1925 to the end of his life, he communicated only with an alphabet board.

Bach, Richard (1936–present): American writer and aviator, best known for his book *Jonathan Livingston Seagull* (1970).

Beecher, Henry Ward (1813–1887): Brilliant preacher in Brooklyn, New York, who did not believe in hell and defended evolution.

Belsekar, Ramesh (1917–2009): Advaita master and president of the Bank of India. He was drawn to the teaching of Ramana Maharshi and Wei Wu Wei.

Bergson, Henri-Louis (1859–1941): Major French philosopher, evolutionist, and friend of William James and Evelyn Underhill. He won the Nobel Prize for literature in 1927 for his book *Creative Evolution.*

Bernard of Clairvaux (1090–1153): French abbot who claimed that whatever he knew about divine things and Holy Scriptures, he learned in the woods and fields.

Berra, Yogi (1915–2015): Famous Yankee baseball catcher known for his tendency toward malapropism (seemingly unintentional witticisms).

Birgersdotter, Birgitta (Saint Bridget of Sweden) (1301–1373): Mystic, visionary, saint, and founder of the Bridgettine nuns and monks. In 1999, Pope John Paul II chose Bridget as a patron saint of Europe.

Blake, William (1757–1827): English poet, painter, engraver, and visionary, and one of the best examples of a true nature poet/mystic.

Boehme, Jacob (1575–1624): German mystic and shoemaker who experienced a religious epiphany in 1600 when a ray of sunlight reflecting in a pewter dish catapulted him into an ecstatic vision of God. His first work, *Aurora,* brought him a following.

Bonaventure, Saint (1221–1274): French Franciscan monk influenced by Aristotle and Augustine. He had a strong influence on the development of the philosophical, theological, and mystical side of the Franciscan Order.

Borchert, Bruno (20th century; dates unknown): Carmelite priest and mystical researcher, and author of *Mysticism: Its History and Challenge.*

Bronowski, Jacob (1908–1974): Science historian and author of *The Ascent of Man.*

Bruno, Giordano (1548–1600): Italian Dominican friar, philosopher, poet, and cosmologist who insisted that the universe was infinite with no center. Tried for heresy, he was burned at the stake in 1600. He is regarded as a martyr to science.

Brunton, Paul (1888–1981): British theosophist best known for his best-selling book, *A Search in Secret India.*

Buck, Pearl S. (1892–1973): American novelist whose book *The Good Earth* was the best-selling book in the United States in 1931 and 1932. She won the Pulitzer Prize in 1932.

Buddha, Gautama (563–480 BCE): Founder of Buddhism and recognized as an enlightened or divine teacher.

Bultmann, Rudolf (1884–1976): German Lutheran theologian who developed the idea of demythologizing—interpreting myths as you would interpret a dream.

Bunyan, John (1628–1688): English writer and preacher best remembered as the author of the Christian allegory, *The Pilgrim's Progress.*

Burke, Edmund (1729–1797): Irish statesman and active politician who opposed the British invasion of the American colonies.

Butterworth, Eric (1918–2003): Senior Minister of the Unity Center of New York City from 1961 to 2003 and a pioneer in the Unity movement.

C

Campbell, Joseph (1904–1984): American mythologist, professor, writer, and orator best known for his work in the fields of comparative mythology and comparative religion.

Carlyle, Thomas (1795–1881): Scottish essayist and historian who said: "A well-written life is almost as rare as a well-spent one." He was a religious non-Christian.

Castaneda, Carlos (1925–1998): American author with a doctorate in anthropology who wrote twelve books on shamanism in Mexico. His first book was *The Teachings of Don Juan* (1968).

Cayce, Edgar (1877–1945): American mystic and parapsychologist. The Association for Research and Enlightenment in Virginia Beach, Virginia, continues Cayce's work to this day. See *The Essential Edgar Cayce* by Mark Thurston.

Chambers, Oswald (1874–1917): Well-known Scottish Protestant minister, lecturer, and author. His best work is *My Utmost for His Highest*.

Chelberg, Rod (1955–present): Medical doctor, ACIM student/teacher, writer, and lecturer.

Chopra, Deepak (1946–present): Popular American author, lecturer, and alternative-medicine advocate.

Chuji, Qiu (1148–1227): Chinese Taoist philosopher.

Coleridge, Samuel Taylor (1772–1834): English poet, philosopher, and theologian who, along with William Wordsworth, was the founder of Romanticism in England.

Connolly, Cyril (1903–1973): English art critic.

Conrad, Joseph (1857–1924): Polish-British writer. Among his best-known works are *Lord Jim* and *Heart of Darkness*.

Crowley, Aleister (1875–1947): English occultist, ceremonial magician, poet, painter, novelist, and mountaineer.

Cousins, Norman (1916–1990): American political journalist, author, professor, and peace activist.

D

da Vinci, Leonardo (1452–1519): Italian polymath whose areas of interest included invention, painting, sculpting, architecture, science, music, math, and more.

Das, Surya (1950–present): American-born Lama in the Tibetan Buddhist tradition. He was born Jeffrey Miller in 1950 on Long Island, New York.

Dass, Ram (born Richard Alpert) (1931–present): American spiritual teacher and author of *Be Here Now* (1971). He is known for his association with Timothy Leary at Harvard in the 1960s.

Davidson, John (1944–present): Oxford scholar and author of *The Gospel of Jesus* and *A Treasury of Mystic Terms*.

de Chardin, Pierre Teilhard (1881–1955): French Jesuit priest and paleontologist who popularized the idea of the noosphere as "a collective web or layer of consciousness that engulfs the universe."

de Chateaubriand, Francois-René (1768–1884): French writer, diplomat, and historian who is considered the founder of Romanticism in French literature.

de Mello, Anthony (1931–1987): Jesuit priest from India. He was psychotherapist who became well known for his books *Contact with God* and *The Song of the Bird*.

Denver, John (1943–1997): American musician, singer-songwriter, activist, and humanitarian who achieved great commercial success from the 1970s until the time of his death.

Descartes, René (1596–1650): French philosopher, mathematician, and scientist often referred to as the father of modern Western philosophy, as much of subsequent philosophy is a response to his work. He is remembered for his statement *Cogito ergo sum*—"I think therefore I am." He said, "Knowledge comes from logical rational deduction. Mind and matter are two clearly distinct substances."

Dickinson, Emily (1830–1886): American poet who, along with Walt Whitman, is regarded as one of the outstanding poets of the 19th century.

Diderot, Denis (1713–1784): French philosopher and editor-in-chief of the seventeen-volume *Encyclopédie*, the first encyclopedia. He did not like organized religion and organized religion did not like him.

Dōgen (1200–1253): Japanese Zen Buddhist master and founder of the Soto School of Zen in Japan. He was a leading religious figure and teacher of *zazen*—a sitting meditation.

Dostoyevsky, Fyodor (1821–1881): Russian novelist and philosopher who explored human psychology during the troubled times of 19th-century Russia.

Dyer, Wayne (1940–2015): American philosopher, self-help author, and motivational speaker. His first book, *Your Erroneous Zones* (1976), sold more than 35 million copies.

E

Eckhart, Meister (1260–1326): Often regarded as the greatest of the medieval Christian mystics. He was a member of the German Dominican Order.

Eddy, Mary Baker (1821–1910): Founder of Christian Science. The Course and Christian Science are similar in the importance they place on the power of the mind to heal all things physical and psychological.

Einstein, Albert (1879–1955): Widely considered one of the greatest, if not the greatest, physicists of all time. He was a true mystic who saw into another dimension and tried to tell us about it.

Emerson, Ralph Waldo (1803–1882): American essayist, lecturer, poet, and leader of the Transcendentalist Movement in the 19th century.

Erikson, Erik (1902–1994): German-born American developmental psychologist.

Estés, Clarissa Pinkola (1945–present): American Jungian psychoanalyst, poet, and post-trauma recovery specialist, who was also an author and lecturer.

F

Fichte, Johann (1762–1814): German Idealist philosopher. He insisted that a study of the ego was fundamental to philosophy.

Ficino, Marsilio (1433–1499): Italian scholar and Catholic priest, and one of the most influential Humanist philosophers of the early Italian Renaissance.

Fillmore, Charles (1854–1931) and Myrtle (1845–1932): Co-founders of the Unity Church in 1889. Myrtle's major work is the collection *Healing Letters*.

Foligno, Angela of (1248–1309): Italian Franciscan who wrote extensively about her mystical revelations. She became known as Mistress of Theologians.

Fowles, John (1926–2005): Philosopher and novelist best known for his novel *The French Lieutenant's Woman.*

Fox, Emmet (1886–1951): Minister of New York's Church of the Healing Christ. Immensely popular as a speaker and author. His book *The Sermon on the Mount* is especially popular in Alcoholics Anonymous circles.

Fox, George (1624–1691): English Dissenter and founder of the Society of Friends, better known as the Quakers.

Frankl, Viktor (1905–1997): Austrian neurologist and psychiatrist, Holocaust survivor, and author of the best-selling book *Man's Search for Meaning.*

Franklin, Benjamin (1706–1790): Deist, Freemason, and a true Renaissance man. He was an elder statesman of the American Revolution and the oldest signer of the Declaration of Independence.

Freeman, James Dillet (1912–2002): American Indian poet and Unity minister.

Freud, Anna (1895–1982): Austrian-British psychoanalyst, the sixth and last child of Sigmund Freud, and founder of psychoanalytic child psychology.

Freud, Sigmund (1856–1939): Austrian neurologist and founder of psychoanalysis.

Fry, Christopher (1907–2005): English playwright and poet.

Fuller, Buckminster (1895–1983): American architect, systems theorist, author, designer, and inventor.

G

Galbraith, John Kenneth (1908–2006): American economist and leading 20th-century liberal.

Gandhi, Mahatma (1869–1948): Exemplary mystic who is called "the Father of India"; he is well known for his nonviolent resistance. He practiced simplicity, vegetarianism, celibacy, and *aparigraha*, or non-possession.

Gangaji (1942–present): Formerly Antoinette Roberson Varner, an American-born spiritual teacher dedicated to sharing the mystical path through direct self-inquiry.

Goethe, Johann Wolfgang von (1749–1832): Although not a German Idealist in the same sense as those who came after him, he was a "man of letters" and a great polymath. "Mysticism" he said, "is the scholarship of the heart."

Goodall, Jane (1934–present): British primatologist and anthropologist, considered the world's leading expert on chimpanzees.

Gurdjieff, G. I. (1872–1949): Greek-Armenian spiritual teacher who developed a path called the Fourth Way.

Guyon, Madame (1648–1717): French mystic and advocate of quietism, a practice considered heretical by the Catholic Church.

Gyatso, Tenzin (1935–present): Current Dalai Lama who travels the world teaching. He was forced to leave Tibet in 1959 and lives as a refugee in India. He received the Nobel Peace Prize in 1989 and is the author of many books.

H

Harding, Douglas (1909–2007): English philosophical writer, mystic, spiritual teacher, and author of *On Having No Head—Zen and the Rediscovery of the Obvious*.

Hart, William (dates unknown): Author of *Vipassana Meditation* (1982).

Hawking, Stephen (1942–present): English theoretical physicist, cosmologist, author, and Director of Research at the Center for Theoretical Cosmology at the University of Cambridge.

Hepburn, Katharine (1907–2003): American actress known for her fierce independence and spirited personality.

Heraclites (540–480 BCE): Greek philosopher and deist who was the first philosopher to create a rational philosophical system. He influenced Socrates (470–399 BCE) and Plato, and is the most-quoted pre-Socratic philosopher.

Heschel, Rabbi Abraham Joshua (1907–1972): Professor of Jewish mysticism at the Jewish Theological Seminary in New York City.

Higgs, Peter (1929–present): British theoretical physicist and Nobel Prize laureate for his work on the mass of subatomic particles.

Hildegard of Bingen (1098–1179): Early German speculative mystic influenced by Augustine. She was greatly respected in her time for her writings, her music, and her art.

Hilton, Walter (1340–1396): English priest and Augustinian canon whose book *The Scale of Perfection* is the first exhaustive work on mystical theology in the English language.

Hofmann, Albert (1906–2008): Swiss chemist and the first person to synthesize, accidently consume, and learn of the psychedelic effects of LSD, which he called "medicine for the soul."

Holmes, Ernest (1887–1960): American New Thought writer and founder of Religious Science, now called the Centers for Spiritual Living. He is especially remembered for his book *The Science of Mind* and for *Science of Mind* magazine.

Hopkins, Gerard Manley (1844–1889): English priest and poet.

Hubbard, Barbara Marx (1929–present): Futurist, author, and lecturer credited with the concept of "The Synergy Engine."

Hubbard, Elbert (1856–1915): American writer, publisher, artist, philosopher, and founder of the Roycroft Artisan Community. His 1901 book *A Message to Garcia* was a bestseller.

Hugo, Victor (1802–1885): Novelist, poet, playwright, human rights campaigner, and critic of the Catholic Church best remembered for *Les Misérables* and *The Hunchback of Notre Dame*. Hugo developed what he called "rationalist deism."

Huineng (7th century): Chinese Chan master.

Huss, John (1371–1415): Pre-Reformation mystic and professor of theology at the University of Prague. Having openly defied the teaching of the Catholic Church, he was publicly strangled and then, not yet dead, burned at the stake.

Huxley, Aldous (1894–1963): English-American author best known for *Brave New World, The Perennial Philosophy,* and *The Doors of Perception,* which explores his mystical experience under the influence of mescaline.

I

Ingelow, Jean (1820–1897): English poet and novelist.

J

James, William (1842–1910): American philosopher, psychologist, and physician, and the first person to teach a course in psychology at Harvard University in 1885.

Jefferson, Thomas (1743–1826): American Founding Father, principle author of the Declaration of Independence, and President of the United States from 1801 to 1809.

Jeffries, Richard (1848–1887): English farm boy and nature mystic.

Jesus (4 BCE–29 CE): Jewish teacher whose life serves as the foundation for Christianity. A mystic who "saw" into the beyond and told us about it. The whole of his message concerns the Kingdom of Heaven. God is his Father and Heaven his Home.

John of the Cross (1541–1591): Student of Teresa of Avila. Canonized by the Catholic Church. He was a mystic and a poet who was celebrated for his deep love of God. "Suffering," he said, "is epistemology. We learn from it." His famous book is *Dark Night of the Soul.*

Jones, Ernest (1879–1958): English psychiatrist, and friend and biographer of Sigmund Freud.

Julian of Norwich (1324–1413): English anchoress who retired from the world to lead an intensely ascetic prayer-oriented life in a little room attached to a cathedral. She wrote *Sixteen Revelations of Divine Love.*

Jung, Carl (1875–1961): Swiss psychiatrist and psychoanalyst who founded analytical psychology.

K

Kabir (1440–1518): One of the great poet-saints of India. Kabir did not want to be classified as Hindu, Muslim, or Sufi. He preferred to be free of organized religions.

Khan, Hazrat Inayat (1887–1927): From one of the most musical families in India. His grandfather was known as the Beethoven of India.

Kalu Rinpoche (1905–1989): Tibetan Buddhist teacher, meditation master, and scholar who taught in the United States.

Kant, Immanuel (1724–1804): German philosopher who is consider a central figure in modern philosophy.

Katagiri, Dainin (1928–1990): American immigrant who became the first abbot of the Minnesota Zen Meditation Center in 1972.

Keller, Helen (1880–1968): American inspirational author and lecturer, and the first deaf-and-blind person to earn a college degree.

Kierkegaard, Søren (1813–1855): Danish theologian regarded by many as the first existential philosopher.

King, Stephen (1947–present): American author of supernatural fiction, science fiction, and fantasy.

Knox, Ronald (1888–1957): English priest, theologian, writer, and broadcaster for BBC Radio.

Kodikal, Deepa (1941–2013): Scientist, musician, family woman, and mystic. She discovered as a child that she could direct her dreams and achieve a *samadhi*-like state of absorption.

Koestler, Arthur (1905–1983): Hungarian-British author and journalist.

Kokushi, Muso (1275–1351): One of the most influential early garden designers in Japan.

Kornfield, Jack (1945–present): Teacher of Vipassana meditation in the Buddhist tradition. *Vipassana* means "the realization of the non-self."

Krishnamurti, Jiddu (1895–1986): Born in India, but spent most of his life in the United States. His primary teaching was the pursuit of freedom from the ego.

L

Laing, R. D. (1927–1989): Scottish psychiatrist who thought that much of mental illness was the result of ordinary people being unable to adjust to an insane world. He called insanity "a perfectly rational adjustment to an insane world."

Lalleshwari (1320–1392): Indian mystic also known as *Lalla* who was also a Hindu poet. Her verses are the earliest known compositions in the Kashmiri language.

Lawrence, Brother (1611–1691): Lay brother of the Carmelites, famous for his book *The Practice of the Presence of God*.

Leibniz, Gottfried Wilhelm (1646–1716): Polymath, deist, and metaphysician. He believed that reason rather than dogma should provide the foundation for belief in God.

Levenson, Lester (1909–1994): Successful business man who had a crash-and-burn mystical experience as a result of two heart attacks. He developed a training program called The Sedona Method, which helped people take responsibility for their lives.

Lewis, C. S. (1889–1963): British writer, poet, academic, theologian, and defender of the Christian faith. He wrote several mythological works, including *The Chronicles of Narnia* and *The Space Trilogy*.

Lilly, John (1915–2001): Researcher of the nature of consciousness using isolation tanks, dolphin communication, and psychotropics.

Lisieux, Thérèse of (1873–1897): French Catholic nun known as The Little Flower of Jesus. She is especially remembered for her memoir *L'histoire d'une âme* ("The Story of a Soul"), a best-seller in the early 20th century.

Livergood, Norman D. (no dates): Look for a list of his books on Amazon.com.

Luther, Martin (1483–1546): German professor of theology, composer, priest, and monk. He was the primary figure in starting the Protestant Reformation in 1517.

M

Ma, Anandamayi (1896–1981): Bangladeshi mystic. "She became," she said, "completely empty with no sense of 'I am.'" "She is," she said, "nobody." She was described as "the most perfect flower the Indian soil ever produced."

Madison, James (1751–1836): American Founding Father who served as the fourth President of the United States.

Maharshi, Ramana (1879–1950): Indian sage who is regarded as a primary teacher of Advaita Vedanta.

Maimonides, Moses (1135–1204): Foremost intellectual figure of medieval Judaism. He lived in Spain and Egypt.

Mandela, Nelson (1918–2013): South African anti-apartheid revolutionary who served as President of South Africa from 1994 to 1999.

Marx, Karl (1818–1883): German philosopher, economist, and revolutionary socialist.

Maugham, W. Somerset (1874–1965): English playwright and novelist. He was one of the most popular writers of the early 20th century. His book *Razor's Edge* is the tale of a young man who goes off to India to find a more meaningful life.

May, Rollo (1909–1994): American psychologist best known for his 1969 book *Love and Will*.

Mencken, H. L. (1880–1956): American journalist and cultural critic known as The Sage of Baltimore.

Merrell-Wolff, Franklin (1887–1985): American mystic, expounder of Advaita Vedanta, and author of *Pathways Through to Space*.

Merton, Thomas (1916–1968): Trappist monk and an acclaimed Catholic writer and social activist. His book *The Seven Storey Mountain* was a *New York Times* bestseller in 1948 and 1949.

Millman, Dan (1946–present): American author and lecturer best known for his book *Way of the Peaceful Warrior*.

Milton, John (1608–1674): English poet best known for his epic poem *Paradise Lost*. His powerful prose and the eloquence of his poetry had a great influence on 18th-century verse.

Mohammad (570–623): Holy Prophet regarded as the founder and central figure of Islam.

Moore, Thomas (1940–present): American psychotherapist, former monk, and writer of popular spiritual books, including the New York Times best-seller, *Care of the Soul*.

Moorjani, Anita (1959–present): *New York Times* bestselling author of *Dying to Be Me*. She continues to write and lecture internationally.

N

Nack, Bonnie (1936–present): Author and student/teacher of *A Course in Miracles*.

Nhat Hanh, Thich (1926–present): Vietnamese Buddhist monk and peace activist. The author of more than 100 books, he travels the world giving talks.

Nietzsche, Friedrich (1844–1900): German philosopher who had little patience for logical proofs about the nature of reality. Flashes of insight, aphoristic expressions, and proclamations characterize his work. "Every philosophy is a foreground philosophy," he said.

Nisargadatta, Maharaj (1897–1981): Indian teacher who said that our true nature is perpetually free, peaceful awareness. He influenced Wei Wu Wei and Jed McKenna.

Nurbakhsh, Javad (1926–2008): master of the Nimatullahi Sufi Order from 1953 to 2008. He was a successful psychiatrist, medical director, and writer who taught that all people are equal when seen truly in the spirit of love.

Nyssa, Gregory of (335–394): Greek Christian bishop and saint who argued for the infinity of God and the eventual salvation of all souls.

O

Orwell, George (1903–1950): English novelist, essayist, and critic. His best-known books, *1984* and *Animal Farm,* pointed out the dangers of social injustice and totalitarianism.

Osho (Bhagwan Shree Rajneesh) (1931–1990): Former professor of philosophy who was perhaps the most prolific of all the Indian teachers, and the funniest. His main emphasis was on nondualism, meditation, and humor.

Otto, Rudolf (1869–1937): Eminent German Lutheran theologian, philosopher, and comparative religionist.

P

Paine, Thomas (1737–1809): English-American political activist and author of *Common Sense* in 1776.

Pascal, Blaise (1623–1662): French mathematician and Christian philosopher. Often sickly, he had a profound near-death experience and, like Julian of Norwich, was from then on subject to states of rapture.

Perron, Mari (1955–present): American author, and first receiver (or scribe) of *A Course of Love.*

Philo of Alexandria (25 BCE–50 CE): Hellenistic Jewish philosopher who lived in the Roman province of Egypt.

Plotinus (205–270): Greek philosopher who is considered the father of Neoplatonism, a philosophy based on the teachings of Plato. He said: "All is one. The Soul is real; and the body exists only for a moment in space/time."

Po, Huang (9th century): Zen master.

Pseudo- Dionysius the Areopagite (5th century): Theologian, philosopher, and Christian mystic. He is called the Pseudo-Dionysius because we do not know who he was. All we have are his writings, the *Corpus Areopagiticum.*

Pythagoras (580–490 BCE): Greek philosopher who founded the religious movement called Pythagoreanism, which emphasizes a mystical relationship between numbers, nature, and the soul. He is best known for the discovery of the Pythagorean theorem and expounding the belief that music is mathematical.

R

Ramakrishna (1836–1886): Indian mystic who taught the Vedanta system of nondualism and sought to experience the truth of Christianity, Hinduism, and Islam.

Ramanujan, Srinivasa (1887–1920): Indian mathematician and autodidact who credited his substantial mathematical capacities to the Divine.

Ramdas, Swami (1884–1963): Indian guru who viewed the world as forms of Ram (God). He thus saw everything that might befall him as the will of God.

Redfield, James (1950–present): American author and screenwriter best known for his novel *The Celestine Prophecy.*

Reid, Forrest (1875–1947): Irish author, and a leading pre-war British novelist who wrote extensively of the experiences of boyhood.

Rilke, Rainer Maria (1875–1926): German mystical poet of the 20th century who focused on the difficulty of trying to express the ineffable in words.

Roberts, Bernadette (1931–present): Devout Catholic nun who left her cloistered order, obtained several degrees, and raised four children. She gives annual retreats at Big Sur in California. She is the author of *The Path to No-Self.*

Roquet, Salvador (1920–1995): Beloved Mexican psychiatrist, public health doctor, and shaman who trained in the psychoanalytic tradition with Erich Fromm. I'm happy to say he was my teacher during the mid-1970s.

Ruiz, Don Miguel (1952–present): Born into a family of healers in Mexico, his mother was a *curandera* (healer) and his grandfather a *nagual* (shaman). A medical doctor himself, Ruiz wrote the popular book *The Four Agreements.*

Rumi, Jalaluddin (1207–1273): Afghani who is the most widely read poet in the world today, and one of the most highly regarded Muslim saints and mystics of all time.

Ruysbroeck, Jan van (1293–1381): Flemish mystic who emphasized detachment, humility, and clarity. He was one of Evelyn Underhill's favorites. In fact, she wrote a whole book on him.

S

Sai Baba, Sathya (1926–2011): Guru, Vedantist, and spiritual leader known for his many apparent materializations.

Saint-Exupéry, Antoine de (1900–1944): French writer, poet, aristocrat, journalist, and pioneering aviator, and a laureate of several literary awards. He is best remembered for *The Little Prince* (*Le Petit Prince*).

Sartre, Jean Paul (1905–1980): French philosopher and a key figure in the philosophy of existentialism.

Schelling, Friedrich Wilhelm Joseph von (1775–1854): Philosopher who stands at the midpoint in the development of German Idealism, between Fichte, his mentor in early years, and G. W. F. Hegel. According to Schelling, nature and consciousness are expressions of absolute reality.

Schopenhauer, Arthur (1788–1860): Student of Plato, Kant, and Fichte, and the first Western philosopher to study Vedanta. The world, he said, "is my representation."

Schrödinger, Erwin (1887–1961): Nobel Prize-winning Austrian quantum physicist made famous by his theory about his cat.

Schucman, Helen (1909–1981): Professor, research psychologist, and the scribe of *A Course in Miracles.*

Schweitzer, Albert (1875–1965): Alsatian theologian, musician, philosopher, and physician who received the 1952 Nobel Peace Prize for his philosophy of "reverence for life." He founded the Lambaréné Hospital in Gabon, Africa.

Seuse, Heinrich (1295–1366): Dominican mystic and student of Meister Eckhart, he was a troubadour and a poet. Eckhart, Suso, and Tauler formed the center of the Rhineland School of mysticism.

Segal, Suzanne (1955–1997): American author of *Collision with the Infinite*, the description of a profound mystical experience—a complete disrobing of the ego—that she underwent in Paris at the age of twenty-seven.

Seneca (4–65): Roman stoic philosopher, statesman, dramatist, and humorist of the Silver Age of Latin literature. He was the teacher of Nero and then was likely killed by Nero.

Shah, Idries (1924–1996): Also known by the pen name Arkon Daraul, he was an author and teacher in the Sufi tradition who wrote over three dozen books on psychology and spirituality.

Shankara (788–820): Indian philosopher who was perhaps the most famous Advaita (non-dual) philosopher of Vedanta. His mysticism is one of reason without dogma or ritual.

Silesius, Angelus (1624–1677): German Catholic priest, poet, physician, and mystic.

Smith, John (1618–1652): Theologian and one of the founders of the Cambridge Platonists.

Smith, Robert (1879–1950): Co-founder of Alcoholics Anonymous along with William Wilson.

Sogyal Rinpoche (1947–present): Tibetan Lama and author of the best-selling *The Tibetan Book of Living and Dying*.

Spinoza, Baruch (1632–1677): Dutch philosopher known as "the world's most sensible mystic." For Spinoza, the intellectual love of God frees man from base desires and thereby confers immortality.

Spong, John Shelby (1931–present): Retired American bishop of the Episcopal Church, a liberal Christian theologian, and religious commentator.

Spurgeon, Charles (1834–1892): Famous English Baptist minister known as "the Prince of Preachers."

Stace, W. T. (1886–1967): British philosopher and professor of philosophy at Princeton University from 1932–1955, best known for his 1960 book *Mysticism and Philosophy*.

Steindl-Rast, Brother David (1926–present): Austrian-born Benedictine monk who, in 1966, was officially delegated to pursue Buddhist-Christian dialogue and began to study Zen.

Steiner, Rudolf (1861–1925): Austrian architect, social reformer, mystic, and esoteric philosopher.

Stowe, Harriet Beecher (1811–1896): American abolitionist and author of *Uncle Tom's Cabin*.

Suzuki, D. T. (1870–1966): Japanese Zen Buddhist who is regarded as the man who brought Zen Buddhism to the West.

Swedenborg, Emanuel (1688–1772): Swedish scientist, philosopher, theologian, Christian mystic, visionary, and an accomplished Renaissance man. He said of himself that he was a "Servant of Jesus Christ."

T

Tagore, Rabindranath (1861–1941): Bengali poet, mystic, philosopher, and the first non-European to win the Nobel Prize in literature. A friend of Evelyn Underhill, they both died in 1941.

Tauler, Johannes (1300–1361): German Dominican mystic who was influenced by Meister Eckhart. He was a part of the Rhineland School of mystics.

Teasdale, Wayne (1945–2004): Catholic monk, author, teacher, and a pioneer in Interfaith Studies.

Tesla, Nikola (1856–1943): Serbian-American inventor, electrical engineer, physicist, and futurist. He is best known for his contributions to the discovery of modern alternating current.

Thakar, Vimala (1921–2009): Indian social activist and spiritual teacher.

Teresa, Mother (1910–1997): Albanian-Indian Roman Catholic nun and missionary who founded the Missionaries of Charity to give "wholehearted free service to the poorest of the poor."

Thetford, William (1923–1988): Psychologist and collaborator with Helen Schucman in the production of *A Course in Miracles*.

Thoreau, Henry David (1817–1862): American essayist, poet, philosopher, naturalist, and leader of the American Transcendental Movement.

Tolkien, J. R. R. (1892–1973): English writer, philologist, poet, and university professor who wrote the best-selling books *The Hobbit, The Lord of the Rings,* and *The Silmarillion*.

Tolle, Eckhart (1948–present): Born in Germany and now living in Vancouver, Canada, he is the author of the best-selling books *The Power of Now* and *A New Earth*.

Tolstoy, Leo (1828–1910): Russian author and a true mystic who is best known for his works *War and Peace* and *Anna Karenina*. A follower of Thoreau, his idea of nonviolent resistance is found in his book *The Kingdom of God Is Within You*.

Traherne, Thomas (1636–1674): English poet, clergyman, theologian, and religious writer.

Twersky, Menachem Nachum (1730–1787): Hasidic rabbi from Ukraine who was a disciple of the Baal Shem Tov. He published one of the first works of Hasidic thought.

U

Underhill, Evelyn (1875–1941): Anglo-Catholic writer and an indefatigable researcher on the topic of mysticism. It was her 1911 book *Mysticism* that I used in teaching my university classes.

V

van Gogh, Vincent (1853–1890): Dutch Post-Impressionist painter and one of the most influential figures in Western art.

Voltaire, François-Marie (1694–1778): French Enlightenment philosopher well known for his attacks on the Catholic Church. Voltaire was an advocate of freedom of religion and of speech.

W

Wang, Zhao (1996–present): Chinese student, young mystic, and computer programmer.

Wapnick, Kenneth (1942-2013): Close friend of Helen Schucman and William Thetford. These three together were the immediate stimulus for the scribing of *A Course in Miracles*.

Watts, Alan (1915–1973): British-born American who was known as an interpreter of Zen Buddhism and Hindu and Chinese philosophy.

Wei Wu Wei (Terence Gray) (1895–1986): English gentleman who dropped out of society in 1958, went to India, studied with Ramana Maharshi, and wrote several books under the pseudonym Wei Wu Wei.

Weil, Andrew (1942–present): American doctor who specializes in alternative medicine, holistic health, and integrative medicine.

Weil, Simone (1909–1943): French philosopher, mystic, and political activist. In Assisi in the spring of 1937, she experienced an unrobing of the ego while visiting the Basilica of Santa Maria degli Angeli, the same church in which Saint Francis of Assisi had prayed.

Weinberg, Steven (1933–present): Theoretical physicist, philosopher, and Noble Laureate in physics.

Wenyan, Yunmen (862–949): Founder of the Yunmen School, one of the five major schools of Chan (Chinese Zen).

Wesley, Charles (1707–1788): John Wesley's younger brother and a leader of the Methodist movement. He is best known for writing more than 6,000 hymns.

Wesley, John (1703–1791): Founder of the Methodist Church, originally a group formed to do a "methodological" study of the scriptures. Born in England, he spent many years in the United States.

White, John (1939–present): Noetic researcher, and author of *The Meeting of Science and Spirit* and *What Is Enlightenment?*

Whitman, Walt (1819–1892): American poet, Transcendentalist, and literary realist.

Wilber, Ken (1945–present): American author of *Integral Psychology* and an integral theorist who attempted to integrate all knowledge.

Williams, Roger (1603–1683): Puritan who was expelled from the Massachusetts colony because of his "new and dangerous ideas." He founded the city of Providence as a refuge offering freedom of conscience. He is a champion of the principle of separation of church and state.

Williamson, Marianne (1952–present): American activist, best-selling author, lecturer, founder of the Peace Alliance, teacher of *A Course in Miracles*, and friend.

Wilson, William (1895–1971): Co-founder, along with Robert Smith (1879–1950), of Alcoholics Anonymous.

Wittgenstein, Ludwig (1889–1951): Austrian-British philosopher who worked primarily in logic, the philosophy of the mind, and the philosophy of language.

Wordsworth, William (1770–1850): English romantic poet who, along with Samuel Taylor Coleridge, launched the Romantic Age in English literature.

Y

Yeshe, Thubten (1935–1984): Tibetan Lama who was considered unconventional in his teaching style.

Yogananda, Paramahansa (1893–1952): Founder of Self-Realization Fellowship. He taught the need for direct experience of mystical truth. "The true basis of religion is not belief, but intuitive experience," he said. His *Autobiography of a Yogi* has been a perennial best-seller.

Z

Zoroaster (ca. 1000 BCE): Prophet of ancient Iran who inaugurated a movement that became the dominant religion in ancient Persia. His dating is uncertain. Scholars say he lived around 1000 BCE, but others put him later, in the 7th and 6th centuries BCE.

Bibliography

A Course in Miracles. CA: Foundation for Inner Peace, 1975, 1992, 2007.

Abhayananda, S. *History of Mysticism: The Unchanging Testament.* Naples, FL: Atma Books, 1987.

Amritanandamayi, Mata. *For My Children.* Mata Amritanandamayi Trust, 1986.

Black Elk, Wallace, and William S. Lyon. *Black Elk: The Sacred Ways of a Lakota.* New York: HarperCollins Publishers, 1991.

Borchert, Bruno. *Mysticism: Its History and Challenge.* York Beach, ME: Samuel Weiser, 1994.

Butler-Bowdon, Tom. *50 Spiritual Classics.* London and Boston: Nicholas Brealey Publishing, 2005.

Carmody, Denise Lardner, and John Tully Carmody. *Mysticism: Holiness East and West.* UK: Oxford University Press, 1996.

Davidson, John. *The Gospel of Jesus: In Search of His Original Teachings.* UK: Element Books, Ltd., 1995.

Eckhart, Meister. *The Essential Sermons,* edited by Bernard McGinn and Edmund Colledge. New York: Paulist Press, 1981. Re-published in paperback, 2005.

Eliade, Mircea. "Mysticism" in *The Encyclopedia of Religion.* Vol. 10, 245–61. New York: Macmillan, 1987.

————. *The Sacred and the Profane.* New York: Houghton Mifflin Harcourt, 1957.

Estés, Clarissa Pinkola. *Women Who Run with the Wolves: Myths and Stories of the Wild Woman Archetype.* New York: Random House, 1995.

Ferguson, John. *An Illustrated Encyclopedia of Mysticism and the Mystery Religions.* New York: Continuum Books, 1977.

Freud, Sigmund. *The Future of an Illusion* (the Norton Library Series). New York: W. W. Norton & Company, 1975.

Gangaji. *The Diamond in Your Pocket: Discovering Your True Radiance.* Boulder, CO: Sounds True, Inc., 2005.

Golas, Thaddeus. *The Lazy Man's Guide to Enlightenment.* Redway, CA: Seed Center, 1971, 1972.

Gunn, J. Alexander. *Bergson and His Philosophy.* London: Methuen and Co., Ltd., 1920.

Hart, William. *Vipassana Meditation: As Taught by S. N. Goenka.* New York: HarperCollins Publishers, 1987.

Harvey, Andrew. *The Essential Mystics: The Soul's Journey into Truth.* Edison, NJ: Book Sales, Inc., 1998.

Hofman, Albert. *LSD: My Problem Child.* Published by the Multidisciplinary Association for Pyschedelic Studies.

Isherwood, Christopher. *Ramakrishna and His Disciples.* Hollywood, CA: Vedanta Press, 1980.

James, William. *The Varieties of Religious Experience.* Cambridge, MA: Harvard University Press, 1987. .

Jung, Carl. *Collected Works.* Princeton, NJ: Princeton University Press, 1979.

————. *Man and His Symbols.* New York: Anchor Books, Doubleday, 1964.

Katz, S. T. *Mysticism and Philosophical Analysis.* UK: Oxford University Press, 1978.

Knox, Ronald. *The Hidden Stream: Mysteries of the Christian Faith.* San Francisco: Ignatius Press, 2002.

Kornfield, Jack. *After the Ecstasy, the Laundry: How the Heart Grows Wise on the Spiritual Path.* New York: Bantam Books, 2000.

Livergood, Norman D. *The Perennial Tradition.* Tempe, AZ: Dandelion Books, 2003.

————. *Portals to Higher Consciousness.* Tempe, AZ: Dandelion Books, 2006.

Maharshi, R. *The Spiritual Teaching of Ramana Maharshi.* Boston: Shambhala Press, 2004.

Maslow, Abraham. *Religions, Values, and Peak-Experiences*. New York: Penguin Books, 1970.

Merton, Thomas. *The Seven Storey Mountain*. New York: Harvest Books, 1948.

McGreal, Ian P. *Great Thinkers of the Eastern World*. New York: HarperResource, 1995.

————. *Great Thinkers of the Western World*. New York: CollinsReference, 1992.

Monroe, R. *Journeys Out of the Body*. New York: Main Street Books, 1992.

Mundy, Jon. *Eternal Life and A Course in Miracles*. New York: Sterling Ethos, 2016.

————. *Living A Course in Miracles*, New York: Sterling Ethos, 2011.

————. *Lesson 101: Perfect Happiness*, New York: Sterling Ethos, 2014.

————. *Missouri Mystic*. Unionville, New York: Royal Fireworks, 2004.

Otto, Rudolf. *The Idea of the Holy*. New York: OUP, 1970, originally published 1917.

Religious Tolerance. *www.religioustolerance.org.*

Roberts, Bernadette. *The Path to No-Self*. Albany, NY: State University of New York Press, 1991.

Sanford, John A. *Dreams: God's Forgotten Language*. San Francisco: HarperSanFrancisco, 1989.

Kavanaugh, Kieran, and Otilio Rodriguez (trans). *The Collected Works of St. Teresa of Avila*. Washington, DC: Institute of Carmelite Studies, 1976.

Schweitzer, Albert. *Paul and His Interpreters: A Critical History*. London: Adams and Charles Black, 1912.

Soelle, Dorothee. *The Silent Cry: Mysticism and Resistance*. Minneapolis, MN: Fortress Press, 1997.

Solomon, Robert C., and Kathleen Higgins. *A Short History of Philosophy*. UK: Oxford University Press, 1996.

Suzuki, D. T. *The Zen Doctrine of No-Mind*. York Beach, ME: Weiser Books, 1991.

Talbot, Michael. *Mysticism and the New Physics*. New York: Penguin Books, 1981.

Thoreau, Henry David. *Letters to a Spiritual Seeker*. New York: W. W. Norton & Co., 2004.

————. *Walden*. Boston: Ticknor and Fields, 1854 (original publication date).

Tolle, Eckhart. *The New Earth: Awakening to Your Life's Purpose*. New York: Penguin Group, Inc., 2005.

————. *The Power of Now: A Guide to Spiritual Enlightenment*. Vancouver, Canada: Namaste Publishing, 1997.

Ullman, Robert, and Judyth Reichenberg-Ullman. *Mystics, Masters, Saints, and Sages: Stories of Enlightenment*. Berkeley, CA: Conari Press, 2001.

Underhill, Evelyn. *Mysticism: A Study in the Nature and Development of Spiritual Consciousness*. (Public Domain) 1911, 1921, and 1955.

————. *Practical Mysticism*. _____: Renaissance Classics, reprint 2002.

Vahle, Neal. *Open at the Top: The Life of Ernest Holmes*. Mill Valley, CA: Open View Press, 1993.

————. *The Unity Movement*. Philadelphia: Templeton Foundation Press, 2002.

Wapnick, Kenneth. *Love Does Not Condemn: The World, the Flesh, and the Devil According to Platonism, Christianity, Gnosticism, and 'A Course in Miracles.'* Foundation for "A Course in Miracles," 1989.

White, John. *What Is Enlightenment? Exploring the Goal of the Spiritual Path*. St. Paul, MN: Paragon House Publishers, 1995.

Wilber, Ken. *Kosmic Consciousness* (audio CD). Boulder, CO: Sounds True, 2003.

————. *No Boundary: Eastern and Western Approaches to Personal Growth*. Boston: Shambhala, 2001.

Woods, R. *Understanding Mysticism*. New York: Continuum International Publishing Group, 1981.

Zaehner, R. C. *Mysticism Sacred and Profane*. UK: Oxford University Press, 1961.

About the Author

Jon Mundy is an author and lecturer, the publisher of *Miracles* magazine, and the Executive Director of All Faiths Seminary in New York City. He taught courses in philosophy and religion from 1967 to 2008 at The New School and the State University of New York, with a specialization in the history of mysticism.

Jon's book *Living A Course in Miracles* has become a perennial bestseller and has been translated into eight languages. Jon met Helen Schucman, the scribe of *A Course in Miracles,* in 1973. Helen introduced him to the Course and served as his counselor until she became ill in 1980.

Jon also appears on occasion as *Dr. Baba Jon Mundane,* a stand-up philosopher/comedian.

If you enjoyed this book, you may enjoy watching regular monthly presentations by Jon on YouTube. You may also enjoy a subscription to *Miracles* magazine.

Visit *www.miraclesmagazine.org.*

To Our Readers